Uncle Paul,
Happy Birthday!
I cncean't remember
if it was Anita Baker
or Anita Bryant. Either
way make something
delicious!

♡ Shib

D1556952

P.S. Great recipe for
Bigot pie in here!
LOL

BLESS THIS FOOD

By Anita Bryant

MINE EYES HAVE SEEN THE GLORY
AMAZING GRACE
BLESS THIS HOUSE

By Anita Bryant and Bob Green

FISHERS OF MEN
LIGHT MY CANDLE

Anita Bryant

BLESS THIS FOOD

THE ANITA BRYANT FAMILY COOKBOOK

DOUBLEDAY & COMPANY, INC.
GARDEN CITY, NEW YORK
1975

ISBN: 0-385-09780-8
Library of Congress Catalog Card Number 74–12677
Copyright © 1975 by Anita Bryant
All Rights Reserved
Printed in the United States of America
First Edition

DEDICATION

To my mother, who gave me the freedom to experiment with various kitchen concoctions when I was knee high to a grasshopper.

To my sister, Sandra, who served as my first official taster and culinary critic.

To my husband, who is the best eater of all and a sheer joy to cook for.

And to my children, who make our family meals the interesting adventure that they are.

READ THIS FIRST

I don't want this to be simply another cookbook full of endless pages of recipes and helpful cooking hints. I have a plan to make this one different and you are a part of this plan.

Many cookbooks are written as an outgrowth of a cooking hobby or strong interest in cooking. Some cookbooks are written as a collection of recipes from various friends and acquaintances of the famous author. The author collects and writes and the reader passively accepts or rejects the recipes and hints, trying a few. But by and large, the book and the recipes remain the author's and the life of the reader remains mainly unchanged.

I'd like very much to change this process, because the things in this book are too important to allow life to go on unchanged. This book is a personal statement from me. It is a wide, open view into my thoughts and opinions as a wife and mother in a Christian household.

On the basis of my still limited experiences in these roles, I have managed to pull together my opinions, thoughts, recipes, and even some of my private times with the source of my strength, God, "for I can do everything God asks me to with the help of Christ who gives the strength and power." (Philippians 4:13)

This book is neither meant to be an academic study in nutrition nor a class in gourmet cooking. Rather it's a story about how one family chooses mundane, everyday experiences to grow as Christ grew, ". . . in wisdom and stature and in favor with God and man."

It seemed that because so many of our Christian growth experiences centered around food and mealtime, it was natural for our story to take the form of a cookbook.

I want you to consider these pages a conversation between two persons interested in and concerned about tomorrow's families—me and you.

My hope is that our time together will be meaningful to you and your family as a series of beginnings in creating a new feeling of Christian love and family togetherness.

The institution of marriage and family is ordained by God. Each family is created in love and is made special for a specific purpose in God's plan.

Take this book. Make it yours. Find God's plan for your family. Use a pencil as you read. Underline thoughts that seem to match your own. Write comments and new personal discoveries in the margins. Write examples of your own family togetherness in the white spaces. I want you to be writing your own family story as you read ours.

Let me suggest you first glance through the book and begin at a point that seems to match a point of need or desire in your family right now. This book is an ongoing account and you need not begin with Chapter 1. Begin where you like.

After you begin to make this book your own, with your own ideas and stories, share it with someone else. That is the purpose for which we have intended it. Bring your own Christian family story to life in the lives of other families you touch. Let the world see God and Christ's love in your family and its togetherness.

If these recipes and suggestions can lead you and your family into a new awareness of God's love and purpose, then, and only then, will my time in preparing this—and your time in reading it—be justified.

This book is like a diary of relationships, friendships, and acquaintances. Many of the recipes are gifts to me from outstanding homemakers, cooks, and chefs. Most of the recipes I have tried. Some I have not, as yet.

I have found, in many cases, that putting these recipes on paper is something like trying to describe a beautiful experience. A part of the real essence is lost as it is put into print. There is often a certain twist of a special wooden spoon, or a particular cooking pot, or a significant flick of the salt shaker, or some other intangible ingredient that simply defies the printed page. Consequently, these recipes may vary from cook to cook.

We have also been faced with trying to translate the terms: dash, some, a little, a pinch, a can, or a lot into standard measures. No doubt, at times, we have selected a slightly inaccurate counterpoint.

My suggestion is for you to do as all good cooks—stir, taste, add to, change, or redo a recipe to suit you and your family.

In a few recipes, you will notice the optional use of a cooking wine or a sherry flavoring. This should in no way be confused with the use of alcohol as a beverage. Cooking wines are in the category of seasonings. When used in cooking, the small alcoholic content is evaporated by the time a dish is fully prepared. The remaining flavor simply adds a richer, fuller body to the food.

CONTENTS

INTRODUCTION

I really believe it was Grandpa Berry who started me on my singing career. He would cuddle the six-month-old Anita Jane on his shoulder in the rocking chair and lovingly command, "Sing, Anita, sing." I "sang," and he applauded. He even "booked" my first performance, at age two. Grandpa made arrangements for me to sing "Jesus Loves Me" at the Baptist church in Barnsdall, Oklahoma.

The rugged Oklahoma oil country was our home—Mother (Anniece Lenora Berry), Daddy (Warren G. Bryant), Sandra, and me. We were a young family. Mother was only eighteen when I was born. Then, a year and a half later, Sandra joined us. Perhaps the intense family pressures were too much for such young parents. Mother and Daddy divorced when I was quite young. Mother, Sandra, and I moved in temporarily with Grandma and Grandpa Berry.

These early days in Tishomingo, Oklahoma, were wonderful days, full of love and warm memories. Grandpa Berry was blind because of a terrible oil field accident. Because of this, Grandpa trusted the Lord as his Savior. This tragedy left him almost helpless and personally destroyed for a while. But eventually, through his new-found faith, Grandpa learned to live with his new life of darkness. He often said he had to get his eyes put out before he could really see. Grandma taught him to garden. He took us on walks into town and took us fishing to catch food for supper. Grandpa Berry taught me much about life and living that serves as the basis for many of my beliefs today.

My cooking days began in Mother and Grandma Berry's kitchen. They allowed me to try all kinds of cooking "experiments." Then Grandpa and Grandma would taste the new dish and brag just like it was the tastiest meal ever. It never occurred to me that they might be speaking more out of love than out of truth.

Mother and Daddy remarried and we moved to Seminole, Oklahoma. There on the high school auditorium stage as a first grader I made my first "public stage appearance" in the high school operetta. Maybe it was the gypsy costume, or the smell of stage make-up, or maybe the sound of applause; I knew immediately that this was meant for me! I wanted more.

We moved to Velma, Oklahoma. At eight, I entered a six-week radio talent show and won each week. Then came my first TV appearance. I went to Oklahoma City and auditioned for the Gizmo Goodkin Talent Show. We didn't even own a TV, so the prospects of appearing on a TV show really shook me up. But I was accepted and I appeared on other shows.

At this point, Mother and Daddy began to realize my dream of becoming a star deserved a second look. After much consideration and deliberation, we moved to Midwest City so I could be near the city. Sandra and I began taking dancing lessons at the Molly O'Day Dance School.

Sandra and I readily launched a full-scale career with performances at plays, schools, clubs, community groups, and TV.

The spell of stardom continued to spin around my head. By this time I had made a public profession of faith in Christ. I truly felt (and feel) a strong sense of God's leadership in pursuing the thing I loved best—singing. I believe God gave me a voice to be used for His glory. He carefully guided me, constantly providing opportunities for each step of development in a career. I simply had to do my best, practice, prepare, and follow Him.

In fact, my whole career is simply a study of God's plan and leadership. As long as I trusted Him for guidance, He miraculously showed me one step at a time. Every time I began to take things into my own hands, or began to walk over people, or became too ambitious, God had ways of putting me in my place.

Mother helped a lot along this line too, keeping my feet planted firmly on solid ground. Mother had marvelous insight into situations and the tendency I had to let things get out of control. With a firm word she would help bring me back to reality and responsibility.

Even though a move to Tulsa threatened to end my career with one fatal blow, things continued to advance. Instead of the move hurting my opportunities, it helped.

Eventually, the chance came for me to fly to New York to be on the "Arthur Godfrey's Talent Scouts." This event marked a special time in my spiritual life. My pastor at that time began to question me about my Christian responsibility as it related to show business. Momentarily, I also began to doubt that God could possibly be in-

volved in *leading* anyone into a show-business career. I prayed very
diligently about this. I thought carefully about all the things that
had gone before. Soon the answer came to me as clearly as the
sound of a human voice. God had given me a voice. As long as I
was completely submissive to His will and used my voice to His
glory, there was no reason to doubt His leadership into show business.

I made the trip to New York with a calm reassurance of God's
will for my life.

Next came the Miss Oklahoma title and the second runner-up
position in the Miss America pageant. Then the appearances on the
"Don McNeill Breakfast Club" and my first million-seller recording
with Carlton Records, "Till There Was You." And finally a contract
as a regular on the "Breakfast Club" radio show.

Later I met Bob Green, who was an important disc jockey from
Miami. Our courtship was long and crazy, spanning the miles be-
tween Chicago and Miami. At last, after many hurdles, I became
Mrs. Bob Green on June 25, 1960.

The early years of our marriage were characterized by strife and
bitter conflict. Only our very great love for the Lord and for each
other sustained us.

Looking back now, we realize we were trying to go it alone—
without complete commitment to God's leadership. Simply getting
married does not necessarily create a Christian home. This is something that has to be developed on a day-by-day basis with prayer and
devotion.

When we had been married three years our little seven-pound,
one-ounce son, Bobby, came to live with us. God sent Bobby to us
through adoption. Seven and one half months later I gave birth to
Gloria Lynn, seven pounds, eleven ounces. Those days with two
little children again gave me opportunity after opportunity to test
God's companionship. I felt if He had led us into this hectic life, He
must surely give us the strength to survive. And He did. Of course,
little did we know, these days were just mild preparation for the coming events.

In 1969 our twins (William Bryant, two pounds, twelve ounces,
and Barbara Elisbet, two pounds, ten ounces) were born prematurely
amid near tragedy. The twins' lives hung in the balance for days. My

recovery was slow and very tedious. My voice seemed to evaporate and my will to work just vanished.

From an emotional rock bottom, I again went to God in prayer. I prayed again for a renewed awareness of the presence of God's love. I felt reassured immediately and began the long road back up to performance level.

And now I sit down, as I have done before, to share these experiences with you. Not because they are unusual or especially worthy of publication. But because it is the story of one girl from Oklahoma and one little family of six diligently seeking and finding God's will for their lives.

PART I

FAVORITE KID-TESTED RECIPES

CHAPTER 1

FOOD IS TO KIDS
WHAT MUSIC IS TO SINGERS

It is not food that makes a meal. At our house a meal is three glasses of spilled Florida orange juice, two excused absences from the table, at least one turned-up nose at the menu, lots of chatter, complaints, laughter, noise, and a few reminders of what we are at the table for.

Some writers refer to this as pleasant surroundings and good company. Frankly, these words are more of a goal than a description, but the idea is important.

Food that is served in a happy, relaxed atmosphere is the most nutritious food, regardless of its actual food value. The psychological impact of mealtime and eating have great effect on the body's use of the nutrients. How we eat and how we eat together are the most important considerations of mealtime.

I am not an expert on nutrition or even an expert cook. But I know that even the most attractive and well-balanced meal loses its value if it is served in the midst of bickering, scolding, or discord. Cooking for a family is indeed a much larger assignment than just providing good healthy food. A big part of preparing a meal for the family is creating an emotional, social, and spiritual climate that can assure a successful mealtime experience.

There has been an advertising slogan in recent years that says, "Nothing says loving like something from the oven." This is something of the feeling I want to express in this book.

Houses are not necessarily homes, and fathers, mothers, and children may not necessarily or automatically make families. It takes a lot of loving, respect, consideration, hard work, and co-operation to become a family. And I am convinced that food is one of the vital keys to the successful development of this family togetherness. Food planning and preparation, eating and feeding are processes that help turn fathers, mothers, and children into loving families.

Going back to the beginning, I remember the first days and weeks of our babies' lives. I remember their little systems of communication were not too refined but were surely effective. They knew what they wanted and were able to communicate this need to me.

And as many parents remember, the first and most intense need any infant communicates is hunger. No adult has ever been hungry like a baby is hungry. It is a painful, totally absorbing hunger. Our babies signaled this hunger by crying. When these early hunger needs were met, it gave our babies (and later the children) a basis for developing a fundamental trust in themselves and their world. Doctors tell us that satisfying this basic human need does more to strengthen the foundation of a strong and healthy self-concept than any other act during these early days.

The twins' early days at home are still vivid in my memory. They were so little when we brought them home from the hospital that they had to be fed every three hours. Now to feed one baby every three hours is a lot of feeding, but two feedings every three hours are one constant job! With the feeding, burping, and changing for each one, I didn't get fifteen consecutive minutes' sleep in a twenty-four-hour period.

We had the feeding assembly line set up in the nursery to cut down on trips to and from the kitchen. We were saving energy every possible way.

We were so thankful for the twins and the fact that they were alive and home with us. It was just a blessing to sit and rock them and sing to them. But it took me several days to realize that this rocking needed to be done other than at feeding time during these early days. The constant rocking during bottle time must have made them seasick, because at the end of each bottle, each twin promptly spit it all right back up. When I stopped the rocking and just enjoyed holding them close, the milk stayed down.

In a few days the nurse came. She was one of the most welcome sights I have ever seen walking through our door. I went to bed and slept for a week.

Food is the earliest communication of love and care between a mother and infant. Eating and being fed are intimately connected with the baby's deepest feelings. It is the most basic interaction between human beings. Making the most of this early mealtime is vital to the baby's basic nutrition.

The baby learns this world is a good and satisfying place. It responds when he feels miserable with hunger. The world (in the form of Mother) is a dependable and trustworthy place.

These early experiences and attitudes also give the basis for a child's beginning spiritual growth. He learns to love and trust people (again in the form of Mother) so he can eventually know love for God. He learns to feel loved by others, so he can understand God's love for him too. He learns what trust is so he can have faith in God.

Food and the feeding process to babies and young children are physical nourishment, but they are also communications of love, a representation of what life will be like.

Now that our children are older, I still feel strongly that eating experiences condition their entire attitude to the world. Not so much because of how nutritious the food is, but with what feelings and attitudes it is given. How a child is being fed, and how he eats, has a larger impact on the personality than any other human experience. Food given without love is not good nutrition but an insult.

One thing that surprised me when I became a mother (and something I continue to be surprised at) is, just because I became a mother and a wife I did not automatically become someone who likes to prepare and serve happy homemaker meals to others. It is hard to meet the demands of mealtime on such a regular basis. So although it is a life commitment for me, I must continually recommit my energy and my intentions to the process.

Another surprise I had as a mother was to notice the difference in how an adult approaches mealtime and food and how a child approaches mealtime and food. Most adults seem to be unaware of what food means to children.

Food is to kids what music is to singers. It is a way of life, it is a communication form, it is an event and an experience. It is a security blanket, it is learning, it is thought, it is habit. It is reward and punishment. Food is a pastime, and an emotional link with Mother and family. It is a time schedule and a sequence to be counted on. Food is real. Food is life and love and sustenance. It represents a large part of all the child knows about love and care.

These loving recipes are ones I have used through the years with my children. I use these special treats when a child needs some particular attention, when there has been a disappointment we need to overcome, during convalescence from an illness, or during long after-noons just for fun. The process of these recipes is the most important thing, and then the product. The process is important because it re-quires the undivided attention of two persons for a length of time—me and my child. And it is important because there is an eatable product (of sorts) at the end, which must be shared by me and my child. And for some strange, heavenly reason these are the magic ingredients to a highly successful parent/child relationship.

INSTANT PUDDING FINGERPAINT

Spread about ½ cup of pudding on a sheet of wax paper or a TV tray. Spread it around with hands and fingers. Use a fork or spoon to make designs. Then lick your fingers and eat the rest.

PRETZELS

1 package active dry yeast   *1 teaspoon salt*
1½ cups warm water   *1 egg*
1 tablespoon sugar   *4 cups flour*

Preheat oven to 425 degrees. Dissolve the package of yeast in ½ cup of the warm water. Mix the remaining water with the sugar and salt and add the yeast water. Add the egg. Stir in the flour add-ing 1 cup at a time.

Prepare a low working area for the child to knead the dough. Work the dough briefly and cut off hunks. Roll hunks into ropes and form into pretzels or alphabet letters. Place on a cookie sheet and bake for 12 to 15 minutes.

Makes about 20 to 25 pretzels, depending on the size you make each one.

SUGAR COOKIES

½ cup butter   *1½ teaspoons baking powder*
1 cup sugar   *pinch salt*
1 egg, beaten   *½ teaspoon vanilla*
1⅓ cups flour

Preheat oven to 350 degrees. Cream butter and sugar. Add egg and mix well. Stir in dry ingredients and vanilla. Chill the dough for 2 to 3 hours or overnight.

Now comes the fun. This basic sugar cookie recipe is limited only by your child's imagination. A few drops of food coloring are fun. Then the dough can be shaped into animal cookies or rolled out and cut with a cookie cutter. Bake 8 to 10 minutes depending on the thickness of the cookie. Decorate the baked cookies with icing, sugar crystals, raisins, chocolate drops, or a dab of jelly.

Makes approximately 2 dozen cookies, depending on size.

PIE DOUGH KISSES

When I was little, we always hung around when Grandma Berry did the baking, especially if she cooked pastry of some kind. The trimmings of crust were called kisses, and we liked to sneak little bites behind her back. My children, like all children, delight in doing the same thing. So occasionally we make a whole recipe of piecrust just to use for fun, with no intention of a pie whatsoever.

Make a piecrust recipe or use a prepared crust and see what you can do.

Cut strips of crust and bake according to the instructions with your recipe. Or twist two strips together. Or braid three strips together. Brush with butter, sprinkle with sugar and cinnamon. Bake and serve.

Make shells of pie dough using the bottom of a cup cake pan to form the shells. Bake and cool. Fill the cups with instant pudding or ice cream.

Roll out dough to thin thickness. Spread with jelly, or sausage, or cheese. Roll up jelly roll fashion. Chill. Slice and bake.

Children enjoy working with dough. Although they can eventually make the dough tough by working it, the process is so satisfying that I really don't mind. The important thing is the time we spend together doing this. I have found that a child who has had an upsetting experience at school or with brothers and sisters finds great comfort in kneading and rolling dough.

GINGERBREAD BOYS

1 cup shortening
1 cup sugar
1 egg
1 cup molasses
2 tablespoons vinegar
5 cups flour

1½ teaspoons baking soda
½ teaspoon salt
2 teaspoons ginger
1 teaspoon cinnamon
1 teaspoon ground cloves

Preheat oven to 375 degrees. Cream shortening and sugar in a large mixing bowl. Stir in egg, molasses, and vinegar. Add dry ingredients, mix well, and chill the dough for several hours.

Roll the dough between two pieces of wax paper that have been lightly floured. Remove the top paper and cut with a cookie cutter or let children shape gingerbread boys by hand. Add decorations as the children desire.

Read the story of the gingerbread boy while the cookies bake for 10 to 12 minutes.

Makes 15 to 20 gingerbread men. It really depends on how many children are sampling the dough as you go along.

CHOCOLATE ETCHING

2 cups marshmallow topping
food coloring
1 box graham crackers

1 package chocolate chips
1 tablespoon butter

Put several spoonfuls of marshmallow topping into two or three separate containers. Small cupcake tins or baby food jars work well. Color each container of topping with a drop or two of food coloring, so that you have three different colors.

Spread this colored topping on the graham crackers. Either mix the colors in a marble effect or put separate colors on each cracker.

Next heat the chocolate chips and butter in the top of a double boiler until smooth. Do not overheat. Use a pastry brush to apply the melted chocolate in a thin layer on top of the marshmallow topping.

Refrigerate for about an hour. Then use the point of some sharp object (knife or toothpick) to etch (scratch) a design in the chocolate. The colors of the marshmallow topping will show through. Children can make initials, names, designs, or pictures—then eat them right up!

Hazel Donaldson is a member of Northwest Baptist Church and is known to be a good cook. When she says this recipe is good, I know I can count on it!

HEAVENLY BITS
Hazel Donaldson

½ pound butter	*2 cups cake flour*
4 tablespoons sugar	*2 cups cut pecans*
½ teaspoon salt	*confectioners' sugar*

Preheat oven to 275 degrees. Mix together the butter, sugar, salt, flour, and pecans. Roll into bite-size balls. Bake on an ungreased cookie sheet about 1 hour.
When done, roll in confectioners' sugar while warm.
Makes about 20 balls.

One of my very favorite persons and teachers is Doris Niles. We used to go over to her house for tea in the afternoon.
Miss Niles reminded me in a recent letter how much her family meant to her. She could date her family ancestry back for more than thirteen generations. She says they were never affluent, but always good, solid citizens.
Miss Niles's grandmother had a famous and popular cookie jar. It was a real surprise to find, after Grandmother Barton's death, her recipe for sugar cookies. It was such a special recipe, made by pinches, scoops, and dabs, that no one really expected ever to find it on paper. Even now, it will take an expert cook to understand "moderate oven" and "until brown."

SOUR CREAM COOKIES
Doris Niles

2 eggs
1 cup sugar
1 cup butter
1 cup sour cream

1 teaspoon soda
pinch salt
nutmeg

Mix together the eggs, sugar, butter, sour cream, soda, and salt. Season to taste with nutmeg. Mix very soft, as soft as possible, with flour. Spread on board and use big, round cookie cutter and cut hole in center. Bake in a moderate oven until brown. Sprinkle with sugar while the cookies are still hot.

DEAR LORD. *Another glass of spilled milk! Dear Lord, how much milk is a mother supposed to clean up in one day! The Bible says to forgive seventy times seven. Does that apply to spilled milk too?*

Is spilled milk really worth the fuss I make over it? O Father of all forgiveness, give me patience to forgive. Help me to understand that I am teaching lessons in forgiveness every time I go for paper towels.

CHAPTER 2

CHRISTIAN FAMILY TOGETHERNESS THROUGH FOOD

The Bible gives countless examples of how God used natural occurrences to communicate His love and care for His people. From the earliest accounts of God's interaction with man, I have been interested in the use of food and mealtimes as object lessons in the faith. The Bible gives much space to food, symbolic uses of food, and mealtime experiences.

I remember the accounts of the wilderness wanderings of the children of Israel. They were miraculously fed with a provisional food called manna. The manna had to be gathered with care and according to God's plan. God used this food and feeding plan to demonstrate His constant care for His chosen people.

And I can imagine that through it all, the parents used these experiences to explain to their children the message of God's love.

Probably one of the more dramatic events in the Jewish household was (and is) the Passover feast. Again, food and mealtime were used to pass on the wonders and plan of God's love as He delivered the ancient Israelites out of bondage in Egypt.

Since this early Passover feast was celebrated by Jesus and even used as the occasion for His commemorating the Lord's Supper, we find a study of this Jewish custom very meaningful to our children. We borrowed the recipe for Matzo Ball Soup from our Jewish friends, and you can use it during the Passover season. We discuss the biblical stories these foods represent. We have found this study helpful in later explaining the observance of the Lord's Supper.

On the negative side there are also biblical accounts of God allowing the withdrawal of food to teach lessons of submission and recommitment. Famine and starvation served to remind the people of their failure to follow God's plan.

Jesus also often used natural everyday experiences to teach great spiritual truths. He caught people in the act of living and introduced them to life more abundant.

Jesus even chose a wedding feast as the background to perform his first earthly sign as the Messiah. At the wedding feast in Cana, Jesus turned the water into wine. (John 2:1–11)

Matthew used food at one of the first evangelism meetings to introduce his friends to the Savior. He called his tax collector fellows together for a feast with Jesus as the guest of honor. (Luke 5:27–29)

Jesus went home and probably ate with Zacchaeus in an effort to teach the equality and importance of each individual. (Luke 19:1–9)

Jesus went often to fellowship meals in the home of his friends, Mary, Martha, and Lazarus. It was on one of these occasions that Jesus stated his philosophy of fellowship as being more important than the service of the food. (Luke 10:38–42) Some of the simplest dinners produce the most desirable feelings of friendship.

Ruth Graham (Mrs. Billy) related the following information to me concerning an appropriate translation of Jesus' message to Martha:

"When I was studying Greek in college, our professor pointed out to us an interesting thought in the story of Jesus, Mary, and Martha. Where Jesus said, 'But one thing is needful,' our professor suggested that might just as well be translated, 'But one dish is needful.' "

Obviously Martha was laying it on and Jesus was suggesting she keep it simple. Some of the sweetest fellowship can be had around the simplest of meals.

Jesus ate with his disciples, shared food with five thousand, and then used food to symbolize his death. He used stories about food, feasts, and eating to demonstrate vital truths of Christianity. (Luke 9:10–17; Luke 14:12–24; John 6:35)

These events in Christ's life vividly became real for us when we attended the Conference on Biblical Prophecy in Jerusalem. Bobby and Gloria went with us for the ten-day trip. Before, during, and after that trip we spent many hours searching God's Word to absorb every detail of Jesus' life on earth. Seeing the geographical locations of so many biblical records left an impact on each of us that we will not ever forget.

I am sure that Christ's methods of teaching as well as what He taught were meant to be examples to us. It is very natural to use everyday family experiences to demonstrate and teach vital spiritual truths.

Each person who claims to be a Christian communicates through words and actions his understanding of God's love and purpose. In the same manner, the family communicates the nature and character of the Christian faith. I sincerely believe it is primarily through this basic family unit that children learn most about what it means to be a Christian. Even though I was a little hesitant at first to take Bobby and Gloria on such a distant trip, I now see how important it was to their understanding of Scripture.

Offering children a daily, authentic example and experience of the Christian faith is a command of God. "O Israel, listen: Jehovah is our God, Jehovah alone. You must love him with *all* your heart, soul, and might. And you must think constantly about these commandments I am giving you today. You must teach them to your children and talk about them when you are at home or out for a walk; at bedtime and the first thing in the morning. (Deuteronomy 6:4–7)

This religious training occurs mainly through the life and actions of each family member as he transacts his daily routine. It is true that we put a lot of emphasis on family devotional time, Bible reading, and prayer. But without the daily *living* example of faith, Christian education is all but impossible for children to grasp. *Not all important messages are given to children in words.* Truth and love must be lived into meaning before they can be clearly understood by childlike minds.

This, of course, puts adult Christians in a constant search of their own. I am continually searching to find renewed meaning in my own Christian experience. Children are quick to recognize sincerity, honesty, and authenticity. My first concern as a Christian parent is for the life of our family where the experience of the Christian faith can be made real.

Forgiveness, tolerance, commitment, understanding, and loving the unlovely are first learned at home.

MATZO BALL SOUP

Only unleavened bread may be eaten during the eight days of Passover. This recalls the day when the children of Israel fled to freedom in such haste they carried only unleavened dough to be baked under the desert sun. Of all the foods prepared for Passover, none is more carefully attended than the matzoth which are the modern-day unleavened bread. Matzoth are thin, flat wafers made of special flour and water. There is also matzo meal and matzo cake meal for preparing other dishes. This meal may be purchased at many large supermarkets and special kosher delicatessens.

4 tablespoons fat	*4 tablespoons chicken soup stock*
4 eggs, slightly beaten	*dash of ginger*
1 cup matzo meal	*2 quarts chicken stock*
2 teaspoons salt	*2 tablespoons chopped parsley*

Mix fat and eggs together. Add matzo meal and salt. Blend well. Add 4 tablespoons soup stock and ginger and mix well.

Bring 2 quarts chicken stock to a boil and reduce heat. Form balls about 1 inch in diameter from the meal mixture.

Drop the balls into the boiling soup. Cover pot and let cook 30 minutes. Garnish with parsley. Makes about 16 matzo balls.

Mina and Philip Braunstein are not only our dear, good friends, but Phil is also our CPA.

Mina is as good a cook as Phil is a manager. She has given me several good Jewish recipes.

NOODLE PUDDING
Mina Braunstein (Mrs. Philip)

1 8-ounce box broad noodles	*1 tablespoon sugar*
2 eggs	*dash of cinnamon*
1 can apples	*1 teaspoon lemon juice*
½ cup white raisins	*1 teaspoon vanilla*

Cook noodles in boiling salted water, strain.

Add well-beaten eggs, apples, raisins, sugar, cinnamon, lemon juice, vanilla, and mix well.

Pour into greased pan, bake until brown in 375-degree oven. Makes 4 servings.

MATZO BALLS
Mina Braunstein (Mrs. Philip)

½ cup water	4 eggs, beaten
½ cup melted shortening	1 cup matzo meal
dash pepper	1 teaspoon salt

Add water, shortening, and pepper to the eggs. Mix well.

Add matzo meal and salt, stir thoroughly, put in refrigerator for 1 hour.

Form into balls, put into soup or boiling water. Cook 20 minutes.

STUFFED BREAST OF VEAL
Mina Braunstein (Mrs. Philip)

6 pounds breast of veal	1 teaspoon garlic powder
1 tablespoon salt	bread stuffing
½ teaspoon pepper	¼ cup fat or shortening

Have butcher cut a pocket in veal.

Preheat oven to 325 degrees. Sprinkle meat in and out with salt, pepper, and garlic powder. Fill pocket with stuffing, sew opening.

Melt fat, put veal in pan, roast in slow oven until meat is tender, approximately 3 hours. Baste every 30 minutes. Brown and serve.

Makes 10 servings.

MEAT KNISHES
Mina Braunstein (Mrs. Philip)

2½ cups sifted flour	½ cup cooking oil
1 teaspoon baking powder	2 tablespoons water
½ teaspoon salt	1 pound ground meat
2 eggs	

Preheat oven to 350 degrees. Sift flour with baking powder and salt. Make a well in center, add eggs, oil, and water. Mix with hands and knead on a lightly floured board until smooth.

Roll out dough as thin as possible on a floured board. Cut dough into 3-inch rounds.

Prepare and mix meat with salt. Fill rounds with meat, moisten edges of dough, and pull together to close filling.

Bake in oven for 35 minutes.

Mary Irwin is the wife of Jim, the astronaut who went to the moon. The Irwins are really dedicated in sharing their faith. Mary seems to be like so many busy mothers who prefer simple but tasty dishes. She reports that Jim will eat anything and the children dislike most everything.

MOON GELATIN
Mary Irwin (Mrs. Jim)

1 package (6 ounces) fruit-
flavored gelatin
1 cup boiling water
1 cup chopped fresh fruit

⅓ cup chopped pecans
1 pint sour cream
maraschino cherries, chopped

Dissolve gelatin in the boiling water; add the fruit and nuts. Pour half the mixture into an 8-inch-square pan; chill until firm. Spread 1 cup of the sour cream over the gelatin in the pan; top with remaining gelatin and chill until firm. Top with remaining 1 cup sour cream and garnish with cherries.

Makes 6 servings (about ⅔ cup each).

Chuck Bird has been my musical conductor and arranger for many years. Working with him and knowing him and his wife Hope are a real pleasure. Hope shared her grandmother's recipe for bread.

Besides bread being the staff of life, and thanking God for our daily bread, what can be nicer than breaking your very own home-made bread with your family?

GRAMMA RHODA'S BREAD
Hope Bird (Mrs. Chuck)

2 cups milk	1 cup warm water
½ cup dark brown sugar, packed	7¼ cups whole-wheat flour
1 tablespoon salt	white flour (for kneading)
¼ cup butter	melted butter
2 packages dry yeast	

Preheat oven to 400 degrees. Scald milk, add sugar, salt, and butter. Cool completely. In large bowl sprinkle yeast over water. When dissolved, stir in cooled milk mixture.

Add half of the whole-wheat flour, beat until smooth. Gradually add remaining wheat flour. At this point, use hands.

Turn out onto floured board. Knead about 4 minutes. Grease the bowl and put the dough back into it, turning the dough to grease all sides. Cover with a towel and let it rise for 1 hour. It should be doubled in size. Turn out dough onto floured board and divide in two. Cover again for 10 to 15 minutes. Roll each into a 9-inch square, then roll up and put into greased 9 × 5-inch loaf pan.

Brush with melted butter. Cover and let them rise again about 45 minutes.

Dough should be rounded at top of pans.

Bake in the middle of your preheated oven for 35 minutes.

Take out of pans immediately and brush tops and sides with melted butter.

Cool a little or a lot. You will enjoy it either way.

Makes 2 loaves.

DEAR LORD, when I come to you at the beginning of each new day, I feel like breathing a sigh of relief. That seems strange—a sigh of relief. But I think it must be a relief when I realize I have the makings of one more day. One more chance to try being a better mother, a better wife, and a better person.

I wonder what all will be required of me today. Will I be nurse, referee, chauffeur, singer, disciplinarian, teacher, tear wiper? Who knows?

Dear Lord, whatever, please don't leave me alone. Be close beside. Keep my voice calm, my nerves collected, and my senses leveled.

Morning is more than a time to get up. It is a time to begin again.

CHAPTER 3

NUTRITION VS. SNACKS

Of all the tasks I have been given on earth, probably the responsibilities of parenthood rest most heavily on my mind. To be so totally responsible for the outcome of a child's physical and spiritual person is an awesome thought, not to mention his emotional self, his social self, and all the other facets of his being.

I am daily grateful for God's guidance and for Bob's companionship in this adventure of parenthood. With the three of us together I feel the chances of success are greater.

One of my firm convictions in parenthood is that I must constantly mother the total child. I can be no more concerned about his company manners at the table than I am about his physical need to sit still only three minutes. I cannot expect best grades in school if I have not insisted on an adequate breakfast. I cannot expect peak performance in any area if I do not see that his physical needs are being met.

It is my God-given duty as a parent to provide for the total care and life enrichment in every phase of life. These little lives represent one of God's most profound miracles. The workings and interdependence of each part of the human body is as intricate a balance as can be found in nature. It is a beautiful gift from God.

Our care of this body and its physical needs is an act of thanksgiving to God. Giving attention to the proper food and rest needs is as much a part of our Christian commitment as prayer.

So it is no wonder that physical nutrition is high on my list of constant concern. Good food habits are as essential as life itself. And like many other lessons in life, they do not happen, they are taught.

Similar to millions of other children in the world, my children learn only what they want to learn. Educators call it motivation. And that has seemed to be the key in my teaching good food habits.

Apparently, getting children to eat brings all mothers to their creative peak in parenting. From my own experience and the suggestions from other mothers who write me, some suggestions seem to surface as the most useful in teaching good eating habits.

Involve children in the planning of menus. Provide them with a list of possible choices and allow them one selection. As they make one entry to the list, you can make an entry. You can promise to eat their gelatin salad with whipped cream if they will eat your hamburger steak selection. In this way, the children become partners in planning.

Allow the children to help prepare some of the more simple dishes. A later chapter of this book will give more detailed ideas for this.

Realize that between-meal snacks are not the forbidden fruit they once were. Small children have small capacities and cannot take in as much at one meal as they may need. Plus the fact that children are fast burners. Their metabolism rate uses energy faster than adults, so they need refueling more often. However, the secret of good nutrition is the substance of these between-meal snacks. Pies, cakes, soft drinks, chips, candies—the usual snack foods—are called empty calorie foods. They do not contain significant food value but do contain abundant calories. They also dull the appetite and therefore are replacement foods rather than additional foods. Keep reading in this chapter for suggestions galore to ease between-meal hunger pains.

Use variety. Variety in food selection, preparation, and service teaches well-balanced eating habits. It's true that children almost always request the same selection—the same old peanut butter sandwich. But if a variety of other selections is offered often enough, his natural curiosity will win over. And if the same old peanut butter jar disappears for a meal or two, it may boost his need to select something else.

Make food interesting. Maybe the reason birthday cakes are so delicious is because we make them so attractive. What if we went to the same amount of trouble making vegetables attractive?

Serve small helpings to small children. The psychological implication of cleaning your plate and asking for more is far better teaching than sitting for twenty minutes trying to make a tiny dent in a heap.

And following close is the need for children to be comfortable while eating. A too big chair at a too big table transfers a child's concentration away from food. And even worse than a too big chair is trying to balance on top of a stack of telephone books in a too big chair at a too big table. We use tall junior chairs for the little children at family meals. Each twin has a low table and child's chair for between-meal snacks.

Keep foods simple. Usually I find my children enjoy food that "is not mixed up." They don't want carrots to touch the meat and they don't want Jell-O to touch the potatoes. So mixing vegetables together or expecting them to eat mixed-up stews and soups is out of the question. When I fix a stew or casserole, I usually arrange the children's plates by putting the bite-size vegetables in separate mole-hills. The same is true with sauces and dressing. Children want to know what's underneath.

Children also seem to prefer raw fruits and vegetables to cooked, which is just great, since that is the vegetable's most natural and nutritious state. Save yourself time and energy and feed the little fellows raw carrots, spinach, beans, and cauliflower. Raw vegetables are crunchier, more fun to eat, more nutritious, and even stimulate gum growth. This makes mothers happy, children happy, and doctors happy.

Avoid making a big deal over food. Food and eating should be a happy, enjoyable experience. Forcing food and forcing unhappy attention on eating sets up super bad feelings, attitudes, and habits. If food has not been eaten in twenty to thirty minutes, I just remove the plate without comment. However, there is an ironclad rule at our house that uneaten meals are never followed with dessert.

Try to gauge mealtime at the height of your child's hunger. We all have different body rhythms and seem to enjoy eating and sleeping more at certain times of the day. If the twins are forced to wait until late evening to eat, I've noticed they are more sleepy and tired than hungry. If I anticipate a late evening meal, I try to feed the children by late afternoon.

Sit down with your children when they eat. Since breakfast and lunch do not always include the total family at our house, it is tempting to sit the kids down to a bowl of cereal and go on about my business. But I have found this to be one of the dearest and most relaxed times to be together. We read a children's devotional, and pray together. Even if I have already eaten, or if I will eat later, I sit and join in conversation with the children while they eat. It seems to show them that I think mealtime is important, too.

In preparation for this book, I spent a great deal of time reviewing nutrition needs and double checking my "handed down" knowledge of food facts.

It was like reviewing some parts of the Bible I haven't read in a while. I was surprised at what I found. And surprised at how far short we fall from meeting the nutritional standard on some days.

For your quick reference, here are the basic four food groups. *Meat:* lean meat, poultry, fish, cheese, and eggs. *Dairy foods:* milk, cheese, ice cream. *Fruits and vegetables. Bread and cereal.*

It is generally accepted by many nutrition experts that everyone needs two to three servings of meat per day, three or four servings of dairy foods, four to five servings of fruits and vegetables, and three to four selections from the bread and cereal group.

Of course the size of the servings varies with age, with little children eating only two or three spoonfuls of each serving.

But you can see, as I did, that the recommended food is a lot of eating for little fellows. Every serving of food (be it snack or mealtime) must count. There really isn't room for "junk" food. Replacing empty calorie snacks with hearty nutritious snack food could double your child's nutrient intake.

Following is a collection of favorite, kid-tested snacks and light meal suggestions. These ideas have two major things going: they are as fun as a candy bar, and they are nutritious.

Cut slices of bologna with cookie cutters. Also cut slices of bread into geometric shapes. Serve only top-quality, all-meat bologna.

Draw a happy face on a paper plate. Serve any kind of good snack food on a special plate and automatically the food becomes special.

Pack a light meal or snack in a school lunch box and eat it outside (or on the kitchen floor spread with a picnic cloth).

Change the usual eating place. A Florida orange eaten outside under a tree tastes much different from an orange eaten at the kitchen table.

Top a serving of breakfast cereal with a scoop of ice milk. Spoon a few sliced strawberries over the top. Serve this in a fancy parfait glass.

Add an egg to a glass of Florida orange juice and put into the blender until frothy. Serve with a straw in a special glass. Call it an orange shake.

Broil a dab of cheese on top of a slice of whole-wheat bread or English muffin.

Be ready with an assortment of vegetables and fruits for snacks.

Serve apples that have been cut in half crosswise instead of lengthwise. Show the children the tiny five-point star in the center of the apple.

There is really no finer or nutritious snack than fresh fruits. Prepare various kinds of fresh or canned fruit such as strawberries, grapes, orange sections, pineapple, apple, and banana. In season, melon balls fit in nicely. Arrange the bite-size fruit on skewers or toothpicks. Serve with powdered sugar or a dish of honey.

Spread a slice of bologna with mayonnaise. Top with a slice of processed cheese. Add another slice of bologna. Add a layer of thin-sliced hamburger pickles. Then top with a last slice of bologna. Cut the stack into one-inch cubes and skewer with toothpicks.

Dip a banana in chocolate fudge topping. Add nuts.

Add ½ teaspoon sugar, ⅛ teaspoon vanilla, and a drop of food color to a glass of milk. Presto! Milkanilla!

HOT SPICY ORANGE JUICE

2 cups apple juice
¾ cup brown sugar
½ teaspoon ground cinnamon
1 cinnamon stick
3 whole cloves
4 cups Florida orange juice
1 cup freshly squeezed lemon juice
fruit slices
whole cloves

Combine the apple juice, sugar, cinnamon, and cloves. Cover and simmer 5 minutes. Do not bring to a hard boil. Add the orange juice and lemon juice. Heat just to serving temperature. Long exposure to heat reduces the vitamin content of citrus fruits. Serve the juice immediately in mugs. Garnish with fruit slices that have been studded with whole cloves.

Makes 12 servings.

ORANGE SMILES

Slice a Florida orange into four sections from the top to bottom of orange (do not slice crosswise). Gently separate the pulp from the peeling for about 1 inch on each end of the slices. Leave the pulp attached in the center of each slice. Serve the Smiles as finger foods.

OATMEAL GOODIES

2 cups quick-cooking oatmeal, uncooked
1⅔ cups buttermilk
2 eggs
1 teaspoon baking soda

1 tablespoon hot water
1 teaspoon salt
½ cup brown sugar
¾ cup sifted all-purpose flour

Preheat oven to 400 degrees and grease muffin tins. About 1 hour in advance of baking time, combine the oatmeal and buttermilk. Let this mixture stand until buttermilk has been absorbed—about 1 hour.

Next, beat the 2 eggs well and set aside. Dissolve soda in the water.

Combine the salt, sugar, flour; add the soda mixture and the beaten eggs. Mix well; add the oatmeal and buttermilk.

Cook in prepared muffin tins or small loaf pans. Bake 20 to 30 minutes.

Makes 15 servings.

EGGS, ETC.

Eggs, being a high source of protein, are good snack foods for children. But no self-respecting child would consider a plain, ordinary egg as a snack, no matter how hungry he was.

But if something special was done to the egg, it might make the choice more tempting.

Mash 4 hard-cooked yolks with a couple of tablespoons of finely chopped ham. Add a dash of sweet pickle juice and a tablespoon mayonnaise. Make a smooth firm paste to fill egg whites.

Mash liver loaf luncheon meat and add to the yolks. Mix with prepared mustard and mayonnaise. Add ½ teaspoon vinegar, salt, and pepper. Replace in whites and sprinkle with paprika.

Other add-ins might be finely chopped anchovies with sour cream, and top eggs with a slice of an olive.

This recipe of Mrs. Billy Graham's falls in her category of "anything-but-fancy." But, as she and I agreed, that is just what you need for a growing family. Ruth also adds wheat germ to this recipe for extra nutrition.

BRAN MUFFINS
Ruth Graham (Mrs. Billy)

6 cups raisin bran flakes (or other suitable cereals and nuts, if desired)
2 cups boiling water
3 cups sugar
1 cup vegetable shortening
4 eggs, beaten
1 quart buttermilk
1 teaspoon salt
4 teaspoons soda
5 cups flour

Preheat oven to 400 degrees. Combine 2 cups of cereal and boiling water in a bowl, stir well, and let cool. Cream sugar and shortening. Add eggs, beat well, stir in buttermilk, salt, and soda. Fold in flour, remaining 4 cups cereal, and the cooled cereal mixture.

These can be baked in tins for 15 to 20 minutes. But the nice part is that you can store them in the refrigerator for several weeks in a covered container and use whenever you like.

This recipe is truly marvelous. When I first tried it, I was amazed at the amount of batter. I baked all I thought we could eat and refrigerated the rest, as Ruth suggested. That bowl of muffin batter was the handiest bowl in my refrigerator—for several weeks. It really does keep well. I often found myself dipping in and baking a few more muffins for breakfast, then a few for snacks, and a few for lunch.

MINT COOLER

3 cups milk
3 tablespoons sugar
finely crushed ice

1½ cups Florida orange juice
mint leaves
orange slices

Combine milk, sugar, and crushed ice in either a shaker or a blender. Place in freezer for 15 to 20 minutes or until ice crystals begin to form around the edges of the container.

Remove and add orange juice. Shake vigorously. Pour into serving glasses, add mint and orange slices.

Makes 6 servings.

DEAR LORD. Dear God, what a price-less treasure you have sent us—this lit-tle child.

Maybe he will be one of the great persons of mankind. Maybe he will be one to heal men's souls or learn to heal men's bodies. Or perhaps our little child will have the mind that can discover a cure for the many hurts and hungers of society.

Maybe this little child will be the daddy who thinks of new ways to tell his little child of your great love.

What a miracle, God, that you should entrust so great a treasure to us! And to think that his future usefulness to you and your service depends so strongly on my care of him now. His physical needs as he grows, his emotional needs as he matures, and his spiritual needs as he seeks—all a part of my daily interaction with him.

Dear Lord, give me constant assur-ance of your guidance.

CHAPTER 4

PEANUT BUTTER—THE STAFF
OF LIFE

I'm not sure why I included an entire chapter in this book on peanut butter. But somehow as I considered families, children, and eating, the image of a big jar of peanut butter stood out like a neon sign in my mind. There is something about peanut butter and kids that just goes together.

I even imagine that the little children growing up in remote jungle civilizations must have some form of peanut butter. Childhood and peanut butter are synonymous. It is the undisputed, top-rated basic food for sandwiches, followed by bologna as a close second.

Of course, as you move into adulthood, maturity brings the knowledge that (1) there are other sandwich materials, and (2) that peanut butter is good in ways other than spread on a slice of bread. (You learn this about the same time you give up bubble gum.)

There are all kinds of recipes that put peanut butter on vegetables, in meat dishes, as part of a soup dish, sauces, dressings, and as food for the birds.

But for the purposes of this chapter we will consider peanut butter as the nutritious staff of life for families with little, middle-sized, and big children.

Each child in our family (and every other child I know) has personality characteristics that make him a truly unique individual. Our children's likes and dislikes seemed to surface at an early age and have persisted through childhood.

One characteristic of each child that will always be outstanding in my mind is the way he wants his peanut butter sandwich fixed. After spreading several thousand peanut butter sandwiches, I am convinced that a child's peanut butter sandwich preference is as much a part of his personality as his hair color.

These are the kinds of peanut butter sandwiches that I know about:

Whole. These are made with two complete slices of bread, peanut butter in between, and the bread slices put back together so that they "match" like they came out of the sack.

Folded. Peanut butter on one half of a slice of bread with the bread folded over exactly in half.

On the half slice. Now, this sandwich is very similar to the previous one. Unless you are a mother, the difference could go completely unnoticed. But the very important difference is that the one slice of bread is cut with a knife and then placed on top of the spread peanut butter—not folded.

Whole, cut. Again the description is very similar, but your little customer will be very quick to point out the difference. This sandwich is fixed like number one, but then it is cut in two with a knife. Whether the cut is made on the straight or on the diagonal is vitally important to a true peanut butter gourmet.

A folded-bread man can *never* bite into a cut sandwich, and a cut-only man cannot *bear* the sight of a folded slice of bread.

Is this silly, trite, undeserving of being published? To me, fixing a peanut butter sandwich *just right* is one of my very favorite things to do. I feel that it is another way I have of saying, "I love you, I think your ideas and preferences are important, just like I think you are important." These are the really priceless treasured things that cement a family together.

Another outstanding characteristic of peanut butter is that it is the one food on earth that is loved (adored) by kids *and* is nutritious. That is some feat! In fact, no other food ranks so high in such a wide range of nutrients.

It was invented as the original health food. A doctor, in 1890, searched for a high-protein food for his patients. He ground up roasted peanuts in a meat grinder, added salt, and fed it to his patients.

So reach for the health jar and try these favorite Green recipes.

MARSHMALLOW STACKS

Spread peanut butter on a saltine cracker. Top with a small square of chocolate from a candy bar. Put a marshmallow on top and toast. Yum!

HONEY BALLS

¼ cup peanut butter
3 tablespoons honey

½ cup non-fat dry milk
½ cup dry cereal, crushed

In a small bowl, combine the peanut butter and honey. Blend in the dry milk; mix well. Grease hands. Using about 2 tablespoons of dough, form into balls. Roll in crushed cereal; chill several hours.
Makes 16 to 18 sweets.

PEANUT BUTTER DOUGH

½ jar peanut butter
2–3 tablespoons honey

2–3 cups non-fat dry milk

Put the peanut butter in a large bowl. Add honey and mix well. Add powdered milk a little at a time. Mix with a large wooden spoon until the batter gets too thick. Continue to mix by hand until the mixture has a dough-like consistency. Now the dough can be shaped or molded into whatever the child wants. Decorate the designs with sprinkles, raisins, or nuts. Chill thoroughly.

PEANUT BUTTER PANCAKES

Add ⅓ cup peanut butter to one recipe of your favorite pancake batter and proceed as directed.

PEANUT BUTTER TARTS

½ cup peanut butter
⅔ cup confectioners' sugar
8 individual tart shells, baked
2 cups milk
⅓ cup flour

½ cup sugar
3 eggs
2 tablespoons butter
1 teaspoon vanilla
chopped peanuts

Preheat oven to 325 degrees. Mix the peanut butter and confectioners' sugar. Spoon about 2 to 3 tablespoons of the mixture into each tart shell. Spread it evenly. In a heavy saucepan, scald milk. Mix flour and sugar. Separate the eggs and beat the egg yolks. Stir flour mixture and the egg yolks into the scalded milk. Cook and stir until the sauce begins to thicken. Add butter and vanilla. Pour over the peanut butter in the tart shells.

Make meringue with the remaining egg whites and top each tart. Sprinkle with a topping of chopped peanuts. Bake until the meringue is lightly browned.

PEANUT BUTTER TOPPING

Often we enjoy crunchy peanut butter straight out of the jar as a topping for ice cream.

If we put this combination in a fancy parfait glass, we call it peanut butter parfait.

At other times I mix 1 part smooth peanut butter with 1 part canned chocolate syrup. This topping for ice cream is absolutely delicious and goes well as a party dish or luncheon dessert. Top each serving with chopped peanuts and a stemmed cherry.

PEANUT BUTTER AND BANANAS

This is a good child recipe given to me by our oldest son, Bobby. We serve it usually when we have children over to visit.

1 cup peanut butter   *2 bananas*
½ cup honey

Mix peanut butter with honey in a small bowl until creamy. Peel bananas and dip them in the peanut butter mix—a bite at a time.

Makes 2 servings.

PEANUT BUTTER SHAPES

This recipe originated in Alabama, a grand and fitting place for a peanut-based recipe to have its origin. Most of the peanuts grown in the United States are grown in the Alabama-Georgia-northern Florida area. So, when a peanut butter recipe comes from this area, I feel confident it uses peanuts to their best advantage.

10 *slices day-old bread*	½ *teaspoon salt*
1 *cup crunchy peanut butter*	½ *cup peanut oil*

Use a small cookie cutter or candy mold to cut two or three shapes out of each slice of bread. Place the cut shapes and the remaining crusts in a slow oven (250 degrees) for 30 minutes.

Roll only the crusts to make crumbs.

Mix peanut butter, salt, and oil together.

Dip the bread shapes into the peanut butter mixture, then into the bread crumbs.

Chill and serve. Makes 25 to 30 small toast shapes. Good served as finger foods for children or as party food for luncheons.

Here is an unusual recipe, but one worthy of your time. Mrs. George McClure of Apopka, Florida, uses this recipe and serves it warm or ice cold, depending on the rest of the menu.

CREAM OF PEANUT SOUP
Mrs. George McClure

1 *medium onion, chopped*	2 *cups smooth peanut butter*
2 *ribs celery, chopped*	1¾ *cups light cream*
¼ *cup butter*	*chopped peanuts*
3 *tablespoons flour*	
2 *quarts chicken stock or canned*	
chicken broth	

Sauté onion and celery in butter until soft. Stir in flour until blended. Add chicken stock, stirring constantly. Bring to boil.

Remove from heat and rub through a sieve. Add peanut butter and cream; stir thoroughly. Return to heat; heat slowly, do not boil.

Garnish with chopped peanuts.

Makes 12 servings.

PEANUT BUTTER SANDWICHES (for adults only)

This recipe is classified for adults only because children usually revolt at the idea of "foreign" additions to their beloved peanut butter.

But a bit of nostalgia, this version of a peanut butter sandwich is quite good.

1 cup peanut butter

½ cup shredded coconut

1 small package cream cheese

½ cup honey

Mix all ingredients together well. Spread on bread slices. Fold or cut the bread just like you used to enjoy it.

DEAR LORD. *Thank you, God, for giving us the beautiful account of Jesus asking for the little children to come to him. I wonder if any of those little round faces who looked upon our loving Christ had ancient Palestine cookie crumbs in the corners of their mouths.*

I look at the little round faces looking at me—the ones with peanut butter on the cheek where the corner of the sandwich reached during the bite.

Thank you, God, for this little peanut butter face and for the little earthly cherub it belongs to.

And, O dear God, may I never get too busy or too unaware to stop and celebrate a peanut butter face.

CHAPTER 5

HAMBURGERS IN FIFTY-SEVEN VARIETIES

Standing tall in family popularity, right alongside peanut butter, is the classic hamburger. If I had to choose between the two, hamburger and peanut butter, for the number-one favorite in our household, I'm afraid I'd be as helpless as a cook who just ran out of salt.

Hamburger is the all-American way. It can be as simple as one plain, dry, meat patty between two slices of bun or as elegant as chopped steak smothered in mushroom sauce. The difference in preference depends on your age. Little fellows at our household have very strong feelings about covering a hamburger patty with anything but catsup.

I often wonder if children are born knowing about hamburgers or if it just comes to them out of the air—like germs. But whatever way, most children I know—and certainly the ones I live with—graduated directly from the baby bottle to hamburgers.

Hamburgers come in no less than fifty-seven varieties. Mothers and Daddies seem to prefer the nice fat, juicy ones that can be made at home. Kids invariably crave the thin, dry hamburgers purchased at a fast food restaurant.

Hamburgers can be made with the cheaper varieties of ground beef, or with ground chuck, or with ground sirloin. The difference in these selections is about enough to pay for the rest of the meal.

Hamburgers can be eaten at a nice family dinner table, or on the patio, driving in the car, sitting in the booth of a hamburger stand, walking out the back door, sitting in the sandbox, or fishing off the dock.

But the real message of hamburgers, to me, is familiarity. Hamburgers are not famous as a quality gourmet food. Nor are hamburgers famous for turning any event into a special occasion. But they are famous for being as all-American as apple pie and as traditional as the Fourth of July. As each child and each adult close their teeth on a big bite of hamburger, they can experience that calm, reassuring feeling, "I think I have done this same thing before." And every hamburger eater can safely vow, "I'm going to do this again." It is part of the process of tradition that binds one week to the next and one generation to another.

A beautiful example of this tradition in family togetherness was related to me by a young Christian mother in Abilene, Texas. Marilee Garner and her husband, Richard, have four young children and are dynamic Christian witnesses in their community. Marilee tells the story:

"My father was a Baptist minister in the West Texas area. Because of the heavy responsibilities connected with Sunday, our Saturday nights were traditionally low-keyed family evenings at home. I can't remember how it started, but the undisputed Saturday night menu was hamburgers—home style. Daddy cooked on the grill, rain or shine or sandstorm. He always carefully patted out each ground meat pattie on wax paper, turning the paper clockwise to get a perfect circle of meat. The ceremony was always the same.

"If we had plans with friends or had dates, the evening always included a stop at our house for Saturday night hamburgers.

"The three of us children married and the new in-laws fell comfortably into the tradition. Daddy turned into Granddaddy and the family menu remained the same.

"Then careers and jobs began separating our family with miles between. It was a painful separation because we had all been so close. At first, Saturday nights were the most lonesome times of the week for my newly formed little family. A big lump came in my throat as I began dinner preparations for that night each week.

"Until one night I discovered we were having hamburgers for Saturday night supper. It felt so right! And I never had to think about the menu from that Saturday on.

"Later I related this story to my sister and brother who lived with their families in distant cities. Would you believe they each had had a similar experience? And without knowing it, each of our separate families had been carrying on the tradition of Saturday night hamburgers.

"Now, on each Saturday night, we all have a sense of closeness, despite the long distances between us, because of a family tradition that began one generation ago."

HAMBURGERS EXTRAORDINARY

Blend these ingredients for a tart teriyaki sauce: ⅓ cup canned consommé, ¼ cup chopped green onions, 3 tablespoons soy sauce, 3 tablespoons lime juice, 3 tablespoons honey, 1 clove garlic, mashed, 2 teaspoons freshly grated ginger. Mix the sauce with ground meat and form hamburger patties.

Spread onion butter on each side of hamburger buns before toasting. Make onion butter with 1 teaspoon toasted dried onions, ¼ teaspoon salt, ¼ teaspoon Worcestershire sauce, ½ cup softened butter.

Mix 1 package blue cheese and ½ cup softened butter. Let stand several hours. Spread on hamburger buns before serving.

To 1 pound ground beef, add 1 chopped onion, 1 cup tomato sauce, dash salt, 2 teaspoons dry mustard, dash chili powder, dash pepper, 2 teaspoons Worcestershire sauce, and 1 cup Wheat Chex. Form into patties and broil. Serve on toasted buns.

Top hamburger patties with Parmesan cheese and sesame seeds.

Combine 1 pound ground beef, ¼ cup French dressing, small chopped onion, salt, and pepper. Fry or grill patties on one side. Turn and top each patty with a cheese slice.

Brown 1 pound ground meat, ½ cup chopped onion. Add 1 can condensed vegetable soup (or substitute bean with bacon, cream of celery, or minestrone soup), 2 tablespoons catsup, dash pepper. Simmer 5 to 10 minutes. Serve hot over hot hamburger buns.

Top hamburger patties with this sauce: 1 small can tomato sauce, 3 tablespoons chopped walnuts, 1 tablespoon brown sugar, dash salt, 1 teaspoon prepared mustard.

Combine 1 envelope onion soup mix, 1½ cups water, ½ cup vinegar, ½ cup butter or margarine, ½ cup sugar, 2 teaspoons prepared mustard, 2 teaspoons salt, 1 teaspoon pepper. Simmer ten minutes. Add 1 cup catsup. Stir and heat. Use as a basting sauce for hamburger patties.

For hamburger patties in a cup-like shape. Fill the cup with canned sliced mushrooms. Top with more ground beef and pinch edges together. Broil as usual.

Form more cup-shaped patties. This time, fill with sliced, stuffed green olives and chopped onion. Broil. Top with sauce made with 1 small can tomato sauce, ⅛ teaspoon oregano, and ¼ teaspoon tarragon. Simmer sauce before basting burger.

Try making a skillet-size hamburger and cut it into serving wedges like a pie.

Hint: Handle hamburger meat lightly so it just holds together. Too much handling makes it tough.

Add onion juice, parsley, and a little lemon juice to the patties before cooking.

Add ½ cup grated Parmesan cheese to ground beef. Then shape into patties.

Form meat around cheese hunks.

Add a slice of tomato to the top of a half-cooked hamburger patty. Top the tomato with chopped parsley and Parmesan cheese.

Mix 4 tablespoons butter and 1 teaspoon capers. Shape into four or five small balls. Freeze for 1 hour. Form ground meat around a caper ball and broil as usual.

HAMBURGER BEANS

2 onions, peeled and chopped	2 tablespoons brown sugar
2 tablespoons bacon drippings	1¼ teaspoons chili powder
2 cups canned tomatoes	3 large cans beans
1 teaspoon garlic powder	3 strips uncooked bacon

Preheat oven to 325 degrees. Sauté onion in bacon fat. Add tomatoes and seasonings. Add beans and mix well. Pour into a baking dish. Lay the bacon slices across the top. Bake for 45 minutes.

Makes 12 servings.

A friend, Mrs. Esther Sonnenberg, sent me this recipe from Osh-kosh, Wisconsin. Mrs. Sonnenberg and her daughter, Bernice, are the kind of cooks who walk into a kitchen and work magic on food, turning every dish into something really delicious. Bernice says the two of them often experiment with different kinds of cooking, "mixing this and fixing that." Others of their recipes appear throughout the book. But this one certainly is a natural addition to any hamburger recipe collection.

BARBECUED HAMBURGER
Mrs. Esther Sonnenberg

1 pound ground beef	*1 tablespoon catsup*
1 small onion, chopped	*1 teaspoon prepared mustard*
1 small green pepper, chopped	*1 teaspoon salt*
2 stalks celery, chopped	*dash pepper*
2 tablespoons oil	*6 hamburger buns*
½ can condensed chicken	
gumbo soup (about ⅔ cup)	

In skillet, cook meat, onion, green pepper, and celery in oil until meat is browned and vegetables are tender; pour off fat. Blend in soup, catsup, mustard, salt, and pepper; heat, stirring occasionally. Serve on buns.
Makes 6 servings.

When you are fixing hamburger for the kids but want something a little more adult for grownups, here is a suggestion. Use basically the same recipe. Shape some of the meat mixture into hamburger patties for the children and use the rest for stuffing a vegetable.

HAMBURGER STUFFING

1 pound ground beef	*1 can stewed tomatoes*
1 medium onion, chopped	*2 tablespoons lemon juice*
½ teaspoon chili powder	*½ cup chopped green olives*
salt and pepper	*with pimiento*
dash garlic salt	*1 cup shredded, Cheddar cheese*
1 cup cooked rice	

Brown meat. Add onion, cook until tender. Add seasonings, rice, tomatoes, lemon juice, and olives. Cover and simmer 5 minutes.

Use this mixture to stuff green peppers, tomatoes, or onions.

For stuffed peppers, select 4 medium-size peppers. Cut off tops and remove insides. Wash and drain.

Precook green peppers in salted water 5 minutes.

Stuff with meat mixture and stand the peppers upright in a baking dish. Bake at 350 degrees for 25 minutes.

Sprinkle the hot peppers with cheese.

For stuffed onions, select 4 large onions. Remove outside skin and cut off stem top. Scoop out insides of onion, leaving about three layers of onion to form cup.

Sprinkle inside of onion with salt. Stuff with meat mixture. Bake at 350 degrees for 25 minutes. Garnish with shredded cheese.

For stuffed tomatoes, follow above directions stuffing 4 large tomatoes with meat mixture and cooking at 350 degrees for 20 minutes.

CHEESE BURGER KABOBS

1 pound ground beef
1 egg
½ cup dry bread crumbs
1 envelope onion soup mix
½ cup water
12 hamburger pickle slices

6 Gruyère cheese cubes (about 1-inch)
6 slices bacon
12 cherry tomatoes
1 medium-size green pepper

Combine beef, egg, bread crumbs, soup mix, and water. Mix well. Shape a heaping tablespoonful of beef mixture into a patty. Place a pickle slice on two sides of a cube of cheese and mold the meat patty around the cheese to form a meatball. Wrap each meatball with a slice of bacon. Secure with a toothpick.

Thread meatballs carefully on a skewer along with two slices of green pepper and cherry tomatoes. Broil or grill about 4 to 10 minutes per slice.

Makes 6 servings.

CRAB BURGERS
Joyce Vinoski (Mrs. Bernie)

1 cup flaked crab meat
¼ cup diced celery
2 tablespoons chopped onion

½ cup shredded Cheddar cheese
½ cup mayonnaise (about)
hamburger buns

Combine crab meat, celery, onion, and cheese. Add mayonnaise. Spread on buttered halved hamburger buns. Broil until hot and brown.

"The first time I ever made these someone thought they looked like cole slaw sandwiches!!"

CONDENSED MILK COOKIES
Joyce Vinoski (Mrs. Bernie)

1 can condensed milk
2 cup graham cracker crumbs
1 cup nuts

1 package (6 ounces) chocolate chips
1 can of coconut or 1 cup

Preheat oven to 350 degrees. Mix all ingredients and flatten on greased cookie sheet. Bake 20 minutes.

"Easy enough for the children to make by themselves. A good top off to hamburgers or crab burgers."

DEAR LORD. O Lord, who made a celebration out of five loaves and two fish, accept our celebrating gratitude for these hamburgers. More importantly, thank you for the realities of our love for each other in this family. Thank you that each mealtime together is a celebration of family togetherness in your tender care.

CHAPTER 6

WHAT DO YOU WANT FOR BREAKFAST?

"This is the day the Lord has made. We will rejoice and be glad in it." (Psalm 118:24)

I try to remember this verse in the mornings as I hear the alarm clock go off. I get up at six o'clock each morning, and for me that isn't easy. I am not an early morning person. But in order to get our household off to a peaceful, even start, this routine seems to work best.

I strongly believe the woman in the family sets the tone of the day for each member of the family. The husband and children simply mirror her introduction to the day.

If I oversleep, wake tired, late, and grumpy, I can count on this same attitude from at least five other people before any of us set foot outside the front door. That is the day we can't find matching socks, at least one shoestring breaks, schoolbooks are nowhere to be found, no one feels like eating, fights and disagreements occur, and the car is late pulling out of the driveway for school. Frankly, I want better than that for my children and husband.

The first item on my daily schedule is private devotional time. During these moments I think about each individual member of the family and pray for their specific needs of the day.

I pray for Bob in his coming daily schedule and responsibilities. I thank God for the miracle of our love and the beauty of our companionship. I pray daily that God will help me grow into a better wife, more devoted to Bob as the head of our household.

I pray for each child and whatever problems he may be facing for that day. I remember when Bobby had a part in a school play. He played the part of the Jamestown preacher Roger Williams. Bobby took the part so seriously and worked very hard memorizing his lines. He prayed that he might do a good job. I can remember taking a little extra time in my private time that morning to pray more specifically for him.

And when Gloria made her singing debut at church recently. She had a series of sore throats and the performance had to be postponed several times. But the evening came. We were out of town but I prayed very specifically for her. The tapes they made for us were splendid. I was surprised at what a good strong voice she was developing already.

Each devotional time ends with a heartful of praise for four healthy children and the divine blessedness of our family. Another Scripture that I enjoy claiming each morning is 1 Thessalonians 5:16–24:

> Always be joyful. Always keep on praying. No matter what happens, always be thankful, for this is God's will for you who belong to Christ Jesus.
>
> Do not smother the Holy Spirit. Do not scoff at those who prophesy, but test everything that is said to be sure it is true, and if it is, then accept it. Keep away from every kind of evil. May the God of peace himself make you entirely pure and devoted to God; and may your spirit and soul and body be kept strong and blameless until that day when our Lord Jesus Christ comes back again.

Then to the kitchen for breakfast.

It is easy to let breakfast get into a dull routine. Somehow mornings are a difficult time for me to apply my creative best to anything. But just as prayer sets the spiritual tone for our day, so breakfast sets our physical tone for the day.

Breakfast is an exceedingly important meal. One third of the recommended nutrients for a day should come at breakfast. Children have a hard, fast-paced morning at school. They really deserve the best send-off I can manage. So, I strive for variety in our breakfast menus to keep interest and appetites alert, and I have to plan in advance in order to do this.

Once at the table, we read portions from a favorite devotional book and pray for each other.

Another important family event in our morning routine is the family prayer time at breakfast. The children, as well as Bob and I, feel free to tell of special needs we will face during the day. We pray for the needs as they are mentioned and it reminds us to think short silent prayers for each other during the day. I feel that of all the family experiences we have, this one is surely among the most rewarding. This custom helps fortify each of us against problems of the day ahead. It teaches the children the value of relying on God for strength and stability during the day. (We often report about answered prayers at the evening meals.) Then off to school and to work and my little family reduces in number rather quickly. I usually drive the children to school myself just to give a little extra moral support for the day.

On Saturdays the children are allowed to plan and prepare their own breakfast. It is a big event for them and one they seem to enjoy from one week to the next. Besides, it lets Mommy and Daddy catch up on a little sleep.

The recipes I have decided to share in this chapter are special favorites and are ones that really help provide variety in breakfast planning. Coupled with your own favorites, you can have menus planned for several weeks.

FRENCH TOAST DE LUXE

3 bananas, sliced
¾ cup Florida orange juice
4 eggs, separated
1 cup half and half

¾ cup flour
10 slices day-old bread
butter
confectioners' sugar

Place bananas in orange juice, set aside. In shallow bowl, beat egg yolks until thick and lemon-colored; add half and half. Gradually add flour, beating constantly, until batter is smooth. Beat egg whites until stiff peaks form; gently fold into yolk mixture. Dip bread in batter. In skillet, melt 1 tablespoon butter; fry each slice of bread 2 to 3 minutes on each side or until golden brown, adding more butter as needed. Serve topped with the sliced bananas and sprinkled with confectioners' sugar.

Makes 10 slices.

BANANA BREAKFAST BREAD

3 cups flour
1 cup sugar
1½ tablespoons baking powder
1½ teaspoons salt

4½ tablespoons melted butter
½ cup milk
4 large eggs, beaten
1½ cups ripe mashed bananas

Preheat oven to 350 degrees. Mix all ingredients in large bowl. Beat at medium speed for 1 minute. Pour into four small loaf pans. Bake for 45 to 50 minutes. Cool on a wire rack before removing from pan.

Since this makes four loaves, I usually use two and freeze two. Then we have extra available for short-notice guests or when I am rushed for time.

We also slice it, spread it with butter, and toast under the broiler.

BREAKFAST EGGS—THREE VARIATIONS

Slice ½ pound cooked ham into julienne strips. Cook in 2 tablespoons butter until heated thoroughly. Lightly beat 8 eggs with a little milk, salt, pepper, and 1 tablespoon chopped chives. Scramble eggs with ham. Avoid overstirring or overcooking.

Add ¼ pound diced Swiss cheese to 6 beaten eggs. Scramble in butter. Add salt and pepper to taste.

Hard-cooked eggs (2 per person) sliced. In individual ovenproof serving dishes, place one layer cooked ham, diced, one layer of sliced eggs. Add 2 tablespoons prepared mustard to a medium white sauce. Pour over ham and eggs. Salt and pepper to taste. Heat in 350-degree oven about 10 minutes. Serve with toast.

ORANGE ALASKA

This dish is certainly more like a dessert than a breakfast food, so there is never any objection to eating it.

3 large Florida oranges	4 egg whites
1 pint vanilla ice milk	½ cup sugar

Preheat oven to 450 degrees. Cut oranges in half; section to remove fruit. Using a spoon, scoop out remaining membrane, leaving shell clean. Fill each shell with ⅓ cup ice milk; top with orange segments and place in freezer.

Beat egg whites until foamy; gradually add sugar, 1 tablespoon at a time, beating well after each addition until stiff peaks form. Cover ice milk and fruit with meringue, making certain to seal edges completely.

Place fruit in an 11 × 7 × 2-inch baking pan; bake 2 to 3 minutes or until meringue is browned. Serve at once.
Makes 6 servings.

SPICED HOT CHOCOLATE

½ cup sugar
½ cup cocoa
1 cup boiling water
⅛ teaspoon salt
8 whole cloves

4 cups milk
1 cup light cream
½ teaspoon vanilla
½ pint cream, whipped
8 cinnamon sticks

Mix sugar, cocoa, and water in a large saucepan. Add salt and cloves. Bring to a boil, reduce heat, and simmer for 3 minutes. Stir constantly. Add milk, light cream, and vanilla. Heat thoroughly.

If you have a blender, froth the drink just a little before pouring into serving cups. Top with a dab of whipped cream and a cinnamon stick.
Makes 8 servings.

GINGERBREAD PANCAKES

1 egg, separated
2¼ cups sifted flour
½ teaspoon salt
1¼ teaspoons soda

2 teaspoons ginger
1 cup dark molasses
½ cup milk
⅓ cup butter, melted

Beat egg white until stiff and set aside. Sift flour, salt, soda, and ginger together.

Combine egg yolk with molasses and milk. Beat well. Gradually add dry ingredients. Add melted butter and mix well. Fold in egg white. Pour small amounts of batter onto grill to make pancakes. Serve with melted butter and favorite syrup.
Makes 6 to 8 pancakes.

WHIPPED ORANGE BUTTER

1 stick butter or margarine
½ cup Florida orange juice
3 tablespoons grated orange rind

⅔ cup confectioners' sugar
1 teaspoon cinnamon

Whip the stick of butter until it is fluffy. Slowly add the remaining ingredients and continue beating until fluffy.

Serve on toast, biscuits, pancakes, or waffles. Keeps well in refrigerator for several days so it can be reused.

JELLY ROLL PANCAKES

1 recipe for your favorite pancakes
milk
2 tablespoons melted butter

1 cup favorite preserves
or
1 pint fresh fruit (pineapple, strawberries, peaches, or apricots)

Add a little extra milk and the melted butter to your pancake recipe to make batter thinner than usual.

Cook as usual, but make the pancakes very thin. Remove from grill and put 2 to 3 tablespoons of preserves or fresh fruit on the pancake. Roll up jelly roll style and secure with a toothpick. These make a good-size single serving. Sprinkle powdered sugar on top.

This recipe is absolutely synonymous in my mind with Grandma Berry. Again, it is one of those recipes that just doesn't fit on paper too well. I'll give it to you just like Grandma gave it to me. With practice, I have been able to do it very nearly like hers.

SODA BISCUITS
Grandma Berry

1½ cups self-rising flour
buttermilk—add small amounts to flour till it is thick enough to make dough.

Preheat oven to 475 degrees.

Use your rolling pin and roll out dough on a floured board to about 1-inch thickness—or more if you like.

Cut into biscuits—put into greased pan.

Bake 15 minutes, or until golden brown on top.

Kay and Don McNeill have visited us at Villa Verde. I love to see them come. It always reminds me of the warm, sweet times I had with them and their family when I worked on the Breakfast Club Show.

I have never known a closer and more dedicated family than the McNeills. They eat well, love the outdoors, and are such whole, happy people. Family togetherness is at its best in the McNeill family.

Kay is a fantastic cook and mother. I have enjoyed this recipe for pancakes and her beautiful prayer.

PANCAKES (Silver Dollar Size)
Kay McNeill (Mrs. Don)

1 cup biscuit mix	1 cup sour cream
1 teaspoon salt	1 cup whipping cream
1 teaspoon baking soda	3 eggs

Mix dry ingredients first—then the rest—beating whites of eggs and yolks separately. Let stand overnight in refrigerator. Cook on griddle at 350 to 400 degrees. Serve with melted butter and heated syrup. Powdered sugar and lemon can also be used.

Leftover batter—add chocolate syrup—cook on griddle—silver-dollar size—serve as dessert. On each pancake put whipped cream or ice cream, top with chocolate fudge sauce. This chocolate pancake batter will keep in refrigerator 2 days.

SHARE A PRAYER

Kay McNeill

O GOD, *we have gathered to* Share a Prayer *with our brothers and sisters, to give greater glory to you, our* Father. *We pray that we may increase our concern for each other's needs and happiness and holiness, to demonstrate to the wayward our* Faith, *to share with those in despair our* Hope, *to give to all who need affection our* Love, *in the conviction that we are all loved by you, our eternal* God. Amen.

CHAPTER 7

VEGETABLES KIDS WILL EAT, MAYBE

Even though your children are positive they like dessert better than vegetables (or *anything* better than vegetables) you can do a lot to change their minds. You just have to give vegetables a little special attention and imagination. For some reason, our finest culinary efforts usually stop just short of vegetables. It is too easy just to "open a can of peas and cook a package of frozen corn."

And, unfortunately, vegetables are considered "necessary" to a balanced diet and dessert is not. So, maybe mothers tend to oversell vegetables. There is that strange something in every child that causes him to do more of what he *wants* to do and less of what he *has* to do. I wonder if years of hearing, "Be sure to eat your broccoli," is the very reason he no longer eats broccoli.

Of course, maybe we spend more time "selling" the vegetables ("I'm sure you want some of this delicious squash!") because the vegetables look and taste as if they need selling. Previously, I mentioned that if we spent as much time on vegetables as we spend on birthday cakes, the results would be more exciting mealtimes.

Try changing your sales pitch. Refrain from mentioning vegetables as "so good for you." Instead, concentrate on making vegetable dishes so marvelous tasting and looking that they are irresistible.

I was looking through an old cookbook from Grandma Berry's days. The printing date is 1875. I wondered what methods were used in her day to add special touches to vegetables. To my surprise, there were very few suggestions for vegetables. Apparently they had only fresh vegetables available during the growing season. So the vegetables were just cooked, fresh from the garden, and that was that. Canned or frozen vegetables were not around for a quick snatch from the shelf. Vegetables were simply just not available long enough for the families to tire of them.

Our recent generations are very fortunate to have not only frozen and canned vegetables available twelve months out of the year, but to have fresh vegetables for many months of the year. Thanks to modern trucking systems, most of today's supermarket produce counters are heavy with excellent vegetable selections year round. Scientific agriculture has created a whole new way of life for present-day families and their eating habits.

And, too, the increase in private family gardening accounts for more and better access to fresher vegetables. So mothers are constantly on the search for new, exciting ways to fix and serve vegetables.

Vegetables have a lot going for them as a type of food. They are the most attractive foods we have. They certainly are more colorful than meats or breads, or cereals or dairy products. They are more interesting in size, shape, and texture than most other classes of foods. Isn't it a wonder, then, that vegetables are so low on children's taste list?

Home economists assure us that all food is good food if it is cooked properly and served attractively. For some reason I usually think of vegetables when I hear that, mainly because there is truly a right way to make the most of vegetables.

Before sharing some of our favorite recipes, a few over-all hints about vegetables might be helpful:

Cook vegetables *only* until they are tender crisp. Overcooking makes flabby and mushy vegetables which are less attractive and less nutritious. Preserve the texture of the fresh vegetable.

Protect the color of the vegetable when you cook it. Long cooking or cooking in hard water turns nice bright colors into dull colors.

Serve vegetables attractively. Arrange together on a platter. Add a garnish of parsley or other vegetables. Consider contrasts in color, shape, and texture when combining vegetables for a menu.

Combine a vegetable with another well-liked food such as cheese, ham, bacon, or a sauce. Or combine a new vegetable with a favorite vegetable. An example is the Orange Sauce recipe which follows in this chapter. It has often turned several vegetables into favorites at our house.

Beware of canned and frozen vegetables! Their easy preparation can lead to the monotonous blahs! Take time to add a little zest with interesting combinations or seasonings.

ORANGE SAUCE

2 tablespoons cornstarch	¼ cup brown sugar
1 can frozen Florida orange juice	1 tablespoon butter
1 can water	

Moisten the cornstarch with half of the water. Smooth to a paste. Mix remaining water, orange juice, and sugar in small saucepan. Bring to a boil and add the cornstarch. Stir constantly and cook until clear and thick. Add butter and pour over vegetable.

This sauce has endless uses. My family has enjoyed it most on cooked carrots, beets, broccoli, and sweet potatoes. I'm sure other vegetables would do just as well. Experiment some on your own.

Makes about 2 cups.

EGGPLANT SOUFFLÉ

1 large eggplant	½ teaspoon black pepper
2 eggs, beaten	1 cup chopped celery
1 medium onion, chopped	1 clove garlic, minced
½ teaspoon salt	½ teaspoon marjoram
½ teaspoon thyme	1 cup grated cheese

Preheat oven to 350 degrees. Peel and chop eggplant. Cook until tender. Mash thoroughly with fork or beat with mixer. Add eggs and continue to beat.

Add other ingredients, reserving enough cheese to cover top. Bake 1 hour. Then sprinkle cheese over top and return to oven for 10 minutes. Serve hot.

Makes 8 servings.

LIMA BEAN CASSEROLE

2 packages frozen lima beans	1 can water chestnuts, drained
salt and pepper	and sliced
1 can cream of mushroom soup	
1 cup sour cream	

Preheat oven to 325 degrees. Cook lima beans according to directions. Add salt and pepper to taste.

Mix mushroom soup and sour cream. Add water chestnuts and lima beans. Pour into a baking dish. Bake covered for 30 minutes. Makes 8 servings.

PICKLED BRUSSELS SPROUTS

2 packages frozen brussels sprouts
1½ cups sugar
2 teaspoons cornstarch

¾ cup red wine vinegar
1 teaspoon salt
1 teaspoon oregano
dash coarse ground pepper

Cook sprouts according to instructions. Drain, reserving ¾ cup of liquid. In a small saucepan combine sugar, cornstarch, vinegar, and seasonings. Add ¾ cup cooking liquid from brussels sprouts. Simmer until sauce begins to thicken. Pour over brussels sprouts. Cover and refrigerate overnight.

Makes 6 to 8 servings.

SQUASH WITH PECANS

1 pound yellow squash
½ cup cooking oil
4 tablespoons butter
2 tablespoons flour

1 cup milk
¾ cup grated, processed cheese
½ cup coarsely chopped pecans

Preheat oven to 325 degrees. Wash squash and cut crosswise into ½-inch slices. Sauté squash in oil for 5 minutes. Drain and set aside.

In separate saucepan, melt butter, stir in flour, and add milk and cheese. Cook over medium low heat, stirring constantly to keep lumps from forming. Add pecans.

Put cooked squash into a shallow baking dish. Pour cheese sauce over. Bake uncovered 20 minutes.

Makes 6 to 8 servings.

CHEESE CAULIFLOWER

1 head cauliflower
boiling water

½ cup sour cream
¾ cup grated Cheddar cheese

Preheat oven to 350 degrees. Remove leaves and cut off tough end of stem of cauliflower. Place in saucepan, head up, in about 1 inch of boiling water. Reduce heat to simmer; cook until just barely tender (15 to 20 minutes, depending upon size). Drain; place in shallow 1-quart casserole. Top with sour cream, sprinkle with cheese, and bake 10 minutes or until cheese melts and is brown and bubbly.

Makes 4 to 6 servings.

ASPARAGUS AND DEVILED EGG SAUCE

1 package (10 ounces) frozen
   whole asparagus spears
3 hard-cooked eggs
⅓ cup mayonnaise

2 teaspoons prepared mustard
1 teaspoon pickle juice
¼ cup finely chopped celery

Cook asparagus as package directs; drain and arrange on serving platter. While asparagus cooks, chop 2 of the hard-cooked eggs and slice 1; set aside. In small bowl, combine remaining ingredients; add the chopped egg. Pour sauce over hot asparagus; garnish with sliced egg.

Makes 3 to 4 servings.

GREEN BEANS AND PEAS

1 package frozen French-style
   beans
1 package frozen green peas

1 can mushroom steak sauce
1 cup sour cream
1 can fried onion rings

This is one of the easiest ways imaginable to dress up frozen green vegetables.

Cook the green beans and peas, following the directions on the package. Drain. Add mushroom steak sauce and sour cream. Blend and heat thoroughly. Top with fried onion rings just before serving.

Makes 8 servings.

This idea is absolutely guaranteed to make vegetable eaters and artist-designers out of your children.

Provide an assortment of raw, cooked, or canned vegetables: chopped celery, thin carrot sticks, slices of pimiento, olives, green peas (cooked), shredded cabbage, pecans, almonds, cauliflowerets, etc.

Allow the children to arrange the vegetables in a design in the bottom of the pan. A face, mosaic, or child picture of any kind will be interesting.

DESIGNER VEGETABLE SALAD

2 *cups vegetables*
1 *package (6 ounces) lemon-*
  flavored gelatin
3 *cups boiling water*

2 *tablespoons vinegar*
¾ *cup mayonnaise*
dash paprika

Arrange vegetables in attractive design on bottom of a 6-cup mold. Dissolve gelatin in boiling water; add vinegar. Carefully spoon enough gelatin into mold just to cover vegetables; chill until set. Chill remaining gelatin until mixture just begins to set (about consistency of unbeaten egg whites). Using electric mixer, beat mayonnaise and paprika into reserved gelatin; spoon over vegetable mixture in mold; chill until set. To serve, unmold onto platter lined with salad greens.

Makes 12 servings (½ cup each).

POTATO SCULPTURE

Preheat oven to 350 degrees. Prepare a package (5 ounces) of instant potatoes according to package directions; cool slightly. Add 2 egg yolks; beat well.

Arrange the potato mixture in a design on an 11 × 7 × 2-inch baking pan. A clown head, a happy face, a house are all fun to begin with.

Color can be added to certain areas by painting on beaten egg with a pastry brush. The potato coated with egg will turn a shiny brown when baked.

Also use little cutouts of cheese, sprinkle small areas with paprika or celery seed to add design.

Bake 15 to 20 minutes or until potatoes are browned.

Makes 8 servings (½ cup each).

A favorite vegetable recipe is from Mrs. Grady Wilson. Wilma and I share a favorite Scripture verse; I like to think about this verse when I have housework or cooking to do. "And whatever you do or say, let it be as a representative of the Lord Jesus, and come with him

into the presence of God the Father to give him your thanks."
(Colossians 3:17)

SQUASH MC DONALD
Wilma Wilson (Mrs. Grady)

yellow crooknecked squash,
    washed and sliced
1 onion, diced
½ teaspoon salt
¼ cup water

1 cup grated Cheddar cheese
1 egg
½ cup milk
buttered cracker crumbs

Preheat oven to 400 degrees. Cook squash and onion in salted
water in covered pan over medium heat until tender, stirring occasionally (about 20 minutes). Drain. Put half of squash into a Pyrex
serving bowl. Add egg and milk combined. Cover with a layer of half
of the cheese. Add remaining squash and fork it in. Sprinkle on
remaining cheese. Cover top with buttered crumbs. Bake until brown
for 30 to 40 minutes.

DEAR LORD, *these mealtimes get so hectic, I really can't remember why we even try to eat together. The teasing and the touching and the spilling get worse with every meal.*

O Lord, if this is family togetherness, deliver me to solitude (temporarily).

Jesus taught patience and long suffering. I'm sure He must have had our mealtimes in mind.

God, giver of all good gifts, please give me the gift of patience to prepare, serve, and endure one more mealtime. And safely lead me to another day when I can give this problem my positive best instead of my negative worst!

PART II

HAPPY BIRTHDAY

CHAPTER 8

HAPPY BIRTHDAYS AT VILLA VERDE

In our family, we are very big on birthdays. They are like a national holiday. The only trouble is we have so many birthdays to celebrate. The household staff is always given a birthday party on their special day. Our two secretaries, Diane Callicutt and Judy Higgins, are on the birthday party list. Jody Dunton (nurse to our twins when they were born) is like family, so we celebrate her birthday like a family member. Then, with four children's birthdays and Bob's and mine, we are in a state of constant birthday celebration.

Family birthdays at Villa Verde are celebrated in two ways. First, we have a family dinner for the honored person. This in itself is a big event. It always includes the household staff, Pedro and Winnie, Coco the cat, Flika the dog, all the children, Bob, and me. The honoree gets to select the menu for the evening—usually hamburgers or spaghetti and meatballs. Then it ends with ice cream and cake.

Following this there is a full-scale party for school friends at a later time. Because of school days and our erratic schedules, it is not always possible to have the party on the birth date, but we have it as soon after as we can.

I used to be very big on themes for the children's birthday parties. The most elaborate birthday party we ever had was for Bobby. We had a pirate treasure hunt on a small island. We went over early and hid treasures all over the island. We found some plastic skeleton heads at a party shop, so we put the "treasures" inside the skulls. The treasures were tickets to a movie later on, small toys, and games. Of course, the "pirate" who found the most got a prize. Everyone got prizes before it was over. Our birthday parties nearly always send children away with far more than they bring.

I also remember a carnival party we had for Gloria. We even set up booths. Each booth was a game. We had things like dart throwing, apple bobbing, ring toss, and bean bag throw.

The decorations and atmosphere were just elaborate. I think I had more fun planning it than the kids had as guests.

I used to spend weeks in preparation for these parties. Now, I must honestly say, we don't do as much of these big-party things as we used to. Somehow you tend to do more for two children than you are able to maintain for four. Even though those big parties were fun, I have learned the children enjoy simple things just as well. I think they would rather have me spend the same amount of my time just doing things with them.

Now the older children seem to enjoy spend-the-night slumber parties or swimming parties or simple cookouts. All with store-bought birthday cakes, of course.

BIRTHDAY GIFTS OF LOVE

Many families we are in contact with seem to be relying more and more on handmade gifts for birthdays and Christmas. It is a lovely idea, since the gift also gives a part of the creator.

I remember a real gift of love I gave Bob for his birthday one year. Since he is especially fond of eating and of Italian food, I cooked him the grandest Italian meal ever. I worked for weeks. I searched the recipe books and planned each course to the letter. I even made egg noodles from scratch. It was truly magnificent. Bob was delighted and still refers to it as one of the best birthdays he ever had. I enjoyed it because it was a real love gift.

Another family we heard from gives word gifts for birthdays. Each family member thinks of all the reasons why he is thankful for and proud of the birthday honoree. At the birthday dinner time, these word gifts are given in the form of a speech, poem, or story. These are recorded on a cassette player and are treasured remembrances for years, long after a store-bought gift would be forgotten.

I wonder if this delightful custom couldn't be expanded to friends also. Can you imagine visiting a friend on her birthday with a verbal gift of how much she has meant to you throughout the year?

Vera Semel, wife of Sandy (one of the producers of our Florida Citrus commercials), shared with us a custom of birthday celebration from her native Holland. There, a person always receives birthday visits from friends. On any birthday, Vera relates, a person could have a dozen or more pop-in calls from good friends. You can imagine her lonely feeling when she didn't find that same custom in America.

The Mancil Ezell family in Nashville, Tennessee, celebrates birthdays by reaching out to others. The birthday honoree spends the day making calls or writing letters to all the special people in his life during the past year. The notes are thank-you letters for friendship, mutual prayer projects, and acts of kindness. Even the children who are too young to write are given help by an older member so the feeling of saying "thank you" is taught early.

BIRTHDAY BARS

3 eggs
1 teaspoon vanilla
¾ cup flour
1 teaspoon baking powder

1 cup sugar
1 pound dates, cut up
1 cup pecans

Preheat oven to 350 degrees. Beat eggs with a fork and add vanilla. Sift flour, baking powder, and sugar together. Mix with dates and pecans. Add the dry ingredients to the eggs. Mix with a large wooden spoon as the mixture will be stiff.

Spread the mixture evenly in a well-greased glass baking dish. The mixture should be no thicker than ½ inch.

Bake for 35 minutes.

Cut into 3 × 1-inch bars and sprinkle with powdered sugar.

DEANA'S CHOCOLATE CHIP COOKIES—Good!
Deana Evans, daughter of Norm and Bobbie Evans

¾ cup brown sugar
¾ cup white sugar
1 cup shortening
2 eggs
1 teaspoon soda
1 teaspoon vanilla

1 teaspoon salt
2 cups flour
1 cup pecans
1 large package (12 ounces)
   chocolate chips

Preheat oven to 375 degrees. Blend together in a large mixing bowl the sugars, shortening, and eggs. Add all remaining ingredients and mix well.

Bake for 10 to 15 minutes.
Deana is eleven and a real cookie "pro"!

Sometimes for a party we freeze colored ice cubes for use in the punch, milk or lemonade. Trays can be colored by dropping in different cake colors, or the cubes can be made decorative by placing mint leaves, cherries, or small orange slices in each cube before freezing.

SUGARED ORANGE RINDS

5 medium Florida oranges (or 3 medium grapefruit)
12 cups water

GLAZE:

3 cups sugar
1⅓ cups water

To make peel, score oranges into quarters. Remove sections of peel and cut into strips about ⅜ inch wide (should have about 3 cups peel). In large saucepan, combine peel with 6 cups of the water. Cook uncovered about 10 minutes; drain, rinse, and repeat with remaining 6 cups water.

Meanwhile, to prepare glaze, in saucepan, combine 2½ cups of the sugar and 1⅓ cups water. Bring to a boil and cook about 10 minutes, or until mixture begins to be syrupy. Add cooked peel and cook over low heat, stirring frequently to prevent sticking, until peel has a glazed, candied appearance. Drain well; toss with remaining ½ cup sugar to coat well. Spread on wax paper to dry; store in an airtight container.

Makes about 3 cups.

LOLLIPOPS

This is one recipe I reserve for close adult supervision. Making lollipops is grand fun for the children, but the boiling liquid needs more child observation than participation.

1 cup sugar   *½ cup water*
½ cup corn syrup   *1 package Kool-Aid*

Mix sugar, corn syrup, and water. Stir until boiling, continue cooking until a hard thread forms. Remove from heat and add Kool-Aid. Pour onto greased platter. Cool to handle. Pull and shape, or snip with scissors.

COCONUT CHEWS

A rich chewy layered cookie bar.

1 cup sifted flour
1 cup firmly packed brown sugar
¼ cup butter
¼ cup shortening
2 eggs, well beaten
½ cup white corn syrup

1 teaspoon vanilla
2 tablespoons flour
1 teaspoon baking powder
½ teaspoon salt
1 cup shredded coconut
1 cup coarsely chopped nuts

Preheat oven to 350 degrees. Combine flour, ½ cup of the sugar, butter, and shortening; mix well. Press firmly into bottom of a 9-inch-square cake pan; bake 10 minutes.

Meanwhile, mix remaining ½ cup sugar with eggs; stir in corn syrup and vanilla. Add remaining ingredients, blending well. Spread evenly over partially baked bottom layer. Bake 25 minutes, or until top is golden brown. Cool; cut into 3 × 1-inch bars.

Makes 27 bars.

FLORIDA CHOCOLATE SAUCE

½ cup frozen Florida orange
juice concentrate
1 package (6 ounces) semisweet
chocolate pieces

¼ cup sugar
1 tablespoon butter

Combine all the ingredients in a small saucepan. Heat slowly and stir constantly until chocolate pieces are melted.

Serve warm over poundcake or ice cream.

PICKING GRAPES

Wash and chill an assortment of fresh grapes. Serve on a plate along with small containers of honey, poppy seed, dressing, and powdered sugar. Party dessert consists of picking grapes and dipping them in the choice of dip.

CRAZY CAKE
Aradith Palmer

3 cups flour
6 tablespoons cocoa
1 teaspoon salt
2 teaspoons soda
2 cups sugar

12 tablespoons cooking oil
2 tablespoons apple cider
   vinegar
2 cups water
2 teaspoons vanilla

Preheat oven to 350 degrees. Sift together the flour, cocoa, salt, and soda. Blend sugar with oil. Add vinegar, water, and vanilla.

Mix well with dry ingredients. Bake for 25 to 30 minutes in greased floured pan (11 × 14 inches) or 2 layer-cake pans.

Very good without icing, but fudge icing may be used.

Any recipe in this book with Joyce Vinoski's name on it is excellent! Joyce and Bernie were our neighbors when we first moved to Florida. Joyce had twins before our twins were born. She and Bernie are just the best parents and make the nicest family imaginable.

Joyce is the best cook ever. Her food is always so light and so delicate, and she seems to cook with the least amount of frustration. Any recipe that Joyce has given me I can believe is excellent.

In fact, so many of the regular recipes I use constantly originated with Joyce. The Florida Citrus Cake (which comes later in the book) came from Joyce.

CHEESE PUFFS
Joyce Vinoski (Mrs. Bernie)

1 loaf firm unsliced white bread
1 package (3 ounces) cream
   cheese

¼ pound sharp Cheddar cheese
½ cup butter or margarine
2 egg whites, stiffly beaten

Preheat oven to 400 degrees. Trim crust from bread, cut bread into 1-inch cubes. Melt cheeses and butter in top of double boiler over hot water until rarebit consistency. Remove from heat.

Fold in egg whites. Dip bread cubes into cheese mixture until well coated. Place on cookie sheet. Refrigerate overnight.

Bake in hot oven 12 to 15 minutes or until puffy and golden brown.

DEAR LORD. Among the brief information given us about Jesus' early childhood is the fact that he grew. "So Jesus grew both tall and wise, and was loved by God and Man." (Luke 2:52)

Birthdays are a time for measuring growth. With our children we like to see how much taller they are and what new skills they have learned in a year. We enjoy comparing last year's snapshots with present birthday pictures and exclaiming over the change.

But birthdays can be a time to measure more than physical growth. I often spend birthday time to reflect over the past year and measure how far I've come, how many hurdles have been overcome, how many spiritual advances have been made.

O Lord, help me never to come to a birthday where I can look back and see no growth in my life. Help each year to bring me closer to you.

CHAPTER 9

BAKING BIRTHDAY CAKES

When my mother was a little girl, all the family had to keep warm by was a coal-oil stove. This is also what Grandma Berry did her cooking on. You can imagine the delicate science of getting and keeping the oven at an even enough temperature to bake a cake.

Cake-baking days were big events. Everyone got in on the act, toting the wood, stirring the batter, and licking the bowl. They started early in the day, especially in the summer, so the kitchen wouldn't get so hot.

If all went well, and the cake turned out good, Grandma would slice it and serve it sparingly to the nine children and Grandpa. *But,* if something happened to cause the cake to fall, she would give the whole thing to the kids to eat with sweet butter.

Mother and the other eight children finally realized they could have an active part in helping the cake fall. It wasn't just what went on inside the stove that caused a cake to stand or fall!

So on cake-baking days, the children would all band together and map their strategy to guarantee a fallen cake. They ran through the kitchen with extra heavy stomps, slammed the kitchen door, and stomped back through the kitchen. With nine kids doing this, I wonder that Grandma ever got a cake to stand.

Now the science of cake baking has about reduced itself to a turn of a knob and the opening of a box. But the motive is probably the same as it was when Grandma baked one-egg cakes. Mothers and wives like to provide a sweet treat for husbands and families. "There is a cake. I made it especially for you."

It may be my imagination, but I believe the cooks I know are beginning to spend more time baking "scratch" cakes than we did several years ago. When box cakes first came out, it was a novelty to bake a cake with so little measuring and mixing.

Then a creative cook here and there began concocting delicious recipes using cake mixes as the basis but adding a few flourishes. These are some of the peaks in cookery in my opinion. It is a way of taking the best of the good life and combining it with the best of the natural way to produce a top-notch product. Now it seems we are continuing to get back to basics even more and feeling real pleasure and satisfaction in the old-fashioned measuring and mixing.

I really don't know what the psychology of it is, but setting a big, beautiful, yummy cake in front of the family makes me feel about ten feet tall inside. If I have put the whole thing together, myself, the good feeling is doubled.

When I was a child, I never knew what a store-bought cake was. Mother always made my favorite cake—chocolate. Of course, the cake was about the best part of my birthdays. We didn't have the elaborate parties my children have now.

For this reason, my children usually get a store-bought cake, because I am so busy working on the rest of the party preparations!

I have accumulated, over the years, cake-baking tips that have been very beneficial in turning out successful cakes. Some of them I remember hearing my mother talk about. Some I have been told by friends, and some I have discovered on my own.

Always measure accurately. With some cooking, it is fun to experiment with measurements, ingredients, and process, but cakes and breads are based on chemical reactions. The ingredients must be absolutely accurate or the chemistry won't work.

Put cake batter in preheated ovens only, so the baking process can begin immediately. The heat is what activates the chemical process. A slowly rising temperature can "kill" the active ingredients.

Use only the kind of pans called for in the recipe, such as loaf, layer, sheet, or tube. Place the pan in the center of the oven with nothing directly above or below it on another rack.

Always let cakes cool before removing from pan. Warm cakes are fragile.

Add eggs one at a time, beating well between each addition.

These are my mother's recipes. Chocolate Pie and Chocolate Cake have always been my favorites.

CHOCOLATE PIE
Lynn Cate (Mrs. George)

1 cup sugar	4 eggs, separated
3 level tablespoons flour	¾ stick margarine
3 heaping tablespoons cocoa	½ cup sugar
dash salt	2 tablespoons vanilla
1 cup milk	

In saucepan, mix 1 cup of sugar, flour, cocoa, and salt. Add half of milk, mix well. Add egg yolks, mix well, then add remainder of milk and margarine. Cook until thick—be sure to keep stirring to keep from sticking. When thick, take off fire. Add the ½ cup of sugar and vanilla. Mix well. Put into baked pie shell. Beat the egg whites to make meringue.

CHOCOLATE CAKE
Lynn Cate (Mrs. George)

2 cups flour	½ cup (1 stick) melted
2 cups sugar	margarine
¾ cup cocoa	1 egg
2 teaspoons baking soda	1 cup boiling water
1 teaspoon baking powder	1 cup milk

Preheat oven to 350 degrees. Sift dry ingredients together, add the remaining ingredients, and beat 2 minutes with mixer.
Bake for 35 minutes.
Use a long baking dish.
Any chocolate icing will do.

FLORIDA ORANGE CAKE
Lynn Cate (Mrs. George)

2 sticks margarine, softened	3 teaspoons baking powder
2 cups sugar	½ teaspoon salt
1 teaspoon cinnamon	3 cups flour
½ teaspoon nutmeg	⅓ cup Florida orange juice
1 tablespoon grated orange rind	1½ cups grated carrots
4 eggs	⅔ cup chopped pecans

Preheat oven to 350 degrees. Grease and flour a tube pan.

Cream margarine and sugar. Add spices and orange rind. Beat eggs well in a separate bowl. Add to the butter and sugar.

Sift baking powder and salt in with the flour. Add to batter alternately with orange juice.

Fold in carrots and nuts.

Bake for 1 hour. Cool and turn out of pan.

FLORIDA ORANGE JUICE GLAZE
Lynn Cate (Mrs. George)

1½ cups confectioners' sugar
1 tablespoon butter, melted
½ teaspoon orange rind

2 to 3 tablespoons Florida orange juice, or more if needed

Combine all ingredients and drizzle over the cooled cake.

Mark and Antoinette Hatfield are to us what riches are to kings. I can't remember what life was like before we became friends with the Hatfields. We thank God for our beautiful association with them.

The Hatfields were instrumental in getting us the family altar that has been so meaningful to our family.

Antoinette, herself a cookbook author, shared a most spectacular recipe with me. The recipe is a special one from her Aunt Dorothy.

AUNT DOROTHY'S CUT A RIBBON CAKE
Antoinette Hatfield (Mrs. Mark)

8 eggs, separated
2 cups sugar
8 teaspoons lemon juice
2 packages unflavored gelatin
½ cup cold water

grated rind of 2 lemons
2 packages ladyfingers
1 cup whipped cream
fresh fruit

Combine egg yolks, sugar, and lemon juice in top of a double boiler. Cook, stirring constantly, until thick. Dissolve gelatin in cold water. Remove mixture from stove, add lemon rind and dissolved gelatin. Cool to room temperature. Beat egg whites until stiff and peaked. Fold into cool yolk mixture.

Line a springform pan with single ladyfingers in an unbroken row around the sides and like spokes of a wheel in the bottom. Pour in lemon mixture and let set overnight in the refrigerator. Remove sides of pan and invert cake on a large plate. Decorate with whipped cream in spaces between ladyfingers (cream may be flavored with a little lemon rind) and fresh fruit (strawberries or peaches). Tie a ribbon around circumference of cake to be cut by the guest of honor.

MOTHER'S COCONUT CAKE
This cake is fit for a king.

2¾ cups instant flour	⅓ cup butter or margarine
1¾ cups sugar	3 eggs
2½ teaspoons baking powder	1¼ cups milk
1 teaspoon salt	1½ teaspoons vanilla

Preheat oven to 350 degrees. Measure all ingredients into a large mixing bowl and blend 30 seconds on low speed of mixer. Beat 3 minutes at medium speed. Pour into three 8-inch greased and floured pans. Bake for 30 to 35 minutes.

FROSTING

2 egg whites	½ teaspoon vanilla
¼ teaspoon cream of tartar	1 pound confectioners' sugar,
2 tablespoons light corn syrup	sifted
2½ tablespoons water	1 cup coconut

Combine egg whites and cream of tartar in medium-size bowl, beat until eggs stand in firm peaks. Combine syrup, water, and vanilla in cup. Add alternately with sugar into egg white mixture, beating well after each addition until it is creamy stiff. Put the frosting on each layer of cake and sprinkle coconut between layers and top.

SOUR CREAM POUNDCAKE
Mary Dale (Mrs. Troy)

2 sticks margarine	6 eggs, separated
2 cups sugar	3 cups flour
1 carton sour cream mixed with	1 teaspoon vanilla
½ teaspoon soda	

Preheat oven to 325 degrees. Cream margarine and 1 cup of the sugar, cream, egg yolks, and flour. Beat egg whites with remaining cup sugar. Fold into batter, add vanilla.

Bake 1 hour in a tube pan.

VANILLA WAFER CAKE
Jane Fortune

2 sticks margarine
2 cups sugar
6 medium eggs
1 box (12 ounces) vanilla
　wafers

½ cup milk
7 ounces angel flake coconut
1 cup chopped pecans

Preheat oven to 300 degrees. Cream margarine, add sugar, and continue creaming. Add eggs one at a time and beat after each addition.

Crush wafer cookies with rolling pin until fine crumbs. Add wafers and milk alternately to eggs, sugar, and butter. Add coconut, then fold in pecans.

Grease and flour tube pan, pour in batter and bake from 1 hour, 15 minutes to 1 hour, 30 minutes, depending on oven. Test with straw. Important to cool in pan.

Recently we worked with Oral Roberts on one of his TV special shows. It was a truly wonderful experience to fellowship with Oral and Evelyn during the days of work.

A very strange experience occurred during that time. I can glorify no one but the Lord. But I am grateful for the opportunities He gives me.

A husband and wife who are associates of Oral were with us. Oral had witnessed to them on many occasions. But, somehow, the warmness of that fellowship meal led me to share the story of God lighting our candle to shine through our total life as He comes in to live through us.

The seeds had been planted before, of course. But the fine associate and his wife trusted the Lord at that meal that day. It was a joyous mealtime experience.

Later, Evelyn sent me the following recipe. It is easy to fix and delicious. The recipe came from a friend of Mrs. Roberts' thirty years ago and has been used as a favorite Roberts recipe since.

RED DEVIL'S FOOD CAKE
Evelyn Roberts (Mrs. Oral)

2 cups sugar
½ cup vegetable shortening or margarine
2 eggs, beaten
½ cup buttermilk
1¼ teaspoons soda

pinch salt
2 cups flour
4 tablespoons cocoa
1 cup boiling water
1 teaspoon vanilla

Preheat oven to 325 degrees. Cream sugar and shortening. Add eggs and beat. Add buttermilk, soda, and salt. Mix, then add flour and cocoa. Add hot water and vanilla last of all. Batter will be thin. Bake 45 minutes to an hour.

ICING

1 egg white
¾ cup white syrup

½ teaspoon vanilla

Beat egg white in mixer bowl until stiff. Add syrup and vanilla.

Mix until so thick you can hardly spread. Color may be added if desired (pink or yellow).

Don't cook.

Cake is best if eaten the day it is baked.

Mother gave me one of her much-used cookbooks. The copyright date is 1940. The recipes are so good and ones that don't seem to be around any more. But the best ones in the book are the ones Mother wrote in the blank pages at the front of the book. Here is one.

SILVER MOON CAKE
Lynn Cate (Mrs. George)

3 cups flour
½ teaspoon salt
3 teaspoons baking powder
⅔ cup butter or other
    shortening

1¾ cups sugar
1 cup milk
1 teaspoon vanilla
5 egg whites

Preheat oven to 375 degrees. Sift flour and salt and baking powder together three times.

Cream butter and sugar until light. Add flour with milk in small amounts, beating after each addition. Add vanilla. Beat egg whites and fold in.

Bake for 20 to 25 minutes.

It is very important to use nothing but Ideal Cocoa in this recipe. Nothing else will do. Look on the specialty shelves of the better markets to find it.

IDEAL CHOCOLATE CAKE

2 cups flour
2 cups sugar
¾ cup Ideal Cocoa
2 teaspoons baking soda
1 teaspoon baking powder

½ cup (1 stick) butter, melted
1 egg
1 cup boiling water
1 cup milk

Preheat oven to 350 degrees. Sift dry ingredients together. Add the remaining ingredients, and beat 2 minutes with electric beater.

Bake for 35 minutes or more.

SPUD AND SPICE CAKE
Mrs. Milford W. Prince

1¾ cups sugar
1 cup cold mashed potatoes
¾ cup soft shortening
1 teaspoon cinnamon
½ teaspoon nutmeg
½ teaspoon salt

3 eggs
1 teaspoon baking soda
1 cup buttermilk
2 cups sifted all-purpose flour
¾ cup walnuts, chopped

Preheat oven to 350 degrees. Combine sugar, potatoes, shortening, spices, and salt. Cream well. Add eggs, beating until blended. Combine baking soda and buttermilk. Add alternately with flour to creamed mixture beginning and ending with flour. Coat walnuts with 2 additional tablespoons flour, stir into batter. Turn into greased and floured 13 × 9 × 2-inch pan. Bake in moderate oven (350 degrees) 50 to 60 minutes. Cool and frost with Quick Caramel Frosting.

QUICK CARAMEL FROSTING

Melt ¼ cup butter or margarine in saucepan, stir in ¾ cup firmly packed brown sugar. Continue cooking over low heat 2 minutes. Add 3 tablespoons milk. Bring to a full boil, cool to lukewarm without stirring. Add 2 cups sifted confectioners' sugar. Beat until smooth and of spreading consistency.

MOTHER'S CHOCOLATE ICEBOX CAKE
Taris Savell

3 squares bittersweet chocolate
½ cup sugar
5 eggs, separated
1 cup butter

1 cup confectioners' sugar
2 dozen ladyfingers, split
whipped cream

Melt the chocolate, add granulated sugar, stirring. When smooth, slowly add well-beaten egg yolks and cook until thickened and smooth, again stirring constantly. Let mixture cool. Cream the butter and confectioners' sugar and add egg mixture, stirring well. Fold in stiffly beaten egg whites.

Line the bottom and sides of a springform with the ladyfingers split in half. Cut the bottom tips straight across so they'll stand more easily. Add a layer of the above filling, cover with another layer of ladyfingers, and repeat until mold is full. The topmost layer should be the filling. Place in refrigerator and chill thoroughly—overnight is best—and prior to serving remove sides of pan and cover with whipped cream. Do not remove the pan bottom.

The only thing it takes to turn a regular cake into a birthday cake is the occasion and a little extra touch.

Now it is possible to spend hours constructing a fantastic baked sculpture with flourishes, extensions, towers, flowers, and even human figures and features.

I, for one, don't have hours and hours to devote to such projects no matter how much satisfaction it might invoke, so when I decorate a cake, I stick to the very simple things that show up well for the time they take.

Drizzle chocolate syrup over the top of white frosted cake.

Gather several small leaves of various shapes; wash and thoroughly dry the leaves. Melt 2 ounces of semisweet chocolate chips along with 1 teaspoon butter. "Paint" the chocolate mixture on the leaves with a small brush. Refrigerate for about 1 hour. Peel off the leaves and use the chocolate leaves to decorate a cake, a dip of ice-cream, or a bowl of pudding.

For the very young set, bake a chocolate cake recipe in small loaf pans instead of layer pans. One recipe should bake 6 small loaves. Frost the cooled cakes and line them up like cars of a train. Use round candy discs for wheels and a gumdrop for the smokestack.

Use store-bought animal crackers to turn a sheet cake into a small zoo.

Bake regular cake batter in flat-bottom ice-cream cones. Pour about ¼ cup of batter into each cone. Follow the directions for baking cupcakes. Frost and decorate with candies and colored sugar. One cake recipe makes about 30 cones.

Bake a hopscotch cake. Cut a sheet cake into small pieces about 4 to 5 inches square. Arrange the squares on a platter in an old-fashioned hopscotch pattern. Use a frosting tube to put numbers on the squares.

Dip a decorative cookie cutter in food coloring, then press it gently into the cake. Repeat the design around the edges or on the top.

Make miniature log rolls (great for a boy's party). Bake twice as many cupcakes as guests. Put two cupcakes together end-to-end and attach with frosting. Frost the sides of the "logs" with chocolate frosting. Texture the frosting with a fork to resemble rough bark.

Bake a poundcake in a tube pan. Fill the center with softened ice cream. Wrap in foil and freeze until firm. Frost with icing or tinted whipped cream.

Use hard candies, gumdrops, licorice, or crumbled peppermint to make designs on frosted cakes.

DEUTERONOMY 8:10

When you have eaten your fill, bless the Lord your God for the good land he has given you.

PART III

LET'S GET OUT OF THE HOUSE

CHAPTER 10

FILLING THE PICNIC BASKET

Of all the customs families indulge in, probably the picnic is the most ancient one of all. Picnics probably date back to the days of cave dwellers. It was the primitive thing to do. Down through the ages, people have always loved taking food outside.

Before and during the time of Christ, the Athens citizens packed bread, fruits, and fish into ancient baskets and ate on hillsides just outside the city. Or other groups might gather in what we might think of as parks, but were actually rich men's olive groves.

Even the Greeks of Bible days were known to stage extravagant outdoor picnics. Greek cooks were very proud and jealous of their picnic specialties.

In more modern times, and moving across the world, the only natural way to eat Polynesian food is outside. In the South Pacific, dinners are always spread picnic style on the ground under a fringe of palm trees.

My ancestors, the American Indians, cooked and ate most of their meals outside.

Outdoor eating is like the call of the wild. When the weather turns warm, and the red ants begin to hatch, the human animal moves his eating outside.

Picnics seem to come in various forms. Stay-at-home-picnics-in-the-yard are one kind. Pack-a-picnic-basket-and-go-somewhere is another kind. Of these two kinds you can further complicate the category by saying there are easy no-fuss picnics, or there can be elaborate Greek-style picnics.

I'm really not one to go fancy on picnics. To me, if you're going to get out of the house, get out the easiest way possible. We usually take something like peanut butter sandwiches with a big basket of fresh fruit and vegetables. At most, sometimes I fix a special salad.

Our own yard is so great for picnics it is tempting to stay home to picnic. But we also enjoy going out on the boat. We go to a little island just past the broad causeway before you get to the inlet. There are several small islands that pop up in that area.

We nicknamed our favorite island Gilligan's Island. We can beach the boat there. We always take marshmallows, hot dogs, baked beans, and maybe potato salad. Since the island is usually covered with litter, we begin our picnic by picking up and cleaning the area. The litter makes a great bonfire. Then we sit around the fire and sing while we roast marshmallows and hot dogs.

If it is a special occasion, or if we have guests, I usually send someone over early to get things looking festive. We take umbrellas for shade and blankets to sit on. Then we all go over later in the day.

Wherever the picnic is staged or whatever the occasion, it is a mystery to me why the food tastes so much better outside than in. Just plain old hot dogs are absolutely delicious when eaten on the beach. And ordinary sandwiches taste like a gourmet's delight under the shade of a big tree. I think it must have something to do with man returning to his natural state of being in the out-of-doors. Gentle breezes, warming rays of the sun, the song of birds, paper plates, the smell of green, and the company of friends at leisure bring on a lulling effect that must surely be divine in nature.

ACTIVITIES FOR PICNICS

Sometimes a picnic with nothing to do is a real treat! Especially if you have had lots to do at home. At other times it is fun to have a change-of-pace activity to really get your mind off things at home.

Take along a large beach ball or basketball. Many kinds of on-the-spot games can be developed with a large ball. Besides, the large muscle activity can be refreshing and relaxing.

Take time to observe God's creation in the world. It can never be equaled for enjoyment and elegant splendor.

Decide to concentrate on only one part of nature. Wild flowers, insects, shells, or leaves make good studies. If you can read up ahead of time on the subject, it can be a real educational experience.

If the day is partly overcast, take time to lie flat down on a blanket or spread. Face the sky and watch the clouds. Find pictures, secret messages, or just interesting designs.

Listen for sounds. Close your eyes and really listen to the different sounds in the area. Name as many as you can.

On your way home, don't forget to thank God for the wonders of creation. Encourage each family member to express his feelings about some aspect of the family outing.

SANDWICHES

Prepare sandwiches for a picnic the day before and freeze in individual plastic wraps. Pack them in the picnic basket while they are still frozen and they will be fresh to eat by mealtime.

For frozen sandwiches, use only cooked egg yolks, peanut butter, cooked chicken, turkey, meat, or fish. Use dairy sour cream or cream cheese for binders instead of mayonnaise or salad dressing. Possible combinations for frozen picnic sandwiches are:

·Hard-cooked egg yolks mashed with sour cream and dill pickle.

·Processed cheese spread with sour cream and a dash of chili powder.

·Cream cheese with chopped green or black olives.

·Chopped chicken with sour cream and pickle relish.

Vary the kinds of bread used for picnic sandwiches.

Pack tomatoes, lettuce, and pickles separately and add to the sandwiches just before eating.

SANDWICH SPREADS

CORNED BEEF

2 cups finely chopped corned beef
½ cup finely chopped cabbage

⅓ cup sour cream
1 tablespoon horseradish

In small bowl, combine all ingredients; mix well. Chill in covered container.

Makes about 2½ cups.

PINEAPPLE AND CHEESE

   2 cups grated American cheese   *1 can (8 ounces) crushed*
   ½ cup mayonnaise   *pineapple, drained*
   ½ cup chopped pecans

Combine ingredients and chill.
Makes about 2½ cups.

CHICKEN ALMOND

   1 cup chopped, cooked chicken   *½ cup mayonnaise*
   ¼ cup slivered almonds   *2 hard-cooked eggs, chopped*
   ¼ teaspoon ground ginger

Combine ingredients and mix well.
Makes 2 cups.

ARTIST IN RESIDENCE SANDWICHES

Make "paint" by mixing a few drops of food coloring in several tablespoons of milk. Two or three different colors of paint will be more fun. Use a small paintbrush to paint a design on one side of a slice of bread. Stripes, circles, faces, stars are good beginnings. Go light on the paint so as not to get the bread soggy.

Dry the bread slice in the toaster for a very few seconds (do not toast). Then spread with your favorite sandwich spread. Of course, with bread like this, it really doesn't matter what goes in between!

HAM AND CHEESE ON RYE

   1 package (3 ounces) cream   *6 slices luncheon meat*
      cheese, softened   *6 slices rye bread*
   1 tablespoon horseradish   *6 stuffed olives*

In small bowl, combine cream cheese and horseradish; mix until smooth. Spread about 1½ teaspoons mixture on each slice of lunch-

eon meat; roll up starting with one corner. Place meat diagonally on slice of bread; bring opposite corners of bread together and fasten with toothpick. Garnish with olive on the toothpick.
Makes 6 sandwiches.

FRIED TOMATO SANDWICHES

2 hard-cooked eggs	2 cups fine cracker crumbs
2 cans deviled ham	⅓ cup grated Parmesan
mayonnaise	cheese
12 tomato slices	butter
2 egg yolks	paprika
2 tablespoons milk	

Chop the hard-cooked eggs fine and mix with the deviled ham. Mix in enough mayonnaise to make a smooth paste. Spread the ham mixture between 2 slices of tomato.

Combine the egg yolks and milk. Dip each sandwich into the batter then into the cracker crumbs mixed with the cheese. Fry in butter until lightly browned. Top with a sprinkle of paprika.

TOASTED WAFFLE SANDWICH

12 slices bread	6 slices cheese
6 tablespoons mayonnaise	2 eggs, well beaten
6 slices ham	

Preheat waffle iron. Spread 6 slices of the bread with 1 tablespoon mayonnaise each. Top each slice with ham, then cheese and remaining bread. Using a pastry brush, coat each side of sandwich with egg mixture. Toast in waffle iron.
Makes 6 sandwiches.

This cooking technique is good for any grilled sandwich. A good variation is to brush the bread with melted butter instead of egg and use cream cheese as a sandwich filling instead of ham and cheese.

FRIED CHICKEN

2 3- to 3½-pound broiler-fryer
    chickens, quartered
1 can (14½ ounces) evaporated
    milk
1¼ cups flour

¼ cup grated Parmesan cheese
1½ teaspoons salt
½ teaspoon paprika
⅛ teaspoon pepper
salad oil

Wash and dry chickens. Place in a 13 × 9 × 2-inch baking pan; cover with evaporated milk. Refrigerate several hours, turning chicken several times.

In bag, combine flour, cheese, and seasonings. Place several pieces of chicken at a time in the bag; shake to coat chicken. In large, heavy skillet, fry chicken in ½ inch oil 20 to 30 minutes or until done. Drain well on paper towels.

Makes 8 servings (¼ chicken each).

PEANUT BUTTER COOKIES

1 cup shortening
1 cup brown sugar
1 cup white sugar
2 eggs
⅛ teaspoon salt

1 cup peanut butter
1 teaspoon vanilla
2 cups flour
1 teaspoon soda

Preheat oven to 350 degrees. Mix all together and roll out on floured board. Cut with cookie cutter. Bake until brown—about 20 minutes. Check after 10 minutes.

These cookies Mother baked for school lunches, if they lasted until the next morning!

CHEESE MOLD

2 cartons (8 ounce each)
    creamed cottage cheese
4 packages (3 ounces each)
    cream cheese
2 cups green seedless grapes,
    halved

1 cup broken pecans
1 tablespoon chopped chives
1 cup heavy cream, whipped
    light

Mash cheeses together till blended. Add everything else gently. Put in oiled ring mold. Put in refrigerator before serving. Garnish with lettuce, apricots, pineapples.

ORANGE AND MINT DRINK
Doris Niles

"I must add a Florida orange juice recipe."

2½ cups water
2 cups sugar
juice of 4 Florida oranges
grated rind of 1 orange

juice of 6 lemons
grated rind of 1 lemon
2 large handfuls mint stalks
*   and leaves*

Boil water and sugar together for 10 minutes. Pour over the fruit juices and rinds. Add mint.

Cover and let stand for 1 hour or more. Strain and put into jars.

To serve, use 5 or 6 tablespoons in a tall glass of crushed ice and water.

Note: Naturally frozen juices may be used.

DEAR LORD. *It was such fun, God, being in your world, seeing new places, feeling the warm wind on my face. The swimming, the fishing, the camping, the picnicking, the standing still of time.*

We all felt so close together and so close to you. I noticed when we got back home today, the usual tense bickering was absent. It seemed to be replaced by a renewed freshness of your love. Thank you, God, for these warm, wonderful family-fun-times in your all outdoors.

CHAPTER 11

SUMMER COOKOUTS

During the summer months in Oklahoma, we would all always get together around the Fourth of July, Memorial Day, and Labor Day. In fact, sometimes we didn't even have to have a holiday—a weekend would do.

The cousins came from every direction, along with aunts, uncles, and even some stray outsiders.

The pattern was always the same as if it had been decreed by law. The women and older girls would all gather in the kitchen and talk "woman talk." The men would all sit around outside. All of us kids would go back and forth. First we would go to the kitchen to hear the lady topics until we were run out, then, out to the men. In my evaluation, the men had more fun. The women just had to stay in the kitchen and do the cooking.

After we had been run out of both circles a few times we would wander off to find our own entertainment, which on more than one occasion was the neighbors' watermelon patch. We were all half starved at having to wait so long for the food to get ready. So those hot watermelons tasted absolutely delicious.

I can remember ice cream—homemade—being a big part of the menu. It was the one event of the food preparation that we kids got to participate in. The women would mix the cream and the men would crank the freezer. We got to sit on the sack and hold the freezer down. The men would all take turns turning the freezer and lightly complain about what hard work it was.

When we got together with the Bryants, I remember my Grandpa Bryant was a great storyteller. The family get-togethers were always dotted with his wild yarns of people and places.

Those were good days. As I look back now, they seem so uncomplicated. Everyone had a fixed role and there didn't seem to be any variation. There weren't too many pressures. People went through life not really questioning or exploring, but rather accepting.

Nowadays, at Villa Verde, we have a cookout at the bare mention of the idea. The relatives don't all assemble, but we are able to share with various sets of friends.

And, thank heavens, the role assignments are different now. I think the men and women mix more. Probably because there are so many do-ahead kinds of foods, we women just don't have to spend all day in the kitchen.

That pattern of socialization seemed to work fine for the Berrys and the Bryants. It reflected the way of life and western culture at that time. Since I am not the kind of housewife who enjoys staying in the kitchen all the time, it won't work for me. I want to participate in the whole party.

Our cookouts are so much more impromptu. I can remember Memorial Day when the state issued the operating license for Fishers of Men, a Christ-centered booking agency. We were so excited. It had taken many months to get the license, so this event definitely called for a celebration.

I simply went to the freezer, found two cuts of meat, some frozen spaghetti, and a few leftovers from the week. Then I invited our dearest friends, Charlie and Marabel Morgan and family, and we had a Memorial Day cookout. A big tossed salad completed the meal.

I really feel this is what summer cookouts are supposed to be. Easy, relaxed, social times that renew and replenish our minds and bodies. They should be done with the least amount of trouble and discord possible so even the cooks enjoy the "night out."

PLANTATION GRILLED CHICKEN
Bernice Sonnenberg
Very good for outdoor cooking.

2 3- to 3½-pound broiler-fryer
   chickens, halved
⅔ cup salad oil
2 teaspoons monosodium
   glutamate

⅓ cup vinegar
2 teaspoons salt
2 teaspoons paprika
½ teaspoon poultry seasoning

Line grill with foil (it radiates heat and eliminates messy clean-up); prepare coals. Place chicken, skin side up, on grill, 3 to 6 inches from source of heat.* Combine remaining ingredients; beat to mix

* Or secure whole chicken to spit of rotisserie and cook according to manufacturer's instructions. Baste chicken frequently as directed.

well. Brush over chicken. Cook chicken, turning once and basting frequently, 45 to 75 minutes or until done.
Makes 4 servings.

FRENCH-FRIED HOT DOGS

Make one recipe of your favorite biscuit mix. Add barbecue seasoning and dry mustard to the batter.

Insert a wooden skewer into enough wieners to serve your number of family members or guests.

Dip the wieners into the thick batter and coat well. Fry in hot fat. Serve with dips such as prepared mustard, catsup, or mayonnaise.

Viki Yancik makes a casserole similar to a recipe I have often used. It is so easy to do, it is a natural for summer cookouts. It can be prepared well in advance.

VAY'S HOT DOGS AND BEANS
Viki Yancik

6 to 8 wieners
⅓ cup brown sugar
⅓ cup prepared mustard
⅓ cup catsup

3 tablespoons vinegar
1 clove garlic
1 large can baked beans
6 strips bacon

Preheat oven to 325 degrees. Slice the wieners in half and line the bottom of a casserole dish. Mix the sugar, mustard, catsup, vinegar, and garlic with the beans. Pour the mixture over the wieners. Top with the strips of uncooked bacon. Bake for 1 hour.
Makes 6 servings.

GRILLED HAMBURGER MEAL

1 tablespoon chili powder
1 tablespoon salt
¾ teaspoon black pepper
1 teaspoon garlic powder
ground beef (allow ¾ pound per
serving)

potatoes
carrots
celery
butter or margarine

Combine dry ingredients and mix well. Use 1 teaspoon of the mixture and ¾ pound beef for each serving. Mix well and shape into patties about 1 inch thick.

Place each patty in the center of a piece of foil. On top of it, place a 1-inch-thick slice of potato, 1 carrot cut in fourths, a piece of celery, and a pat of butter. Wrap and seal.

Grill on a closed grill for 45 minutes to an hour, depending on the intensity of the heat.

Serve with French bread and a green salad.

HOT POT PIE

1½ pounds ground beef
1 onion, chopped
1 can (12 ounces) whole kernel corn
1 can cream of chicken soup
1 can cream of mushroom soup
1 cup sour cream
¼ cup chopped pimiento
¾ teaspoon salt
dash pepper
1 large baked pie shell with cover

Preheat oven to 375 degrees. Brown meat and add remaining ingredients except pie shell. Cover and simmer for 10 minutes.

Pour into pie shell. Place unbaked piecrust cover on and secure edges. Bake until top crust is brown.

Can be baked ahead of time and reheated on a closed grill.

LONGHORN LOAF

1 long loaf Italian bread
1 can bean with bacon soup
½ cup catsup
1 pound ground beef, very lean
¼ cup brown sugar
⅓ cup minced onion
2 cups bread crumbs
1 teaspoon salt
¼ teaspoon pepper
3 large dill pickles
cheese slices

Preheat oven to 375 degrees. Cut a thin slice from top of bread loaf. Scoop out center of bread loaf to form a large bread shell. Use soft center to make crumbs.

Combine crumbs, soup, catsup, beef, brown sugar, onion, and seasonings. Mix well.

Spread half of this meat mixture in the bread shell. Arrange the dill pickles end to end down the center of the meat mixture. Add remaining meat mixture over the dill pickles.

Top with slices of cheese, then cover the cheese slices with top bread slice. Brush with melted butter. Place the bread on a cookie sheet and loosely wrap with foil.

Bake 1½ hours.

Slice crosswise into 1½-inch slices for serving.

WIENER CASSEROLE
Doris Niles

"I have one completely original recipe. I have never seen one akin to it. I had a reason for inventing it, but I can't seem to think up an original name for it. Every Christmas for many years, when my uncle traveled for a packing company in Tennessee, he directed the company to send us a huge box of meat—ham, bacon, smoked tenderloin, sausage, and, to fill empty spaces and to include all the products of the company, the shipment also included packages of wieners. Because I can't bear to see anything go to waste, when we were surfeited with holiday eating, I cooked a prosaic casserole with the wieners as a base. Here it is; it's tasty."

3 cups cooked shell macaroni
1 pound wieners
2 heaping cups grated Cheddar cheese

1 bottle chili sauce
4 slices bacon

Preheat oven to 325 degrees. Alternate in a casserole dish a layer of macaroni, cross-sectioned wieners, and Cheddar cheese to the top (or stir them up if you wish). Pour over this the entire bottle of chili sauce. If it seems too dry, add a little water or catsup.

Spread the bacon slices over the top and bake for about 30 minutes. Brown the bacon briefly under the broiler. This can be prepared ahead of time. The more it is reheated, the better it tastes.

CORNED BEEF BARBECUE

1 can (8 ounces) tomato sauce
    or ½ cup catsup
1 cup chili sauce
¼ cup Worcestershire sauce
¼ cup brown sugar
dash Tabasco sauce
dash soy sauce

2 tablespoons wine vinegar
1 onion, chopped fine
salt and pepper to taste
1 clove garlic, crushed
2 tablespoons chili powder
1 can corned beef

Mix together all ingredients and simmer for 30 minutes. Add small amount of water if necessary.

BERRIES AND CREAM PIE

pastry for single crust pie
4 cups berries
⅓ cup sugar
⅓ cup firmly packed brown
    sugar

4 tablespoons flour
¼ teaspoon salt
½ teaspoon cinnamon
¼ teaspoon nutmeg
1 cup heavy cream

Preheat oven to 400 degrees. Line a 9-inch pie plate with pastry; fill with berries. Combine remaining ingredients; pour over berries; bake 35 to 40 minutes.

PEACHES AND CREAM PIE: Substitute 8 peach halves for berries. Arrange peaches, rounded side up, in pastry-lined pie plate and proceed as above. Makes a 9-inch pie (6 servings).

This most unusual dessert was concocted by Mrs. Minnie Salter for the Ben Hill Griffin family. The flavor is sweet, tangy, and light. I like it because it seems to be a perfect topping to a summer supper. Again, it is a do-ahead treat.

GRAPEFRUIT PUDDING
Mrs. Minnie Salter

1 cup plus 3 tablespoons sugar
4 tablespoons cornstarch
½ teaspoon salt
2 cups milk
3 eggs, separated

3 tablespoons butter or
  margarine
1 teaspoon vanilla
3 or 4 large grapefruits,
  sectioned

Preheat oven to 300 degrees. Mix the cup of sugar, cornstarch, and salt in the top of double boiler. Add milk and beaten egg yolks. Mix well, cook on medium heat until it thickens. Stir constantly. Add butter and vanilla.

Place sections of drained grapefruit in a casserole, pour pudding over fruit. Beat egg whites until stiff. Add the 3 tablespoons of sugar and beat 1 minute. Spread on top of pudding and bake 15 minutes or until brown.

Makes 6 servings.

MOTHER'S APPLE COBBLER
Lynn Cate (Mrs. George)

FILLING:

¾ cup sugar
2 tablespoons flour
½ teaspoon cinnamon
¼ teaspoon salt

5 cups sliced apples
¼ cup water
1 tablespoon butter

BISCUITS:

1 cup flour
1 tablespoon sugar
1½ teaspoons baking powder

½ teaspoon salt
3 tablespoons shortening
½ cup milk

Preheat oven to 400 degrees. In bowl, combine sugar, flour, cinnamon, and salt; toss with apples. Spoon into a shallow 1½-quart casserole. Sprinkle with water; dot with butter. Cover with foil; bake 15 minutes.

Meanwhile, make biscuits: In bowl, combine dry ingredients. Using a pastry blender or two knives, cut in shortening until consistency of coarse corn meal. Add milk; mix well. Drop by spoonfuls onto hot apple mixture to make 6 biscuits. Bake uncovered 25 to 30 minutes or until biscuits are browned.

Makes 6 servings (about ½ cup each).

My father is married to a real super, super cook. Jewel has a blackberry cobbler that is a sensation.

BLACKBERRY COBBLER
Mrs. Jewel Bryant

Cook quart of berries in water to barely cover until well done.

Put berries through strainer to remove seeds. Add sugar to desired sweetness (2 cups or more). Make piecrust, enough to cover bottom and top of deep baking dish. Line bottom of baking dish with crust. Pour in berries and juice. Add several pats of butter and cover with top crust. Cut slits and sprinkle top with sugar. Bake at 350 degrees until crust is brown, approximately 45 minutes. Cool.

Serve with cream topping or ice cream.

From Nassa, Tanzania, East Africa, Miss Edna Jackson sent us this recipe for lime sherbet.

Miss Jackson is a missionary to East Africa. On her visits to the States, she visits our home church, Northwest Baptist, where she was a former member. On her last visit, Bobby was absolutely struck with her stories of the ministry she carries on in Nassa. Since then, he, more faithfully than anyone else in our family, has contributed to this ministry. Bobby sends two dollars a month from his allowance.

We will always think of Miss Jackson and the Tanzania missionaries when we use this recipe.

LIME SHERBET
Edna Jackson

⅓ cup lime juice   2 cups cold milk
1⅓ cups sugar

Mix sugar and juice well, then stir in milk slowly. Pour into an ice tray and freeze.

When frozen, mash up with a spoon, stir, and return to freezer. Makes 4 to 6 servings.

While we were visiting Sandra and Sam Page in Topeka they invited Jan and Ken Carson over for homemade ice cream. Ken is Sam's boss at Sears. Sandra made vanilla ice cream and Jan Carson made this recipe of vanilla-lemon. I have never tasted anything just like it.

VANILLA-LEMON ICE CREAM
Jan Carson (Mrs. Ken)

4 eggs
1½ cups sugar
5 cups milk
2 pints half and half

1 teaspoon salt
3 tablespoons vanilla
1 teaspoon lemon extract

Beat eggs well. Add sugar and continue beating. Add remaining ingredients and mix. Freeze in a gallon home freezer.

The first ice cream was a closely guarded secret of about the year A.D. 64. It is reported to have been made out of snow and fruit juice. The snow was brought by very swift runners from the mountaintops.

VANILLA ICE CREAM
Mary Dale (Mrs. Troy)

6 eggs
1 cup sugar
1 can condensed milk
1 can evaporated milk

1 can water
2 teaspoons vanilla
1 quart milk

Beat eggs on medium-high mixer speed for at least 10 minutes. Add sugar and mix thoroughly. Add two kinds of milk and the can of water. Mix well. Add vanilla.

Pour the mixture into a chilled ice cream freezer container. Add the milk and stir with the dasher. Freeze in a gallon ice cream freezer.

Makes 10 servings.

FRESH FRUIT ICE CREAM

Follow the recipe for Vanilla Ice Cream, adding about 1½ to 2 cups of fresh fruit, cut in very small pieces; or mashed strawberries, peaches, bananas, and oranges are good ice cream fruits.

PEPPERMINT

Stir in about ¾ cup crushed peppermint candy to the Vanilla Ice Cream recipe.

CHOCOLATE

Add 2 ounces melted unsweetened chocolate to the Vanilla Ice Cream recipe.

Bob and I met when I was a regular on the Don McNeill Breakfast Club radio show. The experience on that show was not only a wonderful one professionally, but personally. The families I encountered in connection with that show are friends to this day.

Clifford Peterson was the producer of the show. He and his wife, Eileen, saved me from having one of the loneliest years of my life. They often had me out to their home.

Eileen and Cliff are both good cooks. But Cliff cooks in pinches and dabs, so Eileen contributed this to my recipe files.

STRAWBERRY ICE CREAM
Eileen Peterson (Mrs. Cliff)

Thaw 1 pouch frozen strawberries per directions on package. Add 1 cup sugar to strawberries and 1 pint commercial sour cream.

Whip all together in blender; put in ice tray to set. It takes about 3 hours.

My mother's older sister, Gola Mae Fleming, is one I can remember making such beautiful contributions to our holiday reunions. This recipe has been used for thirty-five years.

STRAWBERRY POP ICE CREAM
Gola Mae Fleming (Mrs. Ernest)

6 eggs
2 cups sugar
2 heaping tablespoons flour
1 quart milk

2 bottles strawberry pop
2 cans evaporated milk
1 teaspoon vanilla
1 quart milk (approximately)

Cream eggs, sugar, and flour together. Add 1 quart milk. Cook in double boiler until custard-like in appearance. Add strawberry pop, canned milk, and vanilla. Pour into 1-gallon freezer container and fill the remaining space with milk. Freeze.

Aunt Marie and Uncle Luther Berry are really more than my aunt and uncle. They are our brother and sister in Christ. Uncle Luther is pastor of Pleasantview Baptist Church, Derby, Kansas. The church has a lot of ice cream fellowships, and Uncle Luther always makes his own recipe of Banana Ice Cream.

LUTHER'S BANANA ICE CREAM
Aunt Marie Berry (Mrs. Luther)

6 eggs
1½ cups sugar
5 bananas
1 can condensed milk

1 can evaporated milk
1 tablespoon wonder flour
1½ teaspoons vanilla
1 quart milk (approximately)

Mix in blender the eggs, sugar, bananas. Add the two kinds of milk, flour, and vanilla. Put in 1-gallon freezer container and finish filling the container with milk.
Freeze and serve.

DEAR LORD. It's a good day, Lord.

Some days just have that special glow about them. I can feel it when I first greet the morning. It is a day where all my attempts will be rewarded. I hope I can have an opportunity to try something big for you today, Lord.

The bay outside my bedroom window is sparkling like a thousand rays of sunshine dancing on the water. It's great to be alive.

Thank you for this special day and for making me feel happy all the way through.

CHAPTER 12

FISH AND FISHING

Right along with sunshine and orange juice, Florida probably provokes just as many thoughts of fresh sea food and fishing.

It is only natural we eat a lot of fish since we can get fresh sea food so easily. It is also nutritious and economical. What more can you require of a good family food?

We go fishing often. But we don't always eat what we catch, for one simple reason—I have to clean what we catch! In a weak moment, I admitted to Bob that Grandma Berry taught me to clean fish. Bob, in his male wisdom, still vows he has no knowledge of how to clean fish. So, to be honest, a lot of the fish we eat comes from the sea food market.

One exception is when we go down by Key Biscayne. Not far from President Nixon's home is an excellent red snapper hole. At certain times of the day, near sunset, a good fisherman can really bring in a lot of beautiful snappers. Those I can clean on the boat, and it doesn't seem nearly as messy as cleaning at home.

Another exception is when any of my family come to visit. They all love to fish. Mother and Daddy George fish right off the dock. With all of us helping, we can clean the catch in no time and have a great fish dinner.

When my brother, Sonny, came for Christmas one year, we bought shrimp bait and fished the entire time he was here.

I think I was born knowing how to fish. Our family was poor and sometimes fishing was our source of food.

We would spend our vacations on fishing trips. The kids would sleep in the car and the adults would sleep in the open air. If we had some relatives to go with us, we would all pool our money and get one tiny cabin. When the mosquitoes got so bad we couldn't stand it, we would all sleep inside the cabin on the floor.

Mainly we cooked what we caught outside on an open fire. If it rained, we could cook inside. I'm not talking about insulated sleeping bags and cooking stoves or lanterns, or any of that fancy camping gear on the market today. I mean we really *roughed* it, long before "roughing it" became stylish.

It is funny that I would look back on those trips as some of the highlights of my life. They were tremendous times. I love the freedom of the outdoors and feel very fortunate to have been raised that way.

I really long for my children to taste that same carefree feeling of the great outdoors. Even now, the grandest vacation we can all have is to go to my dad's Black Jewel Ranch in Sawakwa, Oklahoma, where he raises black Angus cattle. Or to Grandma Cate's house where the children are free to roam in the woods without fear of traffic, people, or harm in any way.

After Bob and I married, I baited Bob's first hook. In the early years we lived in Florida in an apartment that was right on the bay. I could look out there and see those fish flapping around. I just couldn't resist, so we began fishing.

I have a marvelous collection of delicious fish recipes. So many of them have been given to me by some of the best cooks I know.

SNAPPER BONNE FEMME
Joyce Vinoski (Mrs. Bernie)

1 teaspoon salt
⅛ teaspoon pepper
1¼ pounds fish fillets
1 clove garlic
2 tablespoons butter
1 medium onion, minced
2 shallots, minced

½ pound fresh mushrooms, sliced thin
snipped parsley
2 tablespoons butter
½ cup light cream
2 to 3 teaspoons flour

Salt and pepper fish. Stick toothpick in garlic. Melt 2 tablespoons butter in skillet; add onion, shallots, garlic, half the mushrooms; top with fish, remaining mushrooms, and parsley.

Cut a circle of wax paper to fit the skillet, tear a small hole in the center; place paper circle on fish. Cover, bring to a boil; cook for 5 to 10 minutes, or until easily flaked with a fork but still moist. Remove cover, paper, and garlic.

While fish is cooking, make cream sauce with 2 tablespoons butter, cream and flour; season is necessary. Pour sauce over fish, sprinkle with fresh parsley.

Put in broiler to brown if you want.

BALTIMORE IMPERIAL CRAB

1 pound crab meat
1 to 1¼ cups evaporated milk
2 eggs, well beaten
salt and pepper

dry mustard to taste
4 tablespoons or more of
    mayonnaise
pimiento

Combine all these ingredients and let stand about 2 hours. Preheat oven to 350 degrees. Pack in shells, let liquid drain off. Cover with mayonnaise, garnish with pimiento. Bake 15 to 20 minutes. Watch carefully.

Makes 4 servings.

BAKED SALMON STEAKS

2 eggs
2 tablespoons milk
1 tablespoon lemon or lime
    juice
1 teaspoon salt
2 pounds salmon steaks

1½ cups toasted dry bread
    crumbs
⅓ cup melted butter or
    margarine
Lemon or lime wedges

Preheat oven to 350 degrees. In shallow dish, combine eggs, milk, lemon or lime juice, and salt; mix well. Dip fish in egg mixture, then crumbs; shake off excess crumbs and repeat. Place fish in single layer, in well-greased 13 × 9 × 2-inch baking pan. Pour butter over fish; bake 20 to 25 minutes or until fish flakes easily with a fork. Serve garnished with lemon or lime wedges.

Makes 4 servings (½ pound each).

CRAB-LOBSTER CASSEROLE

2 tablespoons butter
2 small onions, chopped fine
1 medium bell pepper, chopped fine
½ cup chopped celery
1 large fresh tomato, peeled, cut into small chunks
1 can mushroom soup

1 cup evaporated milk
½ cup almonds
¼ cup chopped pimiento
½ pound round crackers, crumbled
1 can drained asparagus tips
½ pound lobster meat
½ pound crab meat

Preheat oven to 325 degrees. Sauté in butter the onions, pepper, and celery. Add tomato and cook until tender. Cool and add mushroom soup, milk, almonds, and pimiento. Sprinkle thin layer cracker crumbs in buttered casserole and add the following in layers: asparagus tips, ⅓ mushroom mixture, lobster, ½ remaining mushroom mixture, crab meat, remaining mushroom mixture; cover with cracker crumbs. Bake 30 minutes.

This sounds involved, but it really isn't. Read through the directions carefully before starting to prepare.

RED SNAPPER WITH HOLLANDAISE SAUCE AND MUSHROOMS
Joyce Vinoski (Mrs. Bernie)

1 cup of heavy cream
1 cup of Hollandaise sauce
1 stick plus 2 tablespoons butter
2 to 3 shallots or green onions, minced
6 red snapper fillets (sole or flounder can be substituted)

salt
white pepper
dry white cooking wine or dry vermouth
1 pound fresh mushrooms, sliced thin
1 tablespoon cornstarch

Whip heavy cream, fold the Hollandaise sauce into it and set aside.

In a flameproof dish, enamel or Teflon skillet, melt ½ stick butter —do not brown.

Sprinkle the shallots or onions into the bottom of the dish or pan.

Arrange the fillets in the dish. Salt and pepper lightly. Pour enough wine over the fish to barely cover. Bring to a boil, cover, and poach over high heat 5 to 10 minutes, depending on the thickness of the fillets, or until easily flaked with fork but still moist. Remove from the heat. Gently remove fish to warm platters. Save the liquid. While fish is poaching, sauté sliced mushrooms in ½ stick butter. Top the fish with the sautéed mushrooms. Mix 2 tablespoons soft butter with cornstarch and thicken the fish liquid.

Stir the whipped cream/Hollandaise sauce mixture into the thickened fish liquid and spoon the sauce over the fish and mushrooms.

Broil until golden.

Watch closely.

"Bon appetit."

The Millers are fellow church members at Northwest Baptist.

FLORIDA FISH CHOWDER
Mrs. Paul Miller

1 cup diced potatoes
1 cup sliced carrots
½ cup diced celery
½ teaspoon salt
2 tablespoons butter (or more)
1 medium onion, sliced thin

1 to 2 pounds firm-meat fish, cut into 1-inch pieces
1 teaspoon Worcestershire sauce
1 teaspoon salt
¼ teaspoon pepper
2 to 3 cups milk
paprika

Cook potatoes, carrots, and celery in salted water to cover until almost tender. Melt butter in large stew pan. Add onion and cook over low heat until limp but not brown. Add fish and Worcestershire sauce and cook 1 minute, stirring gently. Add vegetables and water and cook 10 minutes. Add 1 teaspoon salt, pepper, and milk. Heat slowly to boiling. Sprinkle paprika on each bowlful of chowder.

Makes 6 to 8 servings.

Here's a marvelous recipe from Bob's father.

SNOOK (Fish)
Einar Green

Always take skin off of snook before regular cooking, cover fish in pan of water, and bring to a boil, then drain.

Cook in approximately 1 cup water over low heat with 3 to 4 bay leaves, 8 to 10 whole black peppers, and salt. Cook until tender.

Gravy—add approximately 1 cup milk to juice in pan, a little flour for thickness. Chop 1 hard-boiled egg and put in gravy, pour over fish, and serve—or serve on side.

DOLPHIN (Fish)
Einar Green

Season fillets with salt and pepper, then roll in cracker crumbs or crushed corn flakes. Fry in small amount of butter until tender and browned on both sides.

Simon Peter said, "I'm going fishing."

"We'll come too," we all said. We did, but caught nothing all night. At dawn we saw a man standing on the beach but couldn't see who he was.

He called, "Any fish, boys?"

"No," we replied.

Then he said, "Throw out your net on the right-hand side of the boat, and you'll get plenty of them!" So we did, and couldn't draw in the net because of the weight of the fish, there were so many!

When we got there, we saw that a fire was kindled and fish were frying over it, and there was bread.

"Bring some of the fish you've just caught," Jesus said.

"Now come and have some breakfast!" Jesus said;

One day as he was walking along the beach beside the Lake of Galilee, he saw two brothers—Simon, also called Peter, and Andrew—out in a boat fishing with a net, for they were commercial fishermen.

Jesus called out, "Come along with me and I will show you how to fish for the souls of men!" And they left their nets at once and went with him.

God, help us to be better fishers of men than we sometimes are fishermen of the sea. Give us a sense of direction and stewardship in fishing.

PART IV

FOR ADULTS ONLY

CHAPTER 13

DYNAMIC DUO

A Christian family begins at marriage. A relationship is established that serves as a backbone for whatever family members follow.

Marriage partners must have complete acceptance and trust and respect for each other. I am talking about the kind of trust and respect that makes a team. Two persons operating and thinking together for the good of each other and the family.

These attitudes are important because (1) they are what make the marriage relationship real as God intended it to be, and (2) it is the foundation for the family's spiritual development. A couple's love for God is no more effective than their love for each other.

Bob and I first met at a big disc jockey convention in Miami. All the biggest stars were there and all the leading deejays were on hand. I had my million seller, "Till There Was You" on the market, so I was included right along with Connie Francis, Peggy Lee, Pat Boone, and many others.

Joe Carlton of Carlton Records arranged for me to meet the well-known Miami disc jockey, Bob Green, because it was a good professional contact. How little did any of us guess just how beneficial that meeting would be.

I was very dubious of Bob in the beginning. He was so sharp, so friendly, and so handsome. "No one," I thought, "could be all that and be for real."

Bob pursued our courtship against heavy odds: distance, my lack of interest, my family's disapproval, no time to be together. But, thank God, he persisted.

Soon my resistance turned to acceptance and I found myself deeply in love with this big handsome Swede. In order for us to marry, however, I had to make what seemed like, at that time, some real professional sacrifices. On June 25, we were married and left immediately for a show date in New York.

Bob became a Christian the night before our wedding. It was a beautiful way to begin married life. Somehow I must have felt this would automatically guarantee a successful marriage.

Instead of making our marriage an instant success, it proved to be the sustaining factor that brought us through conflict after conflict. Our love for each other and our mutual commitment to Christ were and are the very basis for our marriage.

However, this is only a starting point. On top of Christian love must come lots of hard work at making the marriage satisfying. It takes time, understanding and patience. It takes thought and creativity. In short, marriage is one of the hardest tasks a person can have. I am constantly trying to think of ways to let Bob know I love him. I send him flowers (orchids are his favorite). I send him green plants, I call him during the day to tell him I love him, I send messages in the mail. It makes life fun and marriage more exciting.

As children began to arrive and our business began to expand, the stresses became greater. We have to work harder at maintaining a good marriage relationship. We have found that a major ingredient now is time to be together.

Bob and I have a beautiful advantage in this area. Since our profession calls for so much travel, we have plenty of time for an adult relationship.

It is hard, with four children, to set aside much private time just to sit and talk, or have an adult meal at home.

I am convinced, though, if a husband and wife are home most of the time, they should have a standing date with a good baby sitter. Once or twice a month Mother and Daddy should have time alone to do something they both enjoy. It may be eating out, going to a movie, ball game, or having a fancy private dinner at home. To a marriage, this time is invaluable and certainly money well spent.

Parents have to catch their times when it seems best. Sometimes we even have Saturday morning coffee together before the children get up. We have a little patio area off the kitchen that is just large enough for a table and a couple of chairs. It is a perfect place for time alone to renew friendship.

The recipes I'm including here are a little fancy—not gourmet—but with a few garnishes they certainly rank above food you fix for the children. I hope as you read them you get excited about trying something new for an adult dinner.

Remember, you must really go all out with the extras if you plan to eat at home. Use the good silver, the good china, have candles and flowers. Wear something especially becoming.

Explain to the children that this dinner is for adults only. A special picnic of store-bought hamburgers will be more tempting to them anyway.

UPSIDE DOWN HAM BAKE

1 pound cooked ham, ground
1 small onion, chopped
1 teaspoon prepared mustard
2 cups herb-seasoned croutons
2 eggs, beaten with small
  amount of milk

¼ cup brown sugar
¼ teaspoon ground cloves
½ cup raisins
½ cup chopped pecans
1 small can pineapple slices
parsley

Preheat oven to 400 degrees. Combine ham, onion, and mustard. Soak croutons in egg mixture for a few minutes, then add to ham and mix well.

Line a large loaf pan with foil. Sprinkle brown sugar, cloves, raisins, and nuts over the bottom of the pan. Place the pineapple on top. Press ham mixture on top of pineapple slices to form a loaf. Bake for 1 hour. Turn the loaf out on a platter and serve. Since the loaf looks so pretty, garnish with little parsley sprigs and slice it at the table.

Bob's mother is a good Swedish cook. It is really difficult to select only a few of her recipes to include in a cookbook. Of course, she cooks by pinches, dabs, and tastes, so it is almost impossible to get a recipe of hers on paper.

STUFFED CABBAGE ROLLS (Swedish Kaldomar)
Farmar Green (Mrs. Einar)

> 1 medium head cabbage

FILLING:

> ¼ cup instant rice   1 egg
> ¼ cup water   salt and white pepper
> ¼ cup milk   dry mustard
> 1 pound ground beef

TO FRY:

> 2 tablespoons margarine   2 cups water
> 1 tablespoon brown sugar

Preheat oven to 325 degrees. Discard wilted leaves and cut out core of cabbage. Place cabbage in boiling salted water. Cook until leaves separate. Drain. Cook rice in the ¼ cup water and add milk. Cook until tender. Cool and mix with ground beef, egg, and seasonings. Trim thick center vein of cabbage leaves and put about 2 tablespoons of mixture on each leaf. Fold leaves around meat mixture and fasten with toothpicks. Heat margarine in skillet and brown rolls on all sides. Mix brown sugar and 2 cups water. Pour over rolls.

Place in medium oven about 1 hour. Baste occasionally.

Ed Gerlach and his wife, Doris, are friends of ours from Houston. Ed owns a booking agency and has an orchestra that I sing with when we do a booking in that area. They have a way of making each event an enjoyable experience.

OYSTERS AND WILD RICE
Doris Gerlach (Mrs. Ed)

> 1 cup wild rice   salt and pepper
> 1 cup brown rice   Tabasco sauce
> ½ pound margarine
> 4 dozen raw oysters, well
>   drained

Preheat oven to 300 degrees. Cook all the rice until tender. Add margarine and toss until melted. Place half the rice in a shallow baking dish. Add a layer of all the oysters. Then top with remaining rice. Season with salt, pepper, and Tabasco to taste. Pour sauce over the rice and bake for 45 minutes.

SAUCE:

1 can cream of chicken soup
1 cup light cream
¾ teaspoon thyme

1½ teaspoons curry
onion salt

Mix all ingredients well.

CHICKEN HAWAII STYLE

2 2½-pound broiler-fryer
   chickens, quartered
3 cups pineapple chunks
1 cup pineapple juice

1 cup soy sauce
1 teaspoon ginger
4 small cloves garlic, crushed
shortening

Place chicken in 13 × 9 × 2-inch baking dish. To make marinade, combine pineapple, pineapple juice, soy sauce, ginger, and garlic. Pour over chicken; refrigerate at least 4 hours, turning chicken several times.

Preheat oven to 325 degrees. Drain chicken; reserve marinade. In large heavy skillet, brown chicken in oil; remove to a 13 × 9 × 2-inch baking dish. Add marinade; bake 1 hour or until chicken is tender. Baste several times during baking.

Makes 8 servings (¼ chicken each).

Marabel Morgan does so many things well, it seems like an understatement to talk about her good cooking.

The best thing about Marabel's cooking is that it lives up to her book reputation in every way. In her book, *The Total Woman*, Marabel describes the Christian concept of wives pleasing husbands. Her cooking does just that.

The following recipes are some of Marabel's choice ones.

DELICIOUS ASPARAGUS
Marabel Morgan (Mrs. Charlie)

1 cup grated sharp cheese   *1 cup mushroom soup*
2 cups crumbled saltines   *1 large can asparagus*
½ cup butter   *½ cup almonds*

Preheat oven to 400 degrees. Mix cheese and crackers. Melt butter and soup, then add enough asparagus juice to fill soup can. Put layer of crumbs and cheese in casserole dish, then asparagus spears, then almonds, then a little liquid. Repeat process, ending with crumbs and cheese on top.

Bake for 20 minutes.

Makes 6 servings.

STUFFED MUSHROOMS IN CREAM
Marabel Morgan (Mrs. Charlie)

1 pound very large mushrooms   *1½ teaspoons salt*
⅓ cup butter   *¼ teaspoon pepper*
1 medium onion, chopped fine   *1 tablespoon lemon juice*
2¼ cups soft bread crumbs   *strips of bacon*
1 tablespoon catsup   *½ cup cream*

Preheat oven to 400 degrees. Wash mushrooms, dry well, remove stems and chop, hollow out the crowns. Melt butter, sauté stems and onion. Stir in crumbs and cook 2 minutes. Stir in catsup, salt, pepper, and lemon juice. Stuff mushrooms, garnish tops with narrow strips of bacon to form cross. Bake in glass dish—pour cream over. Bake for 20 minutes.

Makes 6 to 8 servings.

Our association with the Florida Citrus Commission has been a delightful experience from the beginning. Every time we are able to attend a gathering of any kind that includes members of the commission, we come away feeling enriched. These people are so rich in understanding, in fellowship, and in togetherness that it is just a real blessing to be included.

One of the friends we have made in this association gave me a wonderful recipe for overnight vegetable salad. Recipes are like friends—they are more fun if they are shared, and then shared again. This recipe came to me from Betty Hamrick and it came to her from a friend in Texas; now I pass it on to you.

BILLIE REMINGTON OVERNIGHT SALAD
Betty Hamrick (Mrs. David)

1 head lettuce, broken up with fingers	1 pound bacon, fried crisp, then broken up
1 head cauliflower, cut up in flowerets	2 cups salad dressing
1 sweet onion, sliced	⅓ cup Parmesan cheese
	¼ cup sugar

Using large plastic bowl with tight cover, put in ingredients in layers as they are listed. Seal tight. Put in refrigerater overnight. Toss just before serving. If you want to use part of this salad, dip straight down and put in another bowl to mix. This serves quite a group, and is great for family night suppers or buffets. Be sure you give it at least 12 hours so the topping gets crunchy.

ACCORDION DINNER BREAD

1 package hot-roll mix	2½ tablespoons minced scallions
1 egg	sesame seeds
½ cup melted butter or margarine	

ABOUT 3 HOURS BEFORE SERVING:

Prepare hot-roll mix as label directs, but add only ½ cup warm water to yeast; add 1 egg yolk and ¼ cup melted butter, beating well. Knead dough a minute or so or till smooth and elastic, then let it rise in warm place (80 to 85 degrees) for 1 hour, or until doubled in bulk.

On a lightly floured board, roll dough ⅛ inch thick. With 5-inch round cookie cutter, or with edge of 5-inch plate or bowl as guide, make nine or ten circles; shape each circle into an oval.

Brush one of the ovals with melted butter or margarine, sprinkle with a little minced scallion, fold almost in half, place on a greased cookie sheet; then brush the top folded side with melted butter or margarine. Repeat with rest of ovals, making one row, with ovals leaning against each other. Let them rise again about 30 minutes.

Preheat oven to 375 degrees. Brush bread with a beaten egg white; sprinkle with sesame seed; bake 25 minutes or till golden. Cool slightly, then serve, breaking off sections.

Makes 1 loaf.

I could *never* make piecrust until Marabel Morgan gave me her piecrust recipe. It works great—every time!

MARABEL MORGAN'S PIECRUST
Marabel Morgan (Mrs. Charlie)

1 cup flour
½ teaspoon salt
⅓ cup shortening

1 tablespoon butter
1 cup water with ice cubes

In a small bowl, combine flour and salt. Add half the shortening and butter; cut in with pastry blender or two knives until consistency of coarse corn meal. Cut in remaining shortening and butter until mixture looks like large peas. Sprinkle water, 1 tablespoon at a time, over the flour mixture; mix with a fork, adding only enough water to make pastry cling together to form a ball. Roll out pastry on a lightly floured pastry cloth, into a circle about 12 inches in diameter. Flip towel to fold pastry in half; place over 9-inch pie plate. Gently ease pastry into plate; roll under edges and crimp.

Makes pastry for 1 crust (8 or 9 inches).

COCONUT CREAM PIE
Audrey Staton

1 9-inch baked pie shell

FILLING:

⅔ cup sugar
3 tablespoons flour
1½ tablespoons cornstarch
¼ teaspoon salt
2¼ cups milk

2 egg yolks, beaten
1 tablespoon butter
¾ teaspoon vanilla
1 cup shredded coconut

MERINGUE:

2 egg whites   ¼ cup sugar
dash salt   ½ cup shredded coconut

Preheat oven to 325 degrees. In saucepan, combine sugar, flour, cornstarch, and salt. Gradually blend in milk. Cook over medium heat, stirring constantly, until mixture thickens and is smooth. Blend a small amount of the hot mixture into yolks; return to mixture in saucepan and cook 1 minute. Remove from heat; blend in butter, vanilla, and coconut. Pour into baked pie shell.

In small bowl, beat egg whites and salt until foamy. Gradually add sugar, 1 tablespoon at a time, beating well after each addition until stiff peaks form. Spread meringue over filling, making certain to seal edges completely; sprinkle with coconut. Bake 10 to 15 minutes or until meringue and coconut are brown; cool 2 to 3 hours before serving.

Makes a 9-inch pie (6 servings).

CHOCOLATE ANGEL PIE

SHELL:

3 egg whites   ½ teaspoon vanilla
⅛ teaspoon salt   6 tablespoons sugar
¼ teaspoon cream of tartar   ½ cup finely chopped pecans

FILLING:

1 package (4 ounces) German   1 tablespoon vanilla
    sweet chocolate   ½ pint heavy cream
3 tablespoons water

Preheat oven to 300 degrees. In a large bowl, beat egg whites until foamy; add salt, cream of tartar, and vanilla; continue beating until soft peaks form. Gradually add sugar, 1 tablespoon at a time, beating well after each addition until stiff peaks form; fold in nuts. Spread meringue over bottom and sides of well-buttered 9-inch pie plate; build up edges to form a high rim. Bake 50 to 55 minutes or until light brown and crisp to the touch. Cool away from drafts.

In top of double boiler, combine chocolate and water. Place over hot water; cook, stirring until chocolate is melted and mixture is smooth. Remove from heat; add vanilla and cool. Whip heavy cream; fold in the chocolate mixture; spoon into cooled shell and chill. If desired, serve garnished with additional whipped cream.

Makes a 9-inch pie (6 servings).

RECIPE TO PRESERVE A HUSBAND

Be careful in your selection. Do not choose too young, and take only such varieties as have been reared in a good moral atmosphere. When once decided upon and selected, let that part remain forever settled and give your entire thought to preparation for domestic use. Some insist on keeping them in a domestic pickle while others are constantly getting them in hot water. Even poor varieties may be made sweet, tender, and good by garnishing them with patience, well sweetened by smiles, and flavored with kisses. Then wrap well in a mantle of charity, keep warm with a steady fire of domestic devotion, and serve with peaches and cream.

When thus prepared, they will keep for years.

—from the files of Blanche Garner

CHAPTER 14

PARTNERS IN BUSINESS AND PLEASURE

Being partners in business has its joys as well as its strains. Bob and I floundered for one terrible year trying to maintain separate business obligations. We prayed, and the Lord sent an answer. If we joined each other in the same goal, we could each get a lot farther down the road to success.

Bob had exactly what I lacked in my profession—business sense, managerial qualities, and an eye for details. As a team, it would be a perfect match. We realized it would certainly take an unusual marriage to sustain such constant togetherness.

After much prayer and consideration, Bob decided to join me, in my entertainment career, as a personal business manager. It has been a good decision. The business has grown smoothly and steadily. Suddenly the problems of flights, meals, schedules, hotels, and money were not my worries. Bob set up his office at our house. There were two secretaries who were also available to help take up household slack when we got in a tight spot.

Things were smooth sailing and we were, at one time, at the point where we were free to live under less pressure than we had in previous years. The traveling was less, the demands on my energy seemed to be fewer—it was like semiretirement.

But when you are committed to the Lord and His plan for your life, there really isn't any rest. God began to seriously burden Bob's heart about a new venture, one that would again, after thirteen years, throw us into change and a new way of life. It happened like this.

Bob felt badly that we had so many more requests from churches and Christian groups than we could fill. Often the person calling would say, "Well, do you know anyone else we could get?"

Bob began to realize there was no one who seemed to be nurturing Christian talent. There was no one to help churches get in contact with persons who could entertain for banquets, conventions, revivals, etc. Slowly Bob began to dream about Fishers of Men—an agency for Christian performers. It would be a non-profit organization. Whatever income developed would be returned to the ministry in some way. The idea was so good, we began to get excited.

Obstacles we never dreamed of began immediately to block our every effort.

Our very dear friend, Teddy Heard, was supportive in our venture. She and Marabel Morgan became our prayer partners for the business endeavor. This soon became such an important part of our lives and our dreams that I would have been willing to sacrifice anything to see it develop. I have never prayed so earnestly and so long for any one thing. I sincerely felt it would be a beautiful way for Bob to turn his talents into a living witness for the Lord.

The first step was to move Bob's office to a new office building which would be a more fitting spot to conduct a business of this sort. The agency would not compete in any way with a secular agency. This was strictly a ministry for the Lord.

I really was not prepared, however, for what it meant to have Bob move the office out of the house. It nearly destroyed me for a time. Bob had always been at home when I needed him. He had taken care of all the plants, supervised the household staff, and helped care for the children. The secretaries always took care of the phone, the door, all deliveries, and a dozen other chores.

All of a sudden that was gone and I was left in charge of what four persons had been doing. The stress really got to me.

Then, as if the world was beginning to collapse around me, Teddy Heard went in the hospital for rather routine surgery and died soon thereafter. The blow was staggering. We had been so close!

Then the court hassle started over our getting a license to operate Fishers of Men officially. The hassle lasted eight months. I truly believe, considering all things, those were the most difficult eight months of my life. I have rarely withstood such constant struggles.

Nevertheless it brought us to a place of total submission. We are willing to let God's way be ours. Now, I abide in a peace that really passes understanding.

As I sat one day in the office, working on this book, Bob and Charlie Morgan (our friend, prayer partner, and lawyer) came in to report their morning's experience in court. The license for Fishers of

Men had been granted by the state of Florida. We were in business at last! Again, partners in a new venture!

Fishers of Men, by this time, had become a business venture to include more partners than we could name. That is, partners in prayer. Marabel and Charlie Morgan joined us in prayer. Jody Dunton and the Chapmans joined us in prayer. In fact, most of Northwest Baptist Church were partners in this prayer.

For example, on the Saturday night before the court appearance on Monday, Jody was hostessing a dinner at our house. Jody is the nurse who helped introduce our twins to life as they hung in the balance for so long at birth. Since then, she has been as much a part of our family as any of us.

Jody had wanted to have a dinner party for some time, but her small apartment and her guest list just didn't match. She asked if she could stage her dinner at our house. It sounded like fun to me, so we set a date. Jody invited Bro. Bill and Peggy and Charlie and Marabel Morgan.

The dinner was superb in every way, although Jody was convinced it wouldn't be. Midway in the preparation, I noticed Jody was getting so uptight, I wondered if she would make it through the evening. I walked through the kitchen. She looked so distraught, I took her hands in mine and we prayed, asking for God's blessings on the meal and on Jody. Things went beautifully from that point on.

The fellowship and spirit seemed unusually close that night. I could feel the warmness slowly enfolding each of us. Just before the party broke up, I suggested we have a circle of prayer for the Fishers of Men court decision coming up. There, in the living room we all held hands and prayed, oh, so earnestly. I think at that moment I received assurance God would see to it that Fishers of Men would come into being.

How little did Jody know when she planned that dinner that it would turn out to be so significant.

JODY'S MENU
Jody Dunton

Cheese Balls   Tomato Juice Supreme   Mixed Fruit
  Fresh Green Beans   Scalloped Potatoes
Lettuce Cup with Tomatoes   Molded Gelatin
            Cornish Hens
         Chocolate Mousse
         Strawberry Cake

BITE-SIZE CHEESE BALLS
Peggy Noel, Sanford, Florida

8 ounces sharp Cheddar   ½ cup margarine, melted
  cheese, grated   25 stuffed green olives
1¼ cups flour

Mix cheese with flour until crumbly. Add margarine and mix with a fork until moldable. Mold 1 teaspoon of cheese mixture around an olive to form a bite-size ball. Refrigerate for at least an hour or overnight. Bake 2 inches apart on cookie sheet for 15 minutes at 400 degrees. Serve hot.
Makes about 20 to 25 cheese balls.

SCALLOPED POTATOES

6 medium potatoes   1 teaspoon salt
3 tablespoons butter or   ¼ teaspoon pepper
  margarine   2 tablespoons onion, chopped
2 tablespoons flour   fine
1½ cups milk   ¾ cup fine bread crumbs mixed
1 small carton sour cream   with chopped parsley

Preheat oven to 350 degrees.
Slice the potatoes thin. Place half the slices in a shallow baking dish.
Make a white sauce using the butter, flour, milk, sour cream, and seasonings. Pour half the sauce over the layer of potatoes. Sprinkle with 1 tablespoon of the onions. Repeat the layers. Top with the bread crumb mixture.

Cover and bake about 1 hour. Uncover and continue baking until the top is slightly brown.

Makes 6 servings.

CORNISH HENS

4 Cornish hens, split	½ cup melted butter
salt	½ cup lemon juice
pepper	

Preheat oven to 350 degrees. Place hens in large roasting pan, skin side down; season to taste with salt and pepper. Combine butter and lemon juice; use to baste hens every 15 minutes during baking. Bake 20 minutes; turn skin side up and bake 25 to 35 minutes longer or until done. Serve garnished with crab apples and parsley.

Makes 4 servings (1 hen each).

INSTANT CHOCOLATE MOUSSE
Jody Dunton

2 packages chocolate fudge instant pudding mix	1½ pints heavy cream ⅓ cup sugar
2 egg whites	

Prepare pudding as directed on package. Beat egg whites until stiff and fold into pudding.

Whip cream, gradually adding sugar. Fold ⅔ of whipped cream into pudding and refrigerate. Spoon into large glass bowl. To serve, garnish with remaining whipped cream.

Makes 10 to 12 servings.

TWO-LAYER GELATIN SALAD
Jody Dunton

1 package lemon-flavored gelatin	1 cup cold water
1 cup hot water	1 large package cream cheese,
1 small can crushed pineapple with juice	softened

Dissolve gelatin in hot water; add pineapple juice and cold water to make one cup, add cream cheese. Use a blender or mixer to mix well. Chill until partially set. Add pineapple and return to refrigerator.

SECOND LAYER:

2 packages black cherry-
  flavored gelatin
2 cups liquid—water added to
  berry juice

2 cans (8 ounces each) black
  sweet pitted cherries
  (reserve the juice)

Dissolve gelatin in 1 cup hot liquid. Add 1 cup cold liquid. Let cool completely. Add cherries. Carefully pour over first layer. Refrigerate.

Makes 10 to 12 servings.

MRS. MICHAEL'S FROZEN STRAWBERRY CAKE

This is a delicious cake and fast and easy to make, great for family, church suppers, or guests.

CAKE:

1 package (3 ounces)
  strawberry-flavored gelatin
½ cup warm water
1 package (about 1 pound, 3
  ounces) white cake mix

4 eggs
1 cup salad oil
½ cup strawberry juice (from
  frozen strawberries in icing
  below)

STRAWBERRY ICING:

¼ cup butter or margarine,
  softened
1 pound confectioners' sugar

1 package (10 ounces) frozen
  strawberries, drained (use
  juice for cake)

Preheat oven to 350 degrees. Lightly grease a 13 × 9 × 2-inch baking pan. In large bowl, dissolve gelatin in warm water. Add remaining ingredients for cake and beat on high speed of mixer 3 to 4 minutes. Pour into prepared pan; bake 20 to 30 minutes. Cool.

To make frosting, in small bowl mix butter and sugar; blend in strawberries. Spread over cake; cut into 3-inch squares.

Makes 12 servings.

MY PLEA

Dear Lord, I pray you will be my guide
That you will walk right by my side.
That I may place my hand in Thine.
And through my life Thy light will shine.

Help me to walk and talk and live
That unto others I might give
A bit of joy and peace and love
That only comes from Thee above.

My heart cannot contain the song
Of these requests for which I long
O Christ, I pray you will live in me
That through me others may know thee.

by Teddy Moody Heard

CHAPTER 15

DINNER FOR TWO OR TWENTY

Villa Verde (House of the Greens) became our new home in 1968. It is a perfectly charming twenty-nine-room house on the bay. It was a ridiculous jump from where we had been. But it had a charm about it we couldn't resist. There was a lot of fixing and finishing we wanted to do to really put our stamp on the place. The process was fun and frustrating all at the same time.

It wasn't long before we had a yen to have someone in to dinner. A dinner party would be just the kind of celebration we needed to "christen" a new home. So we started to plan the guest list. Immediately we put Joyce and Dr. Bernie Vinoski on the list, somehow we couldn't go any further. We didn't know the Morgans, Jody, or other friends God has given us since that time.

We were traveling a lot in those days and when we returned home after each trip, all we wanted was peace, quiet, and privacy. We were not very outgoing and the friendship list was very limited. Joyce and Bernie were our previous neighbors. They are so even and easy to be with that their friendship was, and is, priceless to us. There just wasn't anyone else at that time with whom we really could share such a momentous occasion. So the guest list stopped about where it started.

A second problem immediately arose. Joyce is just about the best cook I know. Her many contributions to my recipe file and to this book attest to the fact. When I began planning the menu for the evening, I realized all my best possibilities were recipes that Joyce had given me, and, of course, I couldn't serve her back one of her own recipes. I racked my brain trying to decide what to do.

About that time the postman came, bringing my first issue of Gourmet magazine, which Joyce had given me. Inside was this fantastic menu designed to serve twenty people—but it looked so good.

Since the magazine had only just arrived that day, I knew those would be the few recipes I could count on that Joyce had not tried.

The menu started with a twelve-pound salmon, with carrots purée, and veal with mushrooms. It was just a beautiful gourmet meal for a large dinner party. My gourmet cooking experience was so limited, I was afraid to cut down on the recipes. So in a final decision, I took on the whole menu. Fortunately, my luck runs real good on first attempts (and it is a good thing; I needed all the luck I could get at that time).

I started by having to purchase a certain French poaching pan and other special equipment to do just the things the instructions called for. I cooked for a week!

Things began to get more comical as the days went by. The third major problem arrived when I considered the seating arrangement for my "big" dinner party. The dining room at Villa Verde is quite an imposing room, large with a long dining table that can seat twelve to fourteen persons. A dinner party for four was ridiculous-looking, but since the purpose of the event was to celebrate the new house, I wanted the first dinner party staged in the dining room.

The attire was formal and the guests arrived on schedule. Bob sat at one end of the long table and I sat at the other end. The Vinoskis sat on either side. We were all so far apart we could hardly talk. It was so comical we are laughing about it to this day.

Then when I served a six-course meal for twenty-persons, they really couldn't believe it. The meal turned out perfect in every way. I even ended with baked Alaska. The dinner flabbergasted Joyce so badly, it was months before they invited us to dinner. She vowed she could never top a dinner for twenty!

The poached salmon turned out so well that it has now become one of our favorite special-event dishes. In fact, it has become traditional with us at Christmas.

It was a grand night, full of fun and friendship and laughter. It was truly a fitting and joyous opening event to entertaining at Villa Verde.

This story is simply another illustration of how important food, eating, and mealtime events are to the tradition of a family and home. Even though that night was so funny in so many ways, it is one of the times that bonded our friendship with the Vinoskis.

I really don't remember all the exact recipes I used that night. But I am including other favorite recipes that we use for dinner parties.

Since that first dinner party there have been many more. Entertaining is something that comes very naturally for us. We enjoy every aspect.

I plan well in advance for a party, carefully listing every detail. I even list the exact serving dishes I will be using.

I also plan the guest list carefully. I try to include a few "standard" party people. These are the people I can count on to carry the conversation or provide a spark of life if things get dull.

If the party is large or if the schedule preceding the party is rushed, I usually plan to have at least one or two dishes catered—usually the main dish and appetizer, which really relieves the strain.

I insist on preparing all do-ahead dishes. It was customary for hostesses in Grandma Berry's day to spend full time in the kitchen during a company dinner. I frankly don't want to miss out on the fun, so what isn't done when the guests arrive just about goes undone!

Often I feel the whole party reflects my attitude and temperament at the time. A rushed, nervous hostess puts everyone on edge. I like to concentrate my full attention on the guests and their conversation.

I enjoy using fresh flowers for all party occasions. They lend a special atmosphere that seems to show you went to a little extra trouble.

Although we, of course, do not serve alcoholic drinks, we do often enjoy an informal "happy hour" on some occasions. A typical light and bubbly drink for these occasions (Cranberry Cheer) is included in the recipe section of this chapter.

CURRIED NUTS

⅓ cup olive oil
1 tablespoon soy sauce
1 tablespoon curry powder
¼ teaspoon cayenne

3 cups mixed nuts (almonds,
cashews, pecans, peanuts,
and walnuts)

Preheat oven to 300 degrees. In large skillet, combine olive oil, soy sauce, curry powder, and cayenne; bring to a boil. Add the nuts;

mix to coat thoroughly. Line an 11 × 7 × 2-inch baking pan with foil; add nuts and bake about 10 minutes.
Makes 3 cups.

CHEESE 'N' BEEF NIBBLES

½ pound American cheese,
  grated
½ pound sharp Cheddar
  cheese, grated
½ pound butter

2 cups flour
1 teaspoon salt
dash red pepper
½ pound ground meat

Blend cheese and butter. Add all other ingredients *except meat.* Mix well. Roll into rolls 8 inches long and 1½ inches in diameter. Wrap in wax paper and chill for several hours.

Preheat oven to 400 degrees. Slice rolls into ¼-inch slices. Bake on cookie sheet about 10 minutes.

Meanwhile shape ground meat into tiny balls about 1 inch in diameter. Broil the meatballs until done.

Top each cheese wafer with a meatball.

The Florida Citrus commercials have brought us many great friends. Sandy and Vera Semel are prime examples. Sandy is one of the producers of the commercials.

Vera gave me a recipe from her native Holland. This Dutch recipe is served as an appetizer or snack.

BITTER BALLS
Vera Semel (Mrs. Sandy)

"Bitter" means "hearty."

4 tablespoons butter or
  margarine
⅓ cup flour
¾ teaspoon salt
⅛ teaspoon pepper
¼ teaspoon celery salt
1 package unflavored gelatin
½ cup milk
½ cup beef broth

2½ cups coarsely ground cooked
  beef (soup meat)
1 teaspoon grated onion
2 teaspoons finely chopped
  parsley
1 slightly beaten egg, diluted
  with 1 tablespoon water
fine, dry bread crumbs

Melt the butter, blend in flour, salt, pepper, celery salt, and gelatin. Add milk and broth. Cook, stirring until thickened and smooth. Remove from heat.

Add beef, onion, and parsley. Chill in refrigerator for several hours.

Remove from refrigerator and shape into very small balls. Dip into beaten egg and water mixture. Roll in bread crumbs. Deep fry and serve with mustard. (Oil should not be overly hot.)

CHERRY TOMATO TREATS

¾ pound cherry tomatoes
½ to ¾ pound ground beef
1 tablespoon onion, minced
2 tablespoons soy sauce
¼ teaspoon salt
¼ teaspoon pepper

¼ teaspoon marjoram
¼ teaspoon thyme
¼ teaspoon basil
3 tablespoons dried bread crumbs

Cut a thin slice from top and bottom of the tomatoes. Scoop out insides and reserve for adding to the meat mixture later.

Brown the meat and add onion. Drain off fat. Add seasonings and simmer for 5 minutes. Remove from heat and cool slightly. Add bread crumbs and mix. Stuff tomatoes with mixture. Serve warm.

SHRIMP FOR HORS D'OEUVRES
Evelyn Galvin (Mrs. Bill)

2 pounds medium shrimp, cooked and cleaned
1 cup mayonnaise
¼ cup chili sauce
¼ cup salad oil
1 small onion, finely chopped

1 stalk celery with leaves, finely chopped
1 small clove garlic, minced
1 teaspoon celery seed
1 teaspoon dill weed

In container with cover, combine all ingredients; refrigerate overnight. Serve with crackers, melba toast, or small rye bread.
Makes 20 to 25 shrimp.

CRANBERRY CHEER

1 package (3 ounces) cherry-
  flavored gelatin
1 cup boiling water
1 can (6 ounces) frozen
  lemonade

3 cups cold water
1 quart cranberry juice cocktail,
  chilled
1 pint ginger ale, chilled

In small bowl, dissolve gelatin in boiling water; stir in lemonade
until dissolved. Add water and cranberry juice. Place 2 trays ice
cubes (or molded ice ring) in a 3-quart punch bowl; pour punch
over ice. Slowly add ginger ale.

Makes about 10½ cups.

Variation: Substitute 1 can (6 ounces) pineapple-orange juice concentrate for the frozen lemonade.

Many years ago we went to Texas to perform at John Connally's
gubernatorial inauguration. After the ceremony, we all went to Luci
and Pat Nugent's house. Luci fixed scrambled eggs for us. With President and Mrs. Johnson, the secret service, friends, relatives, and
family members, there was a big gang of us, so it took a lot of scrambled eggs.

I tell this to describe what a spontaneous, easy, down-to-earth person Luci is. She did not worry in the least or fuss over a big menu.
She used what she had to make a delightful and special occasion.

But Luci is a marvelous cook and often does long and involved
dishes. Luci often took pride in having her mother and daddy over
to dinner.

She shared the following recipe with me.

SWEET AND SOUR PORK
Luci Johnson Nugent (Mrs. Patrick)

1¼ pounds lean pork, cut in 1½-inch squares ½ inch thick (or cube the pork or leftover pork roast) I like it best cubed!
1 egg, beaten
6 teaspoons cornstarch
3 tablespoons fat
1 cup sugar

1 cup vinegar (½ wine vinegar and ½ regular)
1 cup water
4 teaspoons cornstarch
1 medium green pepper, cut in 1-inch squares
3 or 4 slices pineapple, cut in pieces

Dip pork in egg and place a few pieces at a time in a small paper bag with cornstarch. Coat each piece thoroughly. Cook in very hot oil for 3 minutes, drain on paper. Combine sugar, vinegar, and water; bring to a boil and add paste—4 tablespoons cornstarch and a bit of water. Add pepper; cook gently, no more than 2 minutes, then add pork and pineapple.

It is very important that your pork cook the minimum of time necessary in order to remain moist. For the frying step, I put my pork in a deep-fry basket. If the temperature drops below 375, I remove the basket and wait for it to rise, so I use only the hottest temperature of fat.

A young Yankee skier recently shared this recipe with Dody Sawyer (our friend from Eastman Kodak).

SHRIMP CURRY
Dody Sawyer (Mrs. Bill)

1 20-ounce package frozen shrimp
2 tablespoons butter or margarine
½ large onion, chopped not fine
1 green pepper, chopped not fine

2 fresh tomatoes, cut in small chunks
1 can cream of shrimp soup
4 to 5 teaspoons curry powder
½ cup white cooking wine (optional)
½ pint sour cream

Cook shrimp. In electric fry pan or regular skillet, melt butter, add onion, and cook until yellow; add green pepper, cook until softened; then tomatoes and cook about 2 more minutes. Lower heat, add soup, curry powder, shrimp, and wine. Simmer until piping hot and add sour cream. Be careful not to boil the mixture after cream is added. This is a chunky, fresh tasting curry and can be made in a few minutes.

If the cream has not been added, it can be made early in the day and reheated quickly. Then the cream is added over low heat just before serving. Serve on or with rice of choosing. It is good with chutney on the side.

Makes 6 servings.

BROCCOLI CASSEROLE
Betty Hamrick (Mrs. David)

2 packages chopped broccoli	1 egg, beaten
1 can mushroom soup	1 cup grated Cheddar cheese
1 cup mayonnaise	

Preheat oven to 350 degrees. Cook broccoli 6 minutes; drain. Mix together the broccoli, soup, mayonnaise, egg, and cheese.
Top with Rice Krispies
Bake for ½ hour.

CHERRY PECAN PIE
Doris Gerlach (Mrs. Ed)

1 can sweetened condensed milk	1 ½ 2 can cherries, drained
juice 2 lemons	1 cup chopped pecans
½ pint heavy cream, whipped	2 8-inch baked pastry shells
1 cup sugar	

Mix ingredients together and pour into pastry shells. Place in refrigerator until set.
Makes 2 pies.

Deborah Vinoski is following in her mother's (Joyce's) footsteps as "cook par excellence." She discovered this recipe and made it once for the family. It was such a hit that she now makes it for her mother's dinner parties.

HONEY MOUSSE
Deborah Vinoski

¾ cup liquid honey	*2 cups heavy cream, whipped*
6 egg yolks, lightly beaten	*shaved chocolate*

In top of a double boiler, combine honey with egg yolks. Put the mixture over boiling water, stirring constantly until it coats the spoon.

Set the mixture in a bowl of cracked ice and stir until it is cool.

Fold the honey mixture into the whipped cream.

Transfer the mousse to a serving bowl and freeze without stirring for 3 to 4 hours.

Before serving, sprinkle the edge of the mousse with shaved chocolate.

DEAR LORD. O Lord, I know the Bible says that you are aware of even a sparrow that falls. That gives me great comfort on days like today. Because I know your care must extend to a tired, frustrated worn-out wife and mother, too. There have been so many hands reaching out to me today wanting love, wanting understanding, and wanting attention.

Children, husband, neighbors, friends, career—all wanting a part of me. Dear Lord, help there be enough of me to go around.

CHAPTER 16

DIETS—AN AMERICAN WAY OF LIFE

Bob has been on a diet for so long it is almost a permanent way of life for us. Recently we thought Bob was developing a serious heart condition. After several tests, it was discovered he had problems with the muscles around his heart. This could lead to a heart condition if it is not cared for properly.

The scare of such a possibility gave all of us new incentive to help Bob lose the weight the doctor recommended.

It has been estimated by some experts that there are 79,000,000 adult Americans overweight. Of these, at least 9,500,000 are dieting.

Overweight is a definite contributor to heart disease, which is the number-one killer in the United States.

The main difficulty with dieting for Bob is that he absolutely adores food! No matter the food, the time, or the company, Bob loves to eat. It is not only an obsession, but a genuine enjoyment. To have to give up food, to Bob, is to give up one of his grandest pleasures in life.

A second big difficulty with anyone's dieting is habit. An adult's eating pattern is so firmly established by the time he needs to alter it that it is like learning a whole new way of life. What has been put off as a lack of will power in dieters is really a normal response to lifelong conditioning. Habits are extremely difficult to change, especially a habit that is as psychological as eating.

One estimate indicates that 95 per cent or more of all dieters fail to stay on their diets; or if they lose the recommended weight, they gain it back soon after.

So a word to families who have to live with dieters—don't get discouraged. Praise instead of nag. Help instead of hinder.

To the dieter, I would like to pass on a few of the suggestions we have found helpful with Bob's fight for weight loss.

Begin before it really becomes a problem. A small alteration in eating habits when the margin is five or ten pounds is certainly the easier way to diet. Keep constant check on your weight and never let it get beyond the point of easy control.

Always begin a diet under the care of a doctor. Be sure all physical functions are working properly and there is no physical reason for the overweight. Severe dieting can be very dangerous to some physical conditions if they are not handled properly.

Use proper dieting methods. Too rapid loss is dangerous. It is possible to diet yourself to death. It is also possible to leave out valuable nutrients in crazy dieting practices. Not only do you lose weight, but you could lose your health, too. A slow, steady diet helps establish good, permanent eating habits. A crash diet is obviously not something you can maintain for very long; plus it makes the dieter so miserable that it works against the long-range goal.

Don't get discouraged. Weight loss takes time—lots of time. Your body needs time to readjust itself to reduced intake. Remember, it took months, probably even years, to gather enough excess weight to require dieting. It could take that long or longer to get rid of it.

Reward yourself for successfully reaching a weight goal. But *don't* use food as a reward. Reward yourself with a new outfit in your smaller size, or a new piece of art, or a fishing trip.

Make dieting as much fun as possible. Bland, uninteresting food is death to a dieter. There are too many marvelous alternatives. Maybe the recipes here will help.

HUNGER QUENCHER

1 can (10½ ounces) condensed beef broth
½ soup can water

1 teaspoon horseradish
½ teaspoon dill weed
½ teaspoon chopped parsley

In saucepan, combine all ingredients; heat just to simmering. Makes about 2 cups.

Serve Hunger Quencher with small diet wafers or celery sticks stuffed with the following mixture:

CELERY STUFFING

¾ *cup creamed cottage cheese*   *dash hot pepper sauce*
¼ *cup minced stuffed olives*

In small bowl, combine all ingredients; mix to blend well. Makes about 1 cup.

TOMATO SOUP

2 *beef bouillon cubes*   2 *cups tomato juice*
2 *cups boiling water*   *celery salt*
2 *cups shredded cabbage*   *pepper*
1 *cup thinly sliced celery*
2 *tablespoons chopped celery*
  tops

Dissolve cubes in boiling water. Add cabbage and celery and simmer 15 minutes. Add tomato juice and heat thoroughly. Add seasonings. Serve with melba toast.
Makes 5 servings.

We have been very fortunate to visit the White House on many different occasions. Sometimes the event was formal like a state dinner. Then we would spend the night in the Queen Victoria bedroom. On other visits, we would be personal family guests of President and Mrs. Johnson, and we would stay in the family apartment. No matter the occasion, President Johnson had the beautiful ability to make it seem like old-home week. He was so warm, so friendly, and so informal.

Usually, after all the guests had gone, we would all put on more comfortable clothing and join the Johnsons in their sitting room.

This drink was one of the President's favorites. We would all join him in his late-night diet drink.

THE PRESIDENT'S DIET DRINK
Lyndon B. Johnson
First served to us at the White House, March 14, 1968.

½ cup of skim milk
5 small ice cubes
1 teaspoon liquid Sucaryl
½ teaspoon vanilla extract

3 tablespoons frozen
concentrated Florida orange
juice or fresh Florida orange
juice

Mix ingredients in blender for 1 minute.
Makes 1 serving.

DEVILED SHORT RIBS
Mrs. M. H. Richardson, Florida Citrus Commission

5 to 6 pounds beef short ribs
¼ cup salad oil
1½ tablespoons dry mustard
1 tablespoon salt
½ teaspoon cayenne pepper
¼ teaspoon black pepper
2 beef bouillon cubes

2 cups finely chopped onions
2 tablespoons Worcestershire
sauce
2 tablespoons horseradish
1 tablespoon bottled sauce (for
gravy)

Brown short ribs well in oil in large Dutch oven over medium heat. Stir remaining ingredients and 1½ cups water in and around short ribs. Cover pan and cook over low heat about 2½ hours, or until ribs are fork tender.

Remove ribs to heated platter, skim fat from remaining gravy, add bottled sauce, and serve over ribs.

SPICED ASPARAGUS (for dieters)
Bettie Shepherd (Mrs. David)

2 cans (15 ounces each)
asparagus spears, drained
⅔ cup vinegar
½ cup water
sugar substitute equivalent to ½
cup sugar

1 teaspoon salt
½ teaspoon celery seed
6 whole cloves
2 sticks cinnamon

Place asparagus in shallow 6-cup serving dish. In saucepan, combine remaining ingredients; bring to a boil. Reduce heat; simmer several minutes. Pour over asparagus; cover and refrigerate overnight. Makes about 4 cups (6 to 8 servings).

VERDE VEGETABLE SALAD

1 *package unflavored gelatin*	1 *can small green peas, drained*
2 *packages lemon-flavored*	1 *cup cubed cucumber*
gelatin	1 *cup chopped cabbage*
3 *cups finely chopped celery*	¼ *cup vinegar*
1 *cup chopped almonds*	
1 *cup finely cut stuffed green*	
olives	

Prepare gelatins as directed. Add all the other ingredients. Pour into a well-greased salad mold. When congealed, serve on a lettuce leaf. Top with a dab of mayonnaise and a whole stuffed olive.

But you shouldn't be so concerned about perishable things like food. No, spend your energy seeking the eternal life that I, the Messiah, can give you. For God the Father has sent me for this very purpose.

The true Bread is a Person—the one sent by God from heaven, and he gives life to the world.

Jesus replied, "I am the Bread of Life. No one coming to me will ever be hungry again. Those believing in me will never thirst."

PART V

TAKING FOOD TO CHURCH

CHAPTER 17

FELLOWSHIP DINNERS

The early Christian Church had a number of practices that were meaningful and expressive. Unfortunately, many of these practices have been replaced or redesigned into more modern acts. One of the early church experiences was the love feast. Members of the faith gathered in a common place, ate a meal, and fellowshiped together. Fellowship was of vital importance to the early believers because of the intense persecution they suffered. The Bible speaks of Jesus' followers continuing steadfastly in the doctrine—breaking of bread, praying, and fellowshiping.

Today, the joys of a day-to-day Christian life can be shared in a significant way through the experience of fellowship at the meal table.

The Christian concept of fellowship is described by the Greek word *Koinonia*—literally translated "going shares."

Going shares with covered-dish meals is put into practice by our entire church family once a year.

During the past, this special Sunday was designated as "Old Fashioned Sunday," and we all wore old-fashioned costumes. It was our way to recapture the warm social feelings that seem to characterize the early turn-of-the-century congregations.

In most recent years we decided not to dress in old-fashioned costumes and just concentrated on present-day *koinonia*.

Each family brings enough food for their own family plus a little extra. Since we have so many children who come on the buses, we want to have plenty of food to go around.

Each woman brings her own specialty. I usually take a Florida Citrus Cake among our other things.

Before church a committee of women goes over to the church play yard and sets all the food out on large tables. The church furnishes tea, coffee, soft drinks, and bread. At the end of the service, there it is, tables and tables of luscious homemade goodies under a large tent. Each family has a blanket to sit on.

The process of eating together outside brings out a joyous social side of people that would never show during the normal church activities.

Sometimes it seems that our Sunday attitudes and our Sunday faces match our Sunday clothes. We get all dressed up and seem so prim and proper that no one gets to see the real person.

When we all enter into fellowship over the dinner table, it is easier to let down the regular church "look" and just be ourselves. We always meet people we did not know before. We get to know some persons so much better than we did before. Then we feel we have all "gone shares" in many more ways than food.

ANITA BRYANT'S FLORIDA CITRUS CAKE

First tried for Thanksgiving 1964.

CAKE:

1 package (about 1 pound, 3 ounces) yellow cake mix	4 eggs
1 package (3¾ ounces) instant lemon-flavored pudding mix	¾ cup water
	¾ cup oil

FROSTING:

1½ cups confectioners' sugar	⅓ cup concentrated Florida orange juice
2 tablespoons butter	

Preheat oven to 325 degrees. Grease a 10-inch tube pan. In large mixer bowl, combine all cake ingredients; mix well. Pour into prepared pan; bake 50 minutes or until done.

While cake is baking, in small bowl combine all ingredients for frosting. Spread over hot cake; cool cake in pan.

Makes a 10-inch cake (8 to 10 servings).

HOT CHICKEN SALAD

4 cups cooked cold cut-up
  chicken chunks
2 tablespoons lemon juice
¾ cup mayonnaise
1 teaspoon salt
½ teaspoon monosodium
  glutamate
2 cups chopped celery

4 hard-cooked eggs, sliced
¾ cup cream of chicken soup
1 teaspoon finely minced onion
2 pimientos, cut fine
1 cup grated cheese
1½ cups crushed potato chips
⅔ cup finely chopped toasted
  almonds

Combine all except cheese, potato chips, and almonds. Place in a large rectangular dish.

Top with cheese, potato chips, and almonds.

Let stand overnight in refrigerator.

Bake at 400 degrees for 20 to 25 minutes.

Makes 8 servings.

My sister, Sandra, and her family (husband Sam, daughters Kathy, sixteen, Lisa, ten, and Michelle, eight) attend a church in Topeka that has a nice custom of home suppers once a year. Each neighborhood has a host and hostess to serve the families in their immediate area. It is a way of extending the church fellowship beyond the church property and into the homes of membership.

When Sandra and Sam hosted the fellowship dinner in their neighborhood, she served this recipe of Lasagne.

LASAGNE
Sandra Bryant Page (Mrs. Sam)

1½ pounds ground beef
2 cans spaghetti sauce
1 can cream of mushroom soup
lasagne noodles, cooked and
  drained

½ pound mozzarella cheese,
  sliced
1 pound cottage cheese
Parmesan cheese

Preheat oven to 350 degrees. Cook ground beef in large skillet. Add spaghetti sauce and mushroom soup. Line 8 × 13 × 2-inch glass baking dish with cooked noodles. Spread over noodles ⅓ of the sauce. Arrange sliced cheese and spread with cottage cheese. Repeat. Top with remaining ⅓ of sauce, sprinkle with Parmesan cheese. Bake for 25 to 30 minutes.

VEGETABLE CASSEROLE

1 can hominy, drained
1 can tomatoes
1 package frozen, cut okra
2 teaspoons soy sauce
1 teaspoon celery seed

⅓ cup celery, cut in 1-inch
   pieces
1½ teaspoons salt
dash coarse-ground black pepper

Preheat oven to 350 degrees. Combine all ingredients in casserole dish. Bake uncovered for 1 hour.
Makes 8 servings.

FRANKFURTER SALAD

1 can (16 ounces) cut green
   beans, drained
4 frankfurters, sliced
2 cups raw cauliflowerets

⅔ cup Italian dressing
1 small onion, minced
½ small green pepper, diced
½ teaspoon dry mustard

In large bowl, combine all ingredients; mix well. Place in covered container; refrigerate overnight. Just before serving, toss to mix well.
Makes about 5½ cups (6 servings).

GARLIC GREEN BEANS

½ cup wine vinegar
3 buttons garlic
2 cans French-style green beans
2 teaspoons sugar

½ teaspoon salt
¼ teaspoon red pepper
½ cup corn oil

Place vinegar and garlic in blender and liquefy. Combine all other ingredients and pour over beans. Set mixture in covered container in refrigerator 24 hours before serving.
Serve cold.

Around Northwest Baptist Church when you hear the words "apple pie," almost everyone thinks immediately of Eileen Pope. She always bakes two pies to take to the fellowship dinners. Then she fills the in-between times baking apple pies for Bro. Bill and his family, missionaries home on furlough.

When the Popes' son was fourteen, he commented, "Mom, I will always be able to find someone to wash my clothes and make my bed, but when you go, your apple pie is going to go with you, and I will only have a memory."

Here is the Florida-famous Pope apple pie!

FRESH APPLE PIE
Mrs. Eileen Pope

FILLING:

¾ to 1 cup sugar
2 tablespoons flour
1 teaspoon cinnamon
¼ teaspoon nutmeg
¼ teaspoon salt

4 cups sliced apples (Jonathan or McIntosh)
2 tablespoons ice water
1 teaspoon lemon juice
2 tablespoons butter

PASTRY:

2 cups sifted flour
1 teaspoon salt
¾ cup shortening (¼ cup

margarine, ½ cup vegetable shortening)
¼ cup ice water

Preheat oven to 450 degrees. In large bowl, combine sugar, flour, cinnamon, nutmeg, and salt. Add apples; toss to coat well; set aside.

To make pastry, in small bowl combine flour and salt. Using a pastry blender or two knives, cut in shortening until mixture looks like small peas. Sprinkle ice water, 1 tablespoon at a time, over the flour mixture; mix with fork until pastry clings together to form a ball. Then, using fingers, press dough lightly only until it is smooth. Divide dough in half. Roll out half, on a lightly floured board, until ⅛ inch thick. Gently ease pastry into a 9-inch pie plate. Fill with apple mixture; sprinkle with water and lemon juice; dot with butter. Roll remaining pastry to ⅛-inch thickness. Moisten edge of lower crust with water; top with second crust. Trim upper crust about 1 inch larger than plate; fold upper crust under lower crust edge; seal and flute. Make slits in top crust for steam to escape; sprinkle with sugar or brush with milk to glaze the crust. Bake 10 minutes;

reduce temperature to 400 degrees and bake 35 to 40 minutes or until crust is golden grown.

Makes a 9-inch pie (6 servings).

150-YEAR-OLD POUNDCAKE
Joan Epstein

2⅔ cups sugar	3½ cups flour
8 medium eggs, separated	⅔ cup coffee cream
1 pound sweet butter	1 teaspoon vanilla

Preheat oven to 300 degrees. Measure out 6 level tablespoons sugar, whip egg whites, adding sugar as you whip. Place in refrigerator until needed. Cream butter well, gradually adding remaining sugar and egg yolks (2 at a time).

Add flour and cream alternately to the creamed mixture. Whip until mixture is as light as possible. Takes 10 minutes at low speed on electric mixer.

Still beating at low speed, whip in egg whites just long enough to mix well. Add vanilla at same time.

Pour into slightly greased tube pan, 10 × 4 inches deep, or two pans of smaller size. It should fall one inch after taken from oven. This gives desired waxy texture.

Bake for 1 hour and 25 minutes.

CHERRY DELIGHT
Mrs. Carl Loshinskie

Make graham cracker crust and press into 8 × 12-inch glass or 9 × 13-inch baking pan.

Whip 1 package whipped topping mix.

Blend in 1 8-ounce package cream cheese which has been left out to soften for easy blending.

Add 1 cup confectioners' sugar. Mix together and pour into cooled graham cracker crust. Set in refrigerator about 10 minutes.

Now add 1 21-ounce can cherry pie filling. (You may use blueberry instead.)

The Sunday school classes in our church have a practice of occasionally getting together for lunch. As I correspond and visit with persons from other churches, this seems to meet a need in many churches.

Women seem to have an innate desire to congregate, to exchange family news and stories, and to discuss the latest-in-whatever.

Sometimes these luncheons are at the church and accompany a mission study or Bible study. At other times the meal is staged in a private home. Several women's prayer groups I know meet in homes for meditation and lunch.

The following recipes are better suited to small luncheon groups than larger church gatherings such as the dinner on the grounds.

PINEAPPLE ICE BOX DESSERT

1 small can crushed pineapple
  (artificially sweetened, if you
  count calories)
1 stick margarine
1 cup sugar

1 tablespoon cream
1 egg
crushed vanilla wafers or
  graham crackers

Mix together pineapple, margarine, sugar, cream, and egg, beating well. Bring to boil and boil slowly for 5 minutes, stirring constantly. Pour over ¾ inch of crushed vanilla wafers or graham crackers in baking dish. Sprinkle crumbs over top.

Refrigerate for 6 hours. Cut in squares and serve with whipped topping.

DOLPHIN VICTORY CAKE
Bobbie Evans (Mrs. Norm)

CAKE:

2 cups flour
2 cups sugar
1 teaspoon baking soda
1 teaspoon cinnamon
½ cup shortening
½ cup margarine

¼ cup cocoa
1 cup water
½ cup buttermilk
2 eggs, beaten slightly
1 teaspoon vanilla

ICING:

½ cup margarine   *1 pound confectioners' sugar*
6 tablespoons milk   *1 teaspoon vanilla*
¼ cup cocoa   *1 cup chopped pecans*

Preheat oven to 400 degrees. Grease a 15 × 10 × 1-inch jelly roll pan. Sift flour, sugar, soda, and cinnamon into a large bowl. In saucepan, combine shortening, margarine, cocoa, and water; bring to a boil, stirring constantly, until mixture is smooth. Pour over dry ingredients; mix well. Add remaining cake ingredients; blend well. Pour into prepared pan; bake 20 to 25 minutes.

While cake is baking, prepare icing. In saucepan, combine margarine, milk, and cocoa; bring to a boil, stirring constantly. Add remaining ingredients; beat well. Spread over hot cake; cool in pan. Cut into 3 × 2-inch pieces.

Makes 25 servings.

Pat and Jim Snider are fellow members at Northwest Baptist. Jim is a deacon with Bob and is superintendent of the Sunday school department in which I teach. Jim's Aunt Pauline Pearce shared this recipe with Pat and it has become a family favorite.

FRESH APPLE CAKE
Pat Snider (Mrs. Jim)

2 sticks margarine   *2 teaspoons cinnamon*
2 cups flour   *3 eggs*
1½ cups sugar   *4 cups cut-up fresh apples*
2 teaspoons baking soda   *1 cup chopped nuts*

Preheat oven to 350 degrees. Soften margarine. Mix all ingredients well. Bake uncovered in a large baking dish for 1 to 1½ hours.

MUSHROOMS CALIENTE

2 cups ground beef
1 can condensed cream of
    mushroom soup
1 green chili (more or less to
    taste), chopped fine

corn chips, warmed
1 large onion, chopped
grated cheese

Brown ground meat, using a small amount of corn oil if meat does not have a great deal of fat. Add soup, into which green chili has been chopped. Simmer for 1 hour.

Place corn chips on warmed plates. Cover with a layer of chopped onion. Pour meat and mushroom mixture over onion and corn chips. Sprinkle grated cheese on top.

Green chilies can be bought in small cans. They are very hot—but delicious!

BAKED CHICKEN CASSEROLE

4 whole chicken breasts
½ cup butter
salt
pepper
1 can (10½ ounces) condensed
    cream of chicken soup
½ cup sliced water chestnuts

1 can (4 ounces) sliced
    mushrooms, drained
⅓ cup chopped parsley
¼ cup sliced pitted ripe olives
¼ teaspoon thyme
¼ teaspoon poultry seasoning

Preheat oven to 350 degrees. In skillet brown chicken in butter; remove chicken to 12 × 8 × 2-inch baking dish. Add remaining ingredients to drippings in pan; heat through. Pour over chicken breasts. Cover; bake 25 minutes. Uncover; bake 25 minutes longer. Serve over rice.

Makes 4 servings (1 whole breast each).

STUFFED AVOCADOS

1 cup diced boiled ham
⅓ cup thinly sliced water
    chestnuts
6 small fresh mushrooms, sliced

⅓ cup mayonnaise
3 ripe avocados
lemon juice

Combine ham, water chestnuts, mushrooms, and mayonnaise. Mix well and refrigerate.

Cut avocados in half and peel. Sprinkle with lemon juice. Fill with chilled ham mixture. Serve on a lettuce leaf and garnish with a slice of tomato.

Makes 6 servings.

JODY DUNTON'S CHICKEN CREPES
Jody Dunton

Good for ladies' luncheon, or for several days ahead; freeze them between layers of wax or foil paper to prevent them from sticking. To thaw them, heat in a covered dish in 300-degree oven. You can make the whole dish ahead and freeze it until the day you want to serve it. I usually make the crepes in advance.

BATTER FOR CREPES:

1 cup cold milk
1 cup cold water
4 large eggs
4 tablespoons cooled melted
  butter

½ teaspoon salt
2 cups all-purpose flour, sifted

If you have a blender, put all ingredients in at high speed for 1 minute. If you don't have a blender, put together all ingredients, but halve the liquids, and use electric mixer or rotary beater and beat until smooth; then add rest of liquid and beat until well blended. If there are any lumps, strain through strainer. Refrigerate 3 hours or overnight.

About an hour before cooking crepes, make chicken filling, unless you made them ahead and froze them.

CHICKEN FILLING:

¼ cup butter or margarine
¾ pound mushrooms, chopped
  or 1 can (6 ounces), chopped
  and drained
½ cup chopped green onion

2½ cups diced cooked chicken
½ cup sherry
½ teaspoon salt
dash pepper

Heat butter in large skillet. Add mushrooms and onion; sauté until onion is golden brown—8 to 10 minutes. Add chicken, wine, salt, and pepper. Cook over high heat, stirring frequently, until no liquid remains. Remove from heat.

SAUCE:

¼ cup unsifted all-purpose
flour
⅔ cup sherry
1 10-ounce can condensed
chicken broth

2 cups light cream
½ teaspoon salt
⅛ teaspoon pepper

In medium saucepan, blend flour with sherry. Stir in chicken broth, light cream, salt, and pepper. Over medium heat, bring to boil, stirring constantly. Lower heat, and simmer 2 minutes; stir occasionally. Add half of sauce to chicken filling; stir until well blended. Set filling and rest of sauce aside.

TO COOK CREPES (unless you made them ahead—then just thaw them now):

Heat a 7-inch skillet over medium high heat until a drop of water sizzles and rolls off. Remove skillet from heat; brush lightly with salad oil (use a non-stick or cast-iron skillet). Pour 2 to 2½ tablespoons batter in, tilt pan quickly in all directions to run batter completely over bottom of pan in a thin film. Pour out any that doesn't adhere to pan. Cook over medium heat until lightly brown, turn, and brown other side. Slide onto wire rack or plate and continue with rest of the batter. When you get the hang of it you can keep two pans going at once.

Preheat oven to 425 degrees.

LAST STEP!

½ cup grated natural Swiss cheese

With all three recipes made and oven preheated, place about ¼ cup filling on each crepe; then roll up. Arrange, seam side down, in single layer in buttered 3-quart shallow baking dish. Pour rest of sauce over crepes; sprinkle with grated cheese.

Bake for 15 minutes, or until cheese is bubbly. There is quite a bit

of work involved, but the compliments I've gotten when I serve it
are worth it!

Makes 6 to 8 servings.

FLORIDA SUNSHINE SALAD

Donna Lou Askew (Mrs. Reubin)
Governor's Mansion, Tallahassee, Florida

1 large can apricot nectar
1 large package lemon-flavored
    gelatin
1 large can frozen Florida
    orange juice

1 package cream cheese
1 cup chopped pecans

Heat apricot nectar to boiling point. Dissolve lemon gelatin in
this. Do not dilute. Add can of orange juice undiluted. Make small
balls of the cream cheese to which pecans have been added, add to
mixture, and refrigerate in mold or cupcake pan until jelled.

This is good with fowl, pork, or ham, or at holiday time in place
of cranberry sauce.

FLORIDA WALDORF SALAD

Donna Lou Askew (Mrs. Reubin)
Governor's Mansion, Tallahassee, Florida

SALAD:

½ cup tokay grapes
½ cup unpared cubed tart
    apples
½ cup diced celery
2 tablespoons clear French
    dressing

⅛ teaspoon salt
salad greens
2 tablespoons chopped walnuts

Halve grapes; remove seeds. In small bowl, combine with apples,
celery, French dressing, and salt; toss to coat well. Refrigerate,
covered, 1 hour.

MUSTARD MAYONNAISE:

3 tablespoons mayonnaise
1 tablespoon light cream

⅛ teaspoon dry mustard

To make mayonnaise, combine all ingredients; mix well. To serve, gently mix salad with mustard mayonnaise. Serve on salad greens; sprinkle with walnuts.

Makes about 1½ cups (2 servings).

It is good to say, "Thank you" to the Lord, to sing praises to the God who is above all gods.

Every morning tell him, "Thank you for your kindness," and every evening rejoice in all his faithfulness. Sing his praises, accompanied by music from the harp and lute and lyre. You have done so much for me, O Lord. No wonder I am glad! I sing for joy.

O Lord, what miracles you do!

CHAPTER 18

ENTERTAINING THE DEACONS

Bob is the kind of person who takes decision-making very seriously. He doesn't avoid decisions, he just gives them his most undivided prayer and attention. Sometimes this process causes him to hold back giving his final answer. But when the decision is made, you can count on it being the best decision that can possibly be made.

This is basically what happened when the opportunity came for Bob to become a deacon. Bob really went through some soul searching. He felt himself unworthy of being a deacon. He went to the Deacon Chairman, to our pastor, and expressed his deep concern. Bob told them he felt there were many other men in the congregation more worthy of this office than himself.

Bro. Bill was very wise in his answer to Bob. He told Bob that this very attitude was a good indication of Bob's readiness to be a deacon. Bro. Bill explained that the Lord could never use Bob in any other frame of mind. If Bob ever felt "worthy" enough to be a deacon, it would be at that point that he would become useless.

The standards in the Bible are very strict for deacons. Our church feels very strongly about upholding these qualifications. Therefore, it is becoming more and more difficult to find persons who meet the requirements.

The deacons must be the same sort of good, steady men as the pastors. They must not be heavy drinkers and must not be greedy for money. They must be earnest, wholehearted followers of Christ who is the hidden Source of their faith. Before they are asked to be deacons they should be given other jobs in the church as a test of their character and ability, and if they do well, then they may be chosen as deacons.

Their wives must be thoughtful, not heavy drinkers, not gossipers, but faithful in everything they do. Deacons should have only one wife and they should have happy, obedient families. Those who do well as deacons will be well rewarded both by respect from others and also by developing their own confidence and bold trust in the Lord (1 Timothy 3:8–13).

In addition to these biblical requirements, our church has other qualifications a deacon must meet. For one, a deacon must be a full tither—ten per cent off the top of the income. A deacon does not partake of any alcoholic beverages.

I wanted Bob to become a deacon more than anything in the world. In fact, I had a really hard time not interfering with his thinking and decision. I wanted to be careful that Bob become a deacon because he felt it was God's will for his life, not because he wanted to please me. It was hard not to become a real nag about this. Bob has always been very firm in forcing me to step out with my testimony. I felt like maybe this was my way of wanting to push *him* into a more public testimony.

Bob prayed very diligently. When he finally made the decision, it was because he had committed himself to be the best deacon he knew how to be.

He wrote the most marvelous letter of acceptance to Bro. Bill. He told the pastor that he knew this was a big step up in his Christian life, and it would be a constant challenge to lead him into a deeper Christian commitment.

The ordination service was beautiful. The children were as proud as I. I think they see it as the next best thing to being a preacher.

Bob's decision to be a deacon has had great meaning for all of us. It has led our whole family into new dimensions of the Christian commitment. It has caused us all to dedicate our lives more to the church and the cause of Christ.

At some churches there is the practice of the deacons to have a time of fellowship before, during, or after the regular deacons' meeting. The pastor and deacons of these congregations feel that these fellowship times create a feeling of unity and brotherhood among the deacons.

One church reported that the deacon wives take turns providing refreshments for these times of fellowship.

Other churches have quarterly deacon socials or cookouts. Some churches have yearly retreats where the deacons and their wives leave town for a weekend of spiritual renewal.

These recipes are guaranteed men-pleasers whenever they are used. They go well with coffee or tea and would make good deacon socializers.

ITALIAN CREAM CAKE
Mary Hendricks, the twins' former nurse

CAKE:

½ cup margarine	1 tablespoon baking soda
½ cup shortening	1 tablespoon vanilla
2 cups sugar	2 cups sifted flour
5 eggs, separated	1 can (4 ounces) coconut
1 cup buttermilk	1 cup chopped nuts

ICING:

½ cup margarine	1 pound confectioners' sugar
1 package (8 ounces) cream cheese, softened	1 cup chopped nuts

Preheat oven to 350 degrees. Grease and lightly flour three 9-inch-round cake pans. In large bowl combine margarine, shortening, and sugar; cream until light and fluffy. Add egg yolks, one at a time, beating well after each addition. Combine buttermilk, soda, and vanilla; add alternately with flour, beginning and ending with flour. Blend in coconut and nuts. Beat egg whites until stiff peaks form; gently fold into batter. Carefully spoon batter into prepared pans; bake 30 to 35 minutes. Cool 10 minutes in pan; turn onto wire rack and cool completely.

In small bowl, cream together margarine and cream cheese; blend in sugar and nuts. Spread ⅓ of the frosting over each layer; assemble layers.

Makes a 3-layer 9-inch cake (8 servings).

CHOCOLATE PIE

1 cup sugar	4 eggs, separated
3 level tablespoons flour	¾ stick margarine
3 heaping tablespoons cocoa	½ cup sugar
dash salt	2 tablespoons vanilla
1 cup milk	baked pie shell

Preheat oven to 400 degrees. In saucepan mix one cup of sugar, flour, cocoa, and salt. Add one half of milk, mix well. Add egg yolks, mix well. Then add remainder of milk and margarine and cook until thick. Be sure to keep stirring to prevent sticking. When thick, take off fire, add the ½ cup of sugar and vanilla. Mix well. Pour into baked pie shell, then beat egg whites with mixer or by hand until they stand alone. Add 1 tablespoon of sugar and beat until sugar has dissolved, then spread egg white on chocolate pie, bake in oven until brown—about 5 minutes.

This is a yummy pie—you will want to bake more than one.

Charlie Walker is one of Bob's fellow deacons. He and Bob share the problem of not being able to eat all they would like all the time. But on special occasions, Fredda, Charlie's wife, makes this chocolate poundcake.

Fredda vows she is such an old-fashioned cook that this is one of the few recipes she has ever put on paper.

CHOCOLATE POUNDCAKE
Fredda Walker (Mrs. Charlie)

½ cup shortening	5 tablespoons cocoa
½ cup butter or margarine	1½ cups chopped pecans
3 cups sugar	1 cup milk
5 eggs	2 teaspoons vanilla
3 cups cake flour	2 teaspoons coconut or
½ teaspoon salt	almond flavoring
½ teaspoon baking powder	

Preheat oven to 300 degrees. Cream shortening and butter until smooth. Add sugar. Then add eggs one at a time, mixing between each one.

Sift all dry ingredients together four times. Add gradually to first mixture. Mix thoroughly. Add pecans, milk, vanilla, and other flavoring.

Pour into a well-greased and floured tube pan and bake for 1 hour.

This Scottish recipe came to me from Catherine Marshall. On their initial visit to Scotland, Peter and Catherine encountered this recipe. The Scots evolved this delicious dessert for which one can use leftovers—a trifle of this and a trifle of that.

It is so rich and good it naturally fits into the holiday category of forbidden calories.

SCOTTISH TRIFLE
Catherine Marshall

Line a serving bowl with strips of spongecake (may be slightly dry or stale). Sprinkle 2 tablespoons of sherry flavoring over the cake. Spread with a layer of jam (any flavor).

Now add a layer of pieces of canned fruit such as peaches, pears, etc. Pour cold Boiled Custard over all about 30 minutes before serving time. Just before serving, top with whipped cream and garnish with cherries, strawberries, or the like.

When serving, slice down through the layers so that each portion gets every layer.

BOILED CUSTARD:

3 cups milk	*3 eggs*
⅓ cup sugar	*1 teaspoon vanilla*
1 tablespoon cornstarch	*½ teaspoon almond flavoring*
¼ teaspoon salt	

Heat the milk in top of a double boiler. Meanwhile, mix sugar, cornstarch, and salt. Beat eggs well in separate bowl, then combine with sugar mixture.

Slowly pour very hot milk into egg mixture, beating vigorously with wire whisk or hand beater between each addition. Return to double boiler and cook over simmering water, stirring constantly until mixture begins to thicken. The custard is thick enough when it coats a silver spoon. (If left cooking too long, it will curdle.)

Cool quickly by placing the pan in cool water. Strain and add the vanilla and almond flavoring. Chill thoroughly.

Makes 3½ cups.

Mother, like all good cooks, has learned to take advantage of new packaged short cuts to baking. This recipe combines the short-cut mixes into a homemade delight.

COFFEECAKE
Lynn Cate (Mrs. George)

CAKE:

1 package (about 1 pound, 3 ounces) yellow cake mix	4 eggs
	1 cup water
1 package (3¾ ounces) instant vanilla or lemon-flavored pudding mix	½ cup oil
	2 teaspoons vanilla

NUT FILLING:

½ cup chopped nuts	1 teaspoon cinnamon
½ cup sugar	

Preheat oven to 350 degrees. Grease and lightly flour a 10-inch tube pan. In large mixer bowl, combine all ingredients for cake; mix well.

In another bowl, combine ingredients for nut filling. Fill tube pan with alternating layers of batter and filling, ending with some of the filling mixture. Bake 45 to 50 minutes or until done. Cool in pan.

Makes a 10-inch cake (8 to 10 servings).

This recipe from my good friend Anne Verrocchi is certainly one of her best. It is a favorite with coffee.

SOUR CREAM COFFEECAKE
Anne Verrocchi

CAKE:

½ cup butter, softened	2 cups sifted flour
1 cup sugar	1 teaspoon baking powder
2 large eggs	1 teaspoon salt
1 cup sour cream	1 teaspoon vanilla

TOPPING:

⅓ cup sugar	1 teaspoon cinnamon
⅓ cup chopped pecans	

Preheat oven to 350 degrees. Grease and flour a 9-inch tube pan. In large bowl, combine butter and sugar; cream 5 minutes on high speed of mixer. Add eggs and sour cream; beat 2 minutes. Sift dry ingredients together; add to creamed mixture; blend thoroughly. Blend in vanilla.

Combine ingredients for topping. Pour half the cake batter into the prepared pan; top with half the topping mixture. Add remaining batter and topping, pressing topping into batter slightly. Bake 45 to 55 minutes. Cool; remove from pan.

Makes a 9-inch cake (10 to 12 servings).

Bill Sawyer is vice president of Eastman Kodak Company.

The Sawyers have three children (grown now) and three grandsons. Being in the marketing field has required the Sawyers to move around all over the United States, so Dody has picked up recipes from the four corners.

Dody and I share a friendship verse of Scripture: "Make a joyful noise to the Lord, all the earth, break forth into joyous song and sing praises!"

CHEESECAKE DIVINE
Dody Sawyer (Mrs. Bill)

I started making this in California more than twenty years ago.

CRUMB CRUST:

2½ cups graham cracker
   crumbs
½ cup melted butter

½ cup firmly packed brown
   sugar

FILLING:

2 packages (8 ounces each)
   cream cheese, softened
1 cup sugar

5 eggs, separated
1 teaspoon vanilla

TOPPING:

1 pint sour cream
½ cup sugar

1 teaspoon vanilla

Preheat oven to 350 degrees. In small bowl, combine ingredients for crust. Place in 10-inch springform pan; firmly press mixture against bottom and sides of pan. Chill while making filling.

In small bowl, combine cream cheese, sugar, egg yolks, and vanilla; beat until smooth. In large bowl, beat egg whites until stiff peaks form. Gently fold cheese mixture into whites. Pour into chilled crust; bake 30 minutes or until cake is set in center. Remove from oven.

Blend topping ingredients together; spread over cheesecake. Return to oven and bake 10 minutes. Cool; refrigerate several hours before serving.

Makes a 10-inch cake (10 to 12 servings).

DEAR LORD. I realize that I am so much a part of what Bob is. This new adventure of service will be partly my responsibility, too. Help me to be a good deacon's wife, understanding when the duties of the office sometimes interfere with my personal plans. Help me give support in his spiritual life as well as his personal life so that he will be available for your constant direction and leadership.

PART VI

SOMEONE'S IN THE KITCHEN WITH MOM

CHAPTER 19

THE FAMILY THAT COOKS TOGETHER

Back when I was a little girl in Grandma Berry's kitchen, I loved the big, smelly, noisy bustle of meal preparation. The bigger the occasion, the bigger the activity in her kitchen.

Grandma would start early in the morning to prepare a special dinner if we were having guests or relations. She would peel, cut and season, and change food from one dish to another dish, to a cooking pan, then to a final cooking pan. Each item on the menu would be caressed with the loving care of an expert cook. She could literally love flavor right into a food she was preparing.

During the final cooking Grandma would lift a lid on a steaming pot, lean over to peer inside, then give the contents a stir with a long wooden spoon. Occasionally, this process would be followed by a little tasting sip from the spoon. Then a slight pause, while the taste was carefully evaluated. If the taste was approved, the pot lid would be replaced. If not, another dash of something or other would be added to the cooking food.

I didn't realize what an indelible impression this process had made on me until one day I caught myself with a large wooden spoon mid-air over a pot of gently boiling soup. Tears came to my eyes when I realized how exactly I was mimicking Grandma.

That led to a whole afternoon of warm recall of those beautiful days in Grandma Berry's kitchen.

Cooking wasn't all that went on in that kitchen. There was a little reading, some singing and games, lots of laughing, and playing, and loving.

No matter how busy Grandma was with her cooking, she always had time to stop and love on us when we came in.

There are certain smells that still arrest my attention and recall of that long-ago friendly kitchen. Chocolate is one of them—and corn bread, hot in the big iron skillet.

In the spring, the storms would come, usually blinding, cutting sandstorms that could last for hours at a time. We would all sit in the kitchen listening to the blistering wind carrying half of Oklahoma, grain by grain, to Kansas, and then back again. Somehow the security of the kitchen gave us assurance that the world would still be there when the morning light again brought peace to the plains.

My kitchen today is so different in appearance from Grandma Berry's kitchen. Like most other present-day American women, I have managed to utilize every modern convenience and appliance on the market. I can blend, mash, squeeze, bake, sauté, cream, crush, grate, broil, chop, freeze, slice, and wash dishes at the touch of a button. The children are not even intrigued with such a vast assortment of machinery. They expect it. They can't imagine a kitchen where it does not exist.

At times I wish they had the opportunity of visiting Grandma Berry's kitchen as it was when I was little. I wish they could see and feel and taste the experiences I had there. But this is not possible. So, somehow, I want to recapture that feeling of warm togetherness and reproduce it in my beautiful new all-electric kitchen.

Somehow, I want kitchen-time to be emotionally significant to my children. Kitchen-time can contribute vital ingredients to help a child grow strong and find his own direction in life.

Gathering in Grandma's kitchen was a natural thing. There really were not many other choices. We have to work harder to produce this kitchen togetherness now. I keep many of the children's games, papers, crayons, scissors, and puzzles in the kitchen. This seems to say, "Come be with me, there are fun things to do here." I also encourage any experimenting the children may want to do with simple cooking jobs.

I long to have the same patience with their efforts and messes as Grandma and Mother had with mine. But I'm afraid I fall short sometimes.

Sometimes we plan a meal in which each member of the family can contribute something. This does more to foster a genuinely warm kitchen feeling than nearly any other activity.

We sit down together and make our plans. We decide when each chore needs to be completed in order to get the meal on the table at a certain time. Then we check the ingredients that are needed and review the recipe.

I, of course, do the more difficult tasks, usually the main dish. The children divide the other dishes according to ability.

These recipes are ones that lend themselves beautifully to that procedure. I have tried to include and note the simple, average, and more difficult recipes.

BRAMALOUGH

Frances Bumbalough (Mrs. Harold E.)

1 pound ground chuck	1 can drained green peas
1 small onion, chopped	2 tablespoons butter
2 cans tomato soup	¾ cup cooked macaroni
salt and pepper to taste	¾ cup grated cheese

Preheat oven to 350 degrees. Brown meat. Add onion and cook until tender. Add soup. Mix well and season to taste. Pour mixture in buttered 2-quart casserole dish. Add a layer of peas, butter the macaroni and put layer on the peas. Sprinkle cheese on top. Bake for 30 minutes.

BEEF TARTS

1 pound ground meat	dash marjoram and bay leaves,
1 small onion, chopped	crushed
1 can mushroom soup	8 ready-prepared pastry cups
½ teaspoon salt	2 small tomatoes, sliced
dash pepper	Parmesan cheese

Preheat oven to 300 degrees. Brown meat. Add onion, soup, seasoning, and spices. Simmer for 5 minutes. Remove from heat and cool.

Spoon small amount of meat mixture into pastry cups. Top with tomato slice. Sprinkle with Parmesan cheese. Place on a cookie sheet.

Bake 15 to 20 minutes.

Makes 8 servings.

ORIENTAL BAR-B-CUED RIBS
Taris Savell

*4 pounds spareribs, cut in
serving-size pieces
1 can (10¾ ounces) condensed
cream of tomato soup
2½ tablespoons soy sauce*

*2½ tablespoons honey
½ teaspoon Worcestershire
sauce
3 tablespoons minced onion*

In large heavy pan, cover ribs with water; simmer 1 hour; drain. Meanwhile, in saucepan, combine remaining ingredients. Cover; cook over low heat 10 minutes, stirring occasionally. Place ribs on broiler pan. Broil 6 inches from source of heat for 30 minutes, turning and brushing with sauce every 5 minutes.

Makes 4 servings (1 pound ribs each).

LADY BIRD JOHNSON'S ENCHILADAS

Make chili of your choice.

Preheat oven to 350 degrees.

Take some of the chili meat from the pot with a hand strainer. Chop 1 onion fine, set aside. Grate about 3 cups American cheese, set aside. Fill a 2-quart pot about ¾ full of water, let come to a boil.

Place tortillas, one at a time, in the pot of hot water for 1 second. Keep water very hot.

Place ¼ teaspoon onion, 1 tablespoon chili meat, and 1 tablespoon American cheese on each tortilla, and fold over (roll). Place filled tortillas side by side in an ovenproof dish until the dish is full. Pour about 1 cup chili juice over the enchiladas.

Bake 10 to 12 minutes. Remove from stove and sprinkle with 1½ cups cheese. Return to oven for 5 more minutes.

Serve immediately with a green salad and sherbet, homemade ice cream, or pecan pralines for dessert.

Here is a fun and easy recipe for children.

FRUIT SURPRISE
Esther Pearnan

2 packages strawberry-flavored gelatin
1 ½2 can crushed pineapple and juice

package (10 ounces) frozen strawberries and juice
3 large ripe bananas, mashed
1 container (½ pint) dairy sour cream

Dissolve gelatin in 1½ cups boiling water. Then stir in the crushed pineapple with juice, and the thawed strawberries with juice and mashed bananas. Stir to blend evenly. Pour ½ of the mixture into a dish and place in the refrigerator until firm. Stir and lightly whip the sour cream with a fork. Spread this over the firm gelatin layer. Pour the remaining gelatin mixture over the sour cream. Let it all chill for several hours or overnight.

My mother, Mrs. George Cate, uses this recipe for making lettuce salad.

SHREDDED LETTUCE SALAD
Lynn Cate (Mrs. George)

1 large crisp head lettuce
1 large green pepper

2 large onions
1 cup sugar

Shred vegetables in crock; pour sugar over all.

DRESSING:

1 tablespoon salt
2 tablespoons sugar
1 teaspoon celery seed

1 cup cider vinegar
⅔ cup salad oil

Bring to boil. Pour over vegetables. Cover immediately. Cool. Refrigerate for 4 hours. Keeps several days.

HAMBURGER STROGANOFF
Eileen Peterson (Mrs. Cliff)

⅛ pound butter or margarine
½ cup minced onion
1 pound ground chuck beef
1 clove garlic, minced, or ⅛
    teaspoon garlic powder
2 tablespoons flour
2 teaspoons salt

¼ teaspoon Ac'cent
¼ teaspoon paprika
1 pound mushrooms, sliced, or 1
    can sliced mushrooms,
    drained
1 can cream of chicken soup
1 pint commercial sour cream

In hot butter, sauté onion until golden. Add meat, garlic, flour, salt, Ac'cent, paprika, and mushrooms. Sauté. Add soup; simmer uncovered for 10 to 15 minutes. Stir in sour cream; heat thoroughly. Sprinkle with chopped parsley (or chives or fresh dill). Serve on crisp noodles, rice, or mashed potatoes.

Mary Crutchfield (Mrs. Albin P.) is a friend from our association with the Florida Citrus Commission. She is so sweet to share a recipe with me from her mother-in-law. Mary was given this recipe by Grandmother Crutchfield and now Mary has passed it on to her daughters-in-law.

GRANDMOTHER CRUTCHFIELD'S BREAD
Mary Crutchfield (Mrs. Albin P.)

2 envelopes yeast
2 tablespoons brown sugar
1 can evaporated milk and
    enough very warm water to
    equal one quart

4 cups whole-wheat flour, sifted
8 cups white flour, sifted
2 tablespoons salt
2 to 3 tablespoons melted
    shortening or vegetable oil

Dissolve yeast and sugar in ½ cup warm water. In a large bowl, place the milk/water mixture, add yeast mixture, and mix well with wire whip or beater of some sort. Add two kinds of flour and salt and mix well. (Use your hands—it's fun!) Knead well in bowl, grease top, cover, and let rise to double in size. "Deflate" dough, divide into six equal parts. Knead each part well (about twenty times),

grease, and place in greased pans 9 × 5 inches—two to each pan. Let rise, covered, until double in size. Bake at 325 degrees for 1 hour.
Makes 6 small loaves.

Kids will love working with poppy seed in this recipe.

POPPY SEED DRESSING (for fresh fruit)
Dody Sawyer (Mrs. Bill)

¾ cup sugar	1 cup salad oil
1 teaspoon salt	1 tablespoon minced onion
1 teaspoon dry mustard	4 teaspoons poppy seed
⅓ cup vinegar	

In medium bowl of mixer, combine sugar, salt, and mustard; add vinegar. Gradually add oil, beating constantly on medium speed of mixer. Add onion and poppy seed. Refrigerate in covered container. Before using, shake to blend well. Serve over fresh fruit.
Makes about 2 cups.

APPLE DUMPLINGS
Lynn Cate (Mrs. George)

DUMPLINGS:

pastry for 9-inch crust	1½ teaspoons cinnamon
4 apples, cored	4 teaspoons butter
¼ cup sugar	

SYRUP:

1 cup sugar	¼ teaspoon cinnamon
2 cups water	
3 tablespoons butter or margarine	

Preheat oven to 425 degrees. Roll pastry ⅛ inch thick; cut into four squares. Place 1 apple in center of each pastry square. Combine sugar and cinnamon; fill apples with mixture; dot with butter. Moisten edges of pastry with water; bring all points up over center of apple; pinch edges together. Place in an 11 × 7 × 2-inch baking pan.

In saucepan, combine all ingredients for syrup; bring to boil. Cook about 10 minutes or until sugar dissolves; pour around dumplings; bake 40 to 45 minutes.

Makes 4 servings.

Note: Dumplings can be prepared ahead of time and frozen until ready for use.

A simple recipe from Mother's cooking file. It's just grand for young cooks.

PRALINE SQUARES
Lynn Cate (Mrs. George)

24 graham crackers
1 stick margarine
¼ cup light brown sugar
¼ cup nuts
¼ cup coconut

Preheat oven to 375 degrees. Line a pan with crackers. Heat margarine and sugar 5 minutes on low heat. Add nuts to coconut.

Mix well—spread over crackers.

Bake 10 minutes.

DEAR LORD. Bless my mechanical kitchen. Let the hum of motors only serve as a backup orchestra for the singing of people sounds. Let there be little people and grown-up people, all laughing and being together. Dear Lord, may the food preparation that goes on there be secondary to the life preparation that goes on.

May the warmness that is felt here come more from our hearts than from the oven. Fill this room with the glow of your tender love and care.

CHAPTER 20

RECIPES FOR YOUNG COOKS

Cooking, for children, is fun and educational at the same time. It teaches skills, vocabulary, reasoning, responsibility, and nutrition. Cooking is a task they usually associate with adults, so it is challenging. Cooking provides instant success and reward. There is a product, and the product is usually shared with an interested family. So, cooking is status. Cooking, for children, is also a way of communication. It is a chance they have of saying, "I am more grown up now. Look what I can do."

I can remember cooking all my life. Sometimes it was for fun. Sometimes it was because I had to.

I always helped Mother with the cooking. Actually, after my parents were divorced, when I was twelve, I did all the cooking. Sandra my sister was in charge of cleanup. I would have supper on the table when Mother got home from work. I think this early training was invaluable to me when I set up my own home later.

I was always curious and creative about concocting different things to eat. That's why I never got bored with the job. Of course, half of it wasn't fit to eat, but Sandra was my taster. I'd make her eat part of every new dish. If she liked it, we'd have it for supper. If not, I'd have to start over.

To hear Sandra tell it, eating was even unhealthful at times.

Anita Bryant's Cooking
by Sandra Bryant Page

I really don't like to tell about people's bad points but I would like to let people know that Anita Bryant hasn't always been perfect. She may be a great cook now, but when she was in the sixth and seventh grades I can remember her lunches she fixed for me. Since Mother worked and Anita was "the oldest" she was left in charge. She was pretty good on sandwiches but she liked to experiment. And I was the only one handy to experiment on. She would mix things that couldn't possibly taste good together. I asked her one time what was in it. She told me a little of everything in the cupboard. She called it a soda and made me drink it anyway. And I decided she called it a soda because she put soda in it.

Now I can see myself as just a steppingstone to her good cooking, so maybe it was worth it.

Mother has always been a good cook. Not gourmet foods, but just wholesome family cooking. She gave me a lot to live up to.

There are some simple rules that make children's cooking go much easier:

Start with simple recipes. Even though they may seem too easy, it is better to guarantee success than get tired by overextending. After the first recipes are mastered, there is time to try more difficult things.

Teach children the correct way to do things. Separating eggs, folding, grilling, measuring, browning, etc., are basic cooking tasks. When you learn them correctly the first time, they can later be reused in other recipes.

Help children learn proper words for the techniques they are using. In this way, when they read the next recipe, they can begin to understand the terminology.

Sometimes I have to teach my children to cook as I say—and not as I cook! By now, I take many short cuts and do things the easy way. But these short cuts need to come later for children. Take time to follow each step of the recipe to the letter. Too, I've noticed the tasks that seem routine and unimportant to me are usually great fun to the kids.

Provide the young cooks with the "good" cooking utensils. There is nothing more frustrating than trying to complete the instructions to a recipe when you don't have the necessary equipment to perform the tasks called for.

Bob has a very good practice of lining up all his cooking equipment before he starts on a cooking project. I encourage the children to do as Daddy does in this respect.

Another marvelous practice Bob has in his cooking is to clean as he goes. This, too, is a very good procedure for children. There is something a little discouraging about finishing a nice cooking project and seeing the whole kitchen in a shambles. Just a little cleanup on the way really reduces the load at the end.

Encourage the children to check the list of ingredients *before* beginning a recipe. Many times I have gotten to the end of a cake with everything mixed together, only to discover I was out of vanilla flavoring.

Make sure the children understand kitchen safety rules. Using sharp cutting tools, electric machines, and stoves can be very dangerous if they are not used properly. Set the rules according to the age of the child using the kitchen, then stick to them strictly!

Reserve plenty of time for children's cooking projects. Usually an hour is about the limit of a younger child's attention span in the kitchen, but there is no need to rush the hour. It makes everyone nervous.

Brag like crazy about the finished project. Children (like adults) enjoy being appreciated.

I like to start out with the simple gelatin dishes for the youngest cooks. They are easy enough to make all alone. And they can be made more nutritious by adding fruits or vegetables.

Also, instant puddings are good starters. They can be dolled up with whipped toppings, nuts, and a cherry on top. This really brings praises from the family.

Then you can move to some of the unbaked cookie recipes, and on to more and more complicated projects.

UNBAKED COOKIES

½ cup corn syrup   3 cups Rice Krispies
½ cup peanut butter

Combine syrup and peanut butter. Stir in Rice Krispies. These can be dropped from a teaspoon on wax paper. Let set overnight—if you can.

GRANDMA'S GELATIN
Mrs. M. H. Richardson, Florida Citrus Commission

1 package (3 ounces) mixed fruit-flavored gelatin

1 cup boiling water
1 cup Florida orange juice

In small bowl, dissolve gelatin in boiling water; add orange juice. Pour into a 2-cup mold or 4 individual serving dishes; chill until set.
Makes 4 servings (½ cup each).

OATMEAL COOKIES

⅔ cup butter, softened
¾ cup sugar
3 tablespoons cocoa
1 tablespoon water

½ teaspoon vanilla
2 cups uncooked quick oatmeal
confectioners' sugar

Cream butter and sugar. Add cocoa, water, and vanilla. Blend in oatmeal and roll in confectioners' sugar.
Good for hot summer afternoons when heating the oven seems undesirable.

CANDY COOKIES

2 cups prepared biscuit mix
1 egg

¾ can prepared cake frosting

Preheat oven to 375 degrees.
Mix the three ingredients together. The dough may be heavy enough that Mother will have to help.
Drop by teaspoonfuls on a greased cookie sheet. Bake 10 to 12 minutes.
While the cookies are baking, little cooks may want to finish off the remaining ¼ can of cake frosting with a big mixing spoon.
Decorate the cookies with sugar sprinkles.

ORANGE BLOSSOM PARFAIT

½ pint whipping cream
2 tablespoons confectioners'
   sugar
1 teaspoon vanilla
2 tablespoons Florida orange
   juice

2 cups crushed gingersnaps or
   vanilla wafers
1 can fruit cocktail, drained
1 Florida orange, sectioned

Whip the cream until stiff. Add sugar, vanilla, and orange juice.

Fill parfait glasses by layers. Start with a layer of crushed cookies, then a layer of fruit and a layer of whipped cream. Repeat until glasses are full. Top with an orange section.

CHOCOLATE CREAM PIE

1 package chocolate chips
1 large container of non-dairy
   whipped topping

1 prebaked pie shell

Melt chocolate chips in a double boiler. Fold in whipped topping.

Pour into the pie shell. Top with a sprinkling of nuts or chocolate shavings.

Refrigerate several hours.

GLORIA'S PEANUT BUTTER DROPS

1 cup semisweet chocolate bits
½ cup crunchy peanut butter

1 cup salted peanuts

Melt chocolate bits in the top of a double boiler. Add peanut butter. Blend well. Add peanuts. Cool. Drop by teaspoonfuls on a cookie sheet lined with foil. Chill for several hours and serve.

GLORIA'S FAVORITE BROWNIE RECIPE

A particular favorite of Bobby.

½ cup butter
2 squares (1 ounce each)
   unsweetened chocolate
2 eggs

1 cup sugar
½ cup flour
1 teaspoon baking powder
½ cup chopped peanuts

Preheat oven to 350 degrees. Grease a 9-inch-square baking pan. In saucepan, melt butter and chocolate; blend. Remove from heat; add eggs, one at a time, beating well after each addition. Beat in sugar, then remaining ingredients. Spread in prepared pan; bake 30 minutes; cool. Cut into 1½-inch squares.
Makes 36 brownies.

LEMON CAKE BARS

CRUST:

1 package lemon cake mix   1 egg
1 stick margarine, melted

Mix ingredients and press flat into a large baking dish. Use a spatula or fingers to get an even distribution.

FILLING:

1 package lemon icing mix   2 eggs
1 package (8 ounces) cream   4 tablespoons lemon juice
   cheese

Preheat oven to 350 degrees. Mix all filling ingredients well. Pour over crust, spread evenly. Bake 40 minutes. Cool and cut into 4-inch squares.
Makes 15 to 20 squares.

HOT DOG YUM YUMS
Marabel Morgan (Mrs. Charlie)

1 package (8 ounces) crescent   8 frankfurters
   rolls   1 egg white, beaten slightly
4 teaspoons melted butter   4 teaspoons sesame seeds
4 teaspoons prepared mustard

Preheat oven to 350 degrees. Open rolls; spread each roll with ½ teaspoon butter and ½ teaspoon mustard. Place frankfurter in center of each roll; roll according to directions on package. Place on ungreased baking sheet. Brush each roll with egg white and sprinkle with ½ teaspoon sesame seed. Bake 20 minutes. Makes 8 servings.

Bobby hasn't entered the world of cooking except on a very specialized basis. At this point, snacks seem to be his forte.

GRAPEFRUIT DIPS
Bobby Green

> 1 banana
> ½ cup grapefruit juice
>
> ½ cup wheat germ

Peel banana; dip into grapefruit juice, then wheat germ. Take a bite and repeat the process.
Makes 1 serving.

EASY FRUIT PIE

> 2 cups confectioners' sugar
> 1 package dry whipped topping mix, prepared according to directions
> 1 package (8 ounces) cream cheese
>
> 1 teaspoon vanilla
> 2 pie shells, baked
> canned fruit pie filling

Beat sugar into whipped topping. Add softened cream cheese and vanilla, pour into pie shells. Spread pie filling (blueberry, cherry, peach, lemon) on top.
Chill and serve.
Makes 12 servings.

LEMON OR ORANGE PUDDING
Helen Arn (Mrs. Frank)

> juice and grated rind 1 lemon or 1 orange
> 1 cup milk
>
> 2 eggs
> 1 cup sugar

Preheat oven to 350 degrees. Blend ingredients in blender; pour into 4 custard cups.
Place in pan of water.
Bake for 1 hour.

POPCORN

It is thought that the Inca Indians of South America put corn in specially designed clay pots. The pots were then filled with very hot sand and covered with a lid. The heat from the hot sand caused the corn to pop.

Popcorn is fun always. It can turn an otherwise blah evening into an impromptu party. It is something the children can prepare for themselves. For variation we sometimes add a surprise flavoring to the popped corn.

Melted butter and a dash of cayenne. Then toss with sharp Cheddar cheese, grated.

Caramel ice cream topping makes a good popcorn topping.

Another variation is to sprinkle the hot corn with grated Parmesan cheese and a dash of paprika.

POPCORN BALLS

4 tablespoons butter
1 cup brown sugar
½ cup light corn syrup

1 can sweetened condensed milk
½ teaspoon vanilla

Bring first three ingredients to boil over medium heat. Stir in milk. Simmer, stirring constantly, till mixture reaches soft-ball stage. Stir in vanilla. Pour over popped corn and stir well until all kernels are coated. Butter hands lightly, shape into balls. The few kernels of corn left in the bottom of the popper which do not pop are called old maids.

O LORD, *thank you for the spaces in our family life.*
As I sit here in my quiet solitude
I'm enjoying the temporary space between me and children.
Between me and noise.
Between me and little skinned knees.
Between me and the next meal.
Between me and trouble.
Between me and crises.
Between me and sickness.

CHAPTER 21

MY ITALIAN KITCHEN

Normally, my kitchen is my own private domain. I plan, cook, create, and do my best thinking there. Besides the children, I rarely have anyone else who even wants in.

But, once each year (since 1968) I step back and turn my kingdom over to Anne Verrocchi and her mother, Eva, for what has become a beautiful tradition in food and friendship.

Anne is one of the dearest and most devoted friends and fans I have ever had. Our introduction to Anne began with an invitation to dinner at her house. I was appearing in *Annie, Get Your Gun* in Cohasset, Massachusetts. At that time, we had been on tour for several weeks and a home-cooked meal sounded like a little bit of heaven. Unfortunately, schedules didn't permit such a luxury right then and we had to decline.

But two years later we were back in the Boston area, working with *Guys and Dolls*. It was a hectic week. When Anne appeared with another dinner invitation, we fairly jumped at the chance. Then we not only went to dinner, but made a personal appearance at Verrocchi's Supermarket to autograph some 800 photographs.

It was a grand day. Italian families have a beautiful way of making every occasion a joyous family event. That first dinner, held after the store closed for the day, was served on the Verrocchis' screened patio—and the whole Verrocchi family was there. Mr. and Mrs. Verrocchi, Anne, her sister and her husband, with their two daughters and mother-in-law. Also, Anne's uncle and his girl friend. Bobby and Gloria were traveling with us that summer, and Donna Yurek was there to help us care for the children. In all, at one count, there were fifteen people at the table! I still remember the blessing that Anne gave:

> "Dear Lord, accept my thanks sincere,
> for this food and for these friends so dear.

When they leave, I pray they'll wear a smile
and not have heartburn Italian style."

Shortly after the premature birth of our twins, the Verrocchis visited us at Villa Verde. Anne and her mother reminded me of a traveling Italian market when they arrived. They not only brought all the ingredients for spaghetti, but even a spaghetti machine to make their own!

Bobby and Gloria took turns turning the handle to roll the spaghetti dough. Then each had a turn when it was time to cut the dough into strands.

Eva Verrocchi made the meatballs and spaghetti sauce and Anne did the spaghetti. Then we all ate like it was the last time we would see food.

Bob didn't even pretend to stick to a diet that night. He ate spaghetti with butter, some with grated cheese, and some more with tomato sauce.

An event this special had to be repeated. So, usually in January or February of each year, I step aside for the spaghetti machine. One year Anne added lasagne and another year she added ravioli and eggplant Parmegiana. There is usually date-nut bread with cream cheese, a tossed salad, and homemade cheese spread with crackers.

One year, a few days before the annual dinner, Anne's sister and family came down unexpectedly. Since it was a larger crowd than usual, Anne decided, unknown to me, to do much of the meal preparation ahead of schedule. So she made the spaghetti in the motel and brought it to the house already made.

There is something about the Verrocchi family feeling that is contagious. It seems to bring us all to our peak in fellowship—family style.

That night after dinner, Gloria played the piano for us, the twins did their imitations of Sonny and Cher, and Bob performed an impromptu ballet—in Bermuda shorts, yet!

We love our times with the Verrocchi family. Their food is good, and the dinners together are fun. But most of all, the feeling of fellowship we have during these evenings leaves a glow around us that lasts for weeks.

SPAGHETTI SAUCE A LA VERROCCHI

TIPS TO REMEMBER:

The secret of a savory spaghetti sauce is that it doesn't depend on endless cooking time but on the amount of meat you use. Most any kind of meat will make a good-tasting sauce. I use various combinations. You can substitute thick pork chops or a small piece of roast pork for the sausages. You can use a lean chunk of beef. You can even add a large chicken breast or a meaty lamb shank. These types of meat should be seasoned before adding to the sautéed onion. Naturally, the more meat you use, the more tomato you can use. Increase the other ingredients accordingly.

Leftover sauce can be frozen for later use. Adding water to the sauce will produce a delicious homemade tomato soup. You can serve it plain or with rice or any of the many soup macaroni shapes. You can whip up an authentic pasta e fagioli by adding a can of drained kidney beans or shelled beans to the macaroni soup.

Warm cooked green beans in sauce and serve sprinkled with cheese—they're delicious.

1 medium onion, sliced	1 can (35 ounces) imported
1 clove fresh garlic, sliced in	tomatoes
half lengthwise	1 can (14 ounces) imported
fresh flat-leaf parsley, chopped	tomatoes
¼ cup olive oil	1 can imported tomato paste
1 pound Italian sausages	salt and pepper to taste

In 8-quart saucepan, sauté onion, garlic, and 2 tablespoons parsley leaves in olive oil over low heat until onion is tender.

Add sausages. Cover and simmer slowly 30 to 40 minutes, turning often to prevent onion from sticking to bottom of pan.

Strain tomatoes thoroughly (seeds only add bitter taste) and pour over sausages. Add tomato paste. Refill the can half full of tap water and stir to remove all the paste. Pour this into the pan, too. Stir all, sprinkle with salt and pepper to taste, cover and simmer very slowly, approximately 45 minutes, stirring often.

While sausages and tomatoes are simmering, make the meatballs:

1 to 1¼ pounds fresh lean
  ground chuck or ground
  round
¼ to ½ teaspoon very finely
  minced fresh garlic
1 tablespoon finely chopped
  fresh parsley leaves

1 tablespoon grated imported
  Romano cheese
2 eggs, slightly beaten
salt and pepper
1 4- to 6-inch chunk French
  bread (you can use stale bread)
olive oil

In large bowl, place ground beef, garlic, parsley, cheese, and eggs. Sprinkle with salt and pepper to taste. Soak bread in cool water until soft. Remove crust (it will peel off easily) and squeeze out the water. Add dampened bread to ingredients in bowl and mix all thoroughly. Roll small amounts of mixture between palms of hands to form balls about 2 inches in diameter. Sauté meat balls slowly in heavy skillet with just enough olive oil to cover bottom of pan. Turn several times to brown evenly all around. Cooking time is about 20 minutes.

When tomato sauce has simmered the required 45 minutes, add cooked meatballs. Cover and simmer an additional hour.

Remove meat and spoon sauce over drained cooked spaghetti or macaroni. Sprinkle with grated cheese.

Makes 6 servings.

Anne included these comments with her recipes.

"Perhaps you'd better know that I've been cooking for thirty years —since I was eleven years old. I got the job because my folks were working day and night in their first grocery store and my grandmother, who was taking care of the household chores, was ill. I started by getting dismissed from morning and afternoon school sessions a littler earlier than the other children, so I could put lunch on the table and get supper started.

"I attempted my first homemade spaghetti when I was fifteen years old, and there was no one at home to see if I made an ungodly mess. I distinctly remember getting the spaghetti board that had been in the family for eons, all the ingredients on the table, then bowing my head in a prayer over the board, because I didn't want to fail. It took me three hours that day and my hands were sore for several days, but the spaghetti turned out fine. In those days, we rolled and cut the spaghetti by hand, the cutting being done on a rectangular contraption strung with wire which we kiddingly called the guitar. It did emit an off-key sound when you strummed the wires. It was really a back-breaking job, using that old-fashioned cutter."

HOMEMADE SPAGHETTI

You need a spaghetti-making machine for this.

1 large egg per adult serving   *spaghetti-making machine**
¾ cup flour for each ¼ cup
egg

Break eggs into measuring cup. Sift flour onto large pastry board or formica table top.

Make a well in center of flour and pour eggs into it. With frosting-type spatula, beat eggs gently. Then stir in flour gradually. When egg mixture begins to hold its shape, mix in remaining flour with hands. Form into ball. Scrape board clean, then knead ball, sprinkling board with flour to prevent sticking.

Continue kneading until dough no longer sticks to board, then knead until very smooth. Dough will be stiffer than bread dough. The kneading process may take 30 to 45 minutes to reach proper consistency, depending upon the amount of spaghetti you make.

If you have used more than 3 eggs, divide dough into two or more sections and round up. Place rounds in bowl, cover, and let rest 15 to 20 minutes.

Flatten round with rolling pin until ¼ inch thick. Slice into strips. Feed each strip through roller side of spaghetti machine three times. Set machine guide at desired thickness.

Lay sheets of flattened dough on floured board to dry, turning once or twice. When dough seems dry, try feeding a strip through cutting side of machine. If dough sticks, let dry longer, then try again.

* If you don't have a spaghetti-making machine: Make small rounds of dough after kneading. Let rest 15 to 20 minutes, covered. Then use a rolling pin and roll them to desired thickness, as you'd roll piecrust dough. Sprinkle flour under dough as often as needed to prevent sticking to pastry board or table top. When dough is as thin as you like, cut it into strands with a knife, pizza wheel, or ravioli wheel. Spread on floured board to dry, or cook immediately.

Cut, drop spaghetti into boiling salted water. Cook to desired tenderness. Drain and toss with spaghetti sauce and grated cheese. Top with additional sauce and a final sprinkle of cheese.

CHEESE SPREAD

4 packages (8 ounces) cream
   cheese
1 jar (5 ounces) pimiento
   cheese

1 jar (5 ounces) Roka blue
   cheese
1 jar (5 ounces) Cheddar cheese
   chopped walnut meats

Let all cheeses soften at room temperature. Blend thoroughly. Roll in wax paper as you'd roll icebox cookie dough. Chill until firm. Slice into eight equal sections. Roll each in walnut meats, coating all sides. Wrap in wax paper, then in foil, and store in freezer until ready to use. Remove from freezer several hours before serving. Serve with your favorite crackers or chips.

DEAR LORD. *Thank you, God, for your love.*

The love which understands our family fun times and our everyday problems.

Thank you, God, for the perfect love which accepts us just the way we are, but which gives us power to overcome the imperfect in ourselves.

CHAPTER 22

BOB PUTS ON AN APRON

For Christmas one year Bob gave me a set of gourmet cookbooks. It was like a cook's dream come true—thousands of the most delectable-sounding recipes you can imagine. I could hardly wait to try out a few things. Long before I had time to experiment with some new culinary feat, I noticed Bob interestingly turning the pages.

Something about the recipes reminded him of all the great food we have had all over the world. Sometimes I think eating in those marvelous restaurants is the part Bob likes best about our long trips abroad.

After a while, Bob commented, half to me and half to himself, "You know, Anita, the most famous chefs in the world are men." With that, Bob and the new gourmet cookbook disappeared into the kitchen.

Bob had never cooked before, so I really didn't even have the nerve to look in while he worked.

BOB SPEAKS:

"As I had thumbed through the cookbook, my eye caught on scrambled eggs, of all things! Instantly, I experienced a flashback like they do in the movies. I was working in Palm Beach and went to the Everglades Club. This is a very exclusive club and the event was a formal dinner dance with all the society of the world in attendance. The dance went way into the morning. About 3 A.M. they served scrambled eggs in big copper chafing dishes. Those were undoubtedly the best scrambled eggs I have ever eaten; so I decided to begin my great chef career with scrambled eggs and see if I could match the Everglades eggs on the first try!

"Now I don't mean just scrambled eggs in an old iron skillet—I mean scrambled eggs that have been whipped and coddled in lots of butter and cooked in a French cooking utensil.

"Well, it worked. My scrambled eggs turned out so well I couldn't believe it. I sat right down and ate the whole plateful!

"Good luck went to my head. I decided to try chocolate mousse. First, I read the recipe and got completely organized. I set out everything I would need and lined it up—every spoon, dish, or item that would be used in the process. As I cooked, I cleaned every item as I went along, so when the mousse was safely in its stainless steel bowl, in the refrigerator, the kitchen was completely clean. (I guess that part came more from being in the service than from the French cookbooks.)

"The mousse was absolutely perfect. Maybe a little too rich, but real perfection from the standpoint of texture and appearance. I never knew cooking could be so enjoyable. I felt fantastic when I looked at that big chocolate mousse. Cooking is its own instant reward.

"Why stop now? The next time I had a chance to experiment again I tried shish kabob, which also turned out perfect the first time. It was easy, but it took me all day. I couldn't believe so much had to be done to one piece of meat to produce a dish like that.

"Next came Hungarian goulash. That was really fun because I could use my imagination some. I followed the cookbook directions for the most part, but felt confident in experimenting with the odds and ends. I left out a few of the spices because we are not big on spicy foods. But goulash really gave me a free feeling. I could just pop things in there or leave things out.

"The hardest thing I've ever done was quiche Lorraine. I did the crust and all. The timing on this had to be just right. The crust had to be refrigerated for a couple of minutes and rolled out at the right temperature, just like the cookbook said. It turned out very good. I know, I sat down and ate it on the spot, another instant cooking reward.

"I never cook for guests or because I have to. It is strictly a hobby. Anita is always just flabbergasted at the results.

"Two of my big specialties now are spaghetti and Caesar salad. My hands smell like garlic for weeks after I make Caesar salad, but it is worth it.

"The secret to successful cooking, to me, is having the right utensils, a good recipe, and following it to the letter—no short cuts.

"The fun of cooking is in trying new things and attempting recipes you've never tried before. I think the women who get bored with cooking are the ones who are in a cooking rut. They just fix the same old food in the same old way week after week. If they would just explore a few new cookbooks and try something really fun for a change, not only would cooking be more fun, but mealtime would be more fun, too."

CAESAR SALAD

1 clove garlic, crushed
2 heads romaine or other lettuce
½ cup olive oil
2 eggs

3 tablespoons lemon juice
⅓ cup grated Parmesan cheese
8 to 10 anchovy fillets
1 cup croutons

Use a wooden salad bowl. Rub the sides and bottom of the bowl with garlic. Tear the lettuce into bite-size pieces and put in the bowl. Pour the oil over the greens and gently toss. Break the eggs into the salad and mix. Sprinkle with lemon juice. Add cheese and mix well again. Add salt and pepper to taste. Top with croutons and anchovies.

For main dish salad, add strips of ham, salami, flakes of sea food, or small shrimp.

Makes 6 servings.

CHOCOLATE MOUSSE

½ pound sweet baking
    chocolate
1 cup sugar

½ cup water
8 eggs, separated
2 tablespoons rum flavoring

Melt the chocolate in top of double boiler.

Heat sugar and water in saucepan until in syrup stage. Pour syrup into chocolate in a slow, steady stream, beating constantly.

Add the egg yolks one at a time, beating after each addition. Remove from heat and add flavoring; cool. Beat egg whites until soft peaks form, and fold into chocolate mixture.

Spoon into parfait glasses. Chill overnight.

Makes 8 servings.

CHEESE BLINTZES
Marlene Stone (Mrs. Richard)

FILLING:

1 pound dry cottage cheese
½ pound cream cheese
2 egg yolks
2 tablespoons butter

2 tablespoons sugar
¼ teaspoon salt
cinnamon (optional)

Blend ingredients together. Allow 1 tablespoon filling per blintz.

BATTER:

4 eggs
¼ teaspoon salt
2 tablespoons melted butter

1½ cups flour
2 cups milk

Beat eggs, add salt, butter, and flour. Add milk gradually, beating until smooth. Grease a 7- or 8-inch skillet (I use Teflon) and heat. Pour in about 3 tablespoons batter quickly after taking pan off the heat until you have tilted pan from side to side so that batter covers bottom. Cook until lightly brown and turn out on clean towel. (The uncooked side will be the outside of the blintz.)

Fill and fold pancake into envelope shape.

Brown on both sides in butter and serve with sour cream.

QUICHE LORRAINE

PASTRY:

1 cup flour, sifted
½ teaspoon salt
⅓ cup plus 1 tablespoon
  shortening

2 to 2½ tablespoons ice water

Sift flour before measuring. Then sift flour with salt into a medium-size mixing bowl. Use a pastry blender to cut shortening into flour mixture until the mixture is a coarse corn-meal texture.

Sprinkle the ice water, small amounts at a time, over the pastry.

Toss lightly to moisten all parts of the mixture. Pastry should be moist enough to just stick together.

Shape pastry into a ball, cover with plastic wrap, and refrigerate for an hour or so.

When you are ready to assemble the quiche, remove the pastry and roll it to an 11-inch circle on a lightly floured surface. Use light strokes from the center out to the edge.

Fold pastry in half to line a 9-inch plate. Unfold the pastry and fit it to the plate's contour. Fold under the edge and crimp. Dot the bottom of the shell with butter.

FILLING:

3 large eggs, broken into a 4-cup measure	1½ cups cream
¼ teaspoon salt	6 thick slices bacon, fried crisp and crumbled

Preheat oven to 375 degrees. Mix eggs, salt, and cream. Sprinkle the bacon bits over the bottom of the pie shell. Pour the filling carefully over the bacon, filling to ¼ inch from the top of the crust.

Immediately place the quiche in the preheated oven and bake for 30 to 35 minutes. The quiche is done when an inserted knife comes out clean.

Variation: 1½ cups grated Swiss cheese may be sprinkled over the bacon crumbs before the filling is added. The original, genuine quiche Lorraine had no cheese, but it has become a popular addition for some cooks.

SALMON GRAPEFRUIT MOUSSE

2 cans (1 pound each) salmon	2 teaspoons salt
3 envelopes unflavored gelatin	¼ teaspoon white pepper
1 can (6 ounces) frozen Florida grapefruit juice concentrate, thawed	1½ cups mayonnaise
	1 pint heavy cream
2 tablespoons lime juice	ripe olive slivers
2 tablespoons finely minced onion	grapefruit sections

Drain salmon, add enough water to salmon liquid to make 1½ cups. Sprinkle gelatin over liquid in saucepan to soften. Place over low heat, stirring constantly, until gelatin is dissolved. Remove from heat, stir in undiluted grapefruit juice concentrate. Chill until mixture is slightly thicker than the consistency of unbeaten egg white. While mixture is chilling, flake salmon into a large bowl. Add lime juice, onion, salt, pepper, and mayonnaise. Whip cream and set aside. Using same beater, beat salmon-mayonnaise mixture until smooth. Stir in thickened gelatin-grapefruit mix. Gently fold in whipped cream and turn into two 6-cup molds; chill until firm. Unmold, garnish with ripe olive slivers and serve with grapefruit sections and salad greens.

Makes about 12 servings.

LEMON BUBBLE LOAF

1 cup granulated sugar	½ cup warm water
½ teaspoon mace	3 packages active dry or cake
grated rind 2 lemons	yeast
1 cup milk	2 eggs, well beaten
1 teaspoon salt	5¾ to 6¼ cups sifted flour
¼ cup butter	2 tablespoons melted butter

Combine first three ingredients, using only ½ cup sugar, and set aside. Scald milk and stir in remaining ½ cup sugar, salt, ¼ cup butter. Cool until lukewarm.

In large bowl, measure warm water, sprinkle on yeast, stir until dissolved. Stir in milk mixture, eggs, 3 cups flour, and beat until smooth.

Now, stir in 2½ cups more flour or enough to make a soft dough that cleans side of bowl. Sprinkle board with flour, turn dough out on it and knead until smooth, elastic with small blisters under surface. Place in large, greased bowl, turn to coat all sides, and cover with towel; let rise until double in size.

Poke fingers into dough and punch down. Turn dough onto floured surface, cover, let rest 10 minutes. Preheat oven to 350 degrees. Grease angel loaf pan, 15½ inches long. Cut dough into sixteen equal pieces. Shape pieces into balls, tucking ends under. Place in layer pan, brush with half of melted butter, sprinkle with half lemon mix. Repeat second layer. Let rise until double. Bake for 35 minutes or till done. Cool in pan 5 minutes, then turn out on wire racks.

I bless the holy name of God with all my heart. Yes, I will bless the Lord and not forget the glorious things he does for me.

He forgives all my sins. He heals me. He ransoms me from hell. He surrounds me with lovingkindness and tender mercies. He fills my life with good things! My youth is renewed like the eagle's!

CHAPTER 23

MAKING FRIDAYS SPECIAL

In government and high society, dinner is a play of protocol. The food is nutritious and fancy. At our house, dinner is by far our most social of all meals but far from fancy. Even though it may be a simple menu, it is our happiest gathering. Rather than a study in manners, it is a practical family setting. It is the meal at which we are able to be together as a family, the day's work done.

A well-planned dinner should complete the family nutrition quota for the day. It should be a satisfying experience to pave the way to a restful night's sleep. A hungry (nutritionally hungry) child does not go to bed happy.

Dinner should be enjoyed for its own sake. I try to make it relaxed, a pleasant time for each person. We try to make our dinners a time for happy discussions, telling what each one has seen or learned during the day. We include any amusing experience or interesting events of school or work. It is sometimes the time for family discussions, planning a family trip. But it most surely is not a time for lectures, or mention of problems, or discussion of poor behavior.

I'd like to think every day at Villa Verde is a special day. It is special because we are all together, because we live free in the United States, and because we are children of God. Sometimes we like to celebrate these facts by turning a regular night meal into a special occasion. But on Fridays we designate a family holiday. Fridays are always family night with our family.

Now really all you need to make Friday's dinner a special occasion is the idea. Everything else remains practically the same, except for one or two slight variations.

For example, sometimes we get out the good dishes and use them just for fun—because this Friday is special. On another Friday, we might eat in the dining room or in the outside gallery. You might get your ideas from these suggestions:

Tuck a fresh flower in the napkin ring for each family member.

Wear dress-up clothing for Friday night supper. Maybe real Sunday dress-up clothes, or funny costume dress-up clothing.

Use a tape recorder and secretly record the Friday night dinner conversation. Play it back after dinner.

Make a special centerpiece for dinner, using vegetables, fruits, or other convenient things.

Ask each family member to take a turn letting other members guess his favorite things: color, food, subject in school, time of year, song, Scripture verse.

Play "You Are What I Like Best About Being Me." Ask each family member to describe what he likes best about a brother, sister, or parent.

Encourage personal testimonies about, "What I like best about being in this family."

Allow the children to plan "dinner entertainment" for a family dinner; songs, poems, dances are beginning numbers.

Entertaining comes naturally to our children. They are all real hams. So making a Friday night "appearance" of a family dinner is a real treat. I try always to be a good audience (since I know what this means to an entertainer) even if it is a six-year-old performer.

Again, include the children in the planning and preparation of some of the dinner.

I can remember one Friday when we were getting ready to have a special family dinner. I decided to make one of our favorite family desserts—Florida Citrus Cake. The experience helped our twins learn an important lesson.

Since Bob is on a strict low-calorie diet, I had to make a separate dessert for him—low-calorie chocolate pudding.

Several things were going on that day and I was trying to get through, so I asked Billy to help stir the chocolate. That upset Barbara because she likes chocolate and likes to stir pudding. Billy, of course, would not relinquish the big spoon, because in his mind he had been given a task and intended to complete it. In a moment we had a full-scale battle over stirring the chocolate pudding.

Briefly, as mothers do, I contemplated how to make something good and positive out of the situation. So I said, "Barbara, your special job is to help Mommie with the Florida Citrus Cake." Quickly, I set her to work greasing the pan, putting in the eggs, and stirring the batter.

As we worked, I talked to the children and used this experience as an illustration that every person has his own important job to do in life. God planned it that way. When a task has been assigned, it needs to be completed by the person who received the assignment. There are enough jobs for us all to keep busy in our family.

I went a step further to relate this to the larger family of God. God appoints each of us to serve Him in special ways. We are obligated as Christians to do what He calls us to do. But nowhere in God's plan does it call us to do everyone else's job, too.

Even though Barbara wanted to do Billy's job, because she liked chocolate better, she realized that her job was just as important. At the end of the day everyone received praise for doing his job well.

That was really a special Friday family dinner and everyone in the family benefited from Billy and Barbara's work. Daddy was happy—not as happy as had he been eating Florida Citrus Cake, but happy that Billy did his job well; and the rest of the family benefited from Barbara doing her job well.

The McKinnon family in Miami Shores, Florida, share our idea about making Fridays special. They, too, have a family night on Fridays.

The children perform for the family by tumbling, singing, playing the piano, reciting poems, or acting out a charade. They report that they do things alone, in pairs, or all together. They close the evening by sharing prayers in the living room.

Marion McKinnon sent me an old family recipe she often serves for these Friday night family dinners. It is a brown sauce to go over your favorite meat loaf.

SHARP BROWN SAUCE FOR MEAT LOAF
Mrs. Marion McKinnon

½ cup butter
1 tablespoon flour
6 tablespoons water
3 tablespoons catsup or chili
  sauce

3 tablespoons vinegar
1 tablespoon chopped onion
1 small clove garlic, crushed
salt
pepper

In saucepan, melt butter; blend in flour to make a smooth paste. Blend in remaining ingredients, salt and pepper to taste; cook over medium heat, stirring constantly, until mixture thickens. Pour over meat loaf before baking.
Makes about 1 cup.

FRENCH-FRIED LIVER

One of our favorite family recipes is for liver, believe it or not. I ask the butcher to cut the liver into very thin, match-size strips.
I salt, pepper, and roll the strips in flour, then fry them in hot oil. They fry crisp and good. Often I fry a few slices of onion separately and mix in with the liver strips.

PINEAPPLE SALAD

1 package lemon-flavored gelatin
2 cups boiling water
1 cup crushed pineapple, well
  drained (save liquid)

8 marshmallows, chopped
3 bananas, diced

Dissolve gelatin in boiling water. Chill until partially set. Add pineapple, marshmallows, and bananas.
Refrigerate to set completely.

TOPPING:

reserved liquid from pineapple
2 tablespoons cornstarch
½ cup sugar

1 egg yolk, well beaten
⅔ cup whipped cream
grated sharp cheese

Add water to pineapple juice to make 1 cup. Mix in cornstarch and sugar. Add egg yolk and cook over low heat. Stir constantly until thick.

Cool completely and add whipped cream. Spread this dressing over firm gelatin.

Sprinkle with cheese. Cover and return to refrigerator.

BROWN RICE CASSEROLE

1 cup uncooked rice	1 small can mushrooms
2 cans beef consommé	1 stick margarine
1 small onion, chopped fine	

Preheat oven to 300 degrees. Combine all ingredients in baking dish. Bake uncovered in oven for 1½ hours.

Cover the last 15 minutes of baking time.

Makes 6 servings.

Colonel Sanders isn't the only cook in the Sanders family. Mrs. Sanders has a wonderful recipe for potato rolls.

MRS. HARLAND SANDERS' REFRIGERATOR ROLLS

1 cup shortening	10 to 12 cups flour
1 cup sugar	2 teaspoons salt
1 cup mashed potatoes	1 teaspoon soda
1 quart milk	2 teaspoons baking powder
1 cake yeast	

Cream the shortening and sugar until it is light and fluffy. Then add the potatoes and cream some more. Heat the milk to lukewarm, dissolve the yeast in it. Pour it into the shortening, sugar, and potatoes. Add enough flour (approximately 4 cups) to make it like cake dough. Stir in the salt. Let rise 2 hours, then stir in balance of flour (approximately 6 to 7 cups) soda and baking powder to make it like biscuit dough; knead it some. Refrigerate ½ hour. Preheat oven to 450 degrees. Make dough into rolls, let rise double their size. Bake for about 15 minutes, or until golden. The remainder can be used during the next five or six days.

BROWN SUGAR FRUIT DESSERT

1 Florida orange
1 lemon
½ cup light brown sugar, well
    packed
¼ teaspoon ground nutmeg
1 can (8 ounces) apricots
1 can (8 ounces) pears

1 can (8 ounces) sliced peaches
1 can (8 ounces) pineapple
    tidbits
1 can (17 ounces) pitted bing
    cherries
commercial sour cream

Preheat oven to 250 degrees. Grate the rind from the orange and lemon. Add to brown sugar with nutmeg. Cut orange and lemon into very thin slices.

Drain and combine fruits.

Butter a 1-quart casserole and arrange fruits in layers, sprinkling each layer with some of the brown sugar mixture.

Bake for 30 minutes. Serve warm with sour cream on top.

Makes 6 to 8 servings.

LET'S CELEBRATE

Let's face it—some Fridays are certainly more special than others. There are times when we not only feel like having a family dinner, but we feel like really celebrating. Hallelujah! Peace and joy amongst us all!

I keep a cabinet in the office full of instant party equipment. If an event occurs which needs to be celebrated, we can have a full-scale party in an instant. I have decorations, matched sets of paper plates and napkins, small favors for different age groups, balloons, the whole thing.

Life is a parade of good happenings. Learn to be aware of God's blessings in small daily experiences. Then celebrate with live jubilation.

EVENTS TO MAKE MERRY

The first lost tooth of a child and his coming visit by the tooth fairy.

A tennis victory.

Good news from distant friends.

Good report cards from school.

The longest day of the year.

A stick-to-Dad's-diet celebration.

The first flower of spring.

The first snowfall of winter.

(Of course, we can't celebrate those last two things in Florida, but they sound like great reasons for a party in other parts of the country.)

I don't know what your family has to celebrate, but you do. Notice it and praise God with joyous family times.

VICTORY FAVORITES

Copied from the flyleaf of Mother's old cookbook.

½ package yeast
¼ cup lukewarm water
¼ teaspoon honey or corn
  syrup
¾ cup scalded milk
1 teaspoon salt

6 tablespoons honey or ½ cup
  corn syrup
3½ cups flour (approximately)
1 egg, well beaten
⅓ cup melted butter

Dissolve yeast in lukewarm water and add ¼ teaspoon honey or syrup. Let stand 5 minutes. Put milk, salt, and remaining sweetening into bowl and let cool.

When milk is lukewarm, add softened yeast, 1½ cups flour. Beat until smooth. Add egg, butter, and flour to handle.

Knead into a smooth elastic dough, keeping it as soft as possible. Let dough rise in covered greased bowl in moderately warm oven until double in bulk (2 hours).

Push dough down and let rise again. Turn dough onto a slightly floured board, roll rectangular sheet ⅓ inch thick by 12 inches wide.

Brush top of dough with melted butter, then spread with prune filling.

Roll one side of dough to center of rectangle, then roll opposite side to center. Cut into ¾-inch slices. Place in greased shallow pan. Let rise until light.

Bake 20 minutes in moderate oven. Brush tops with milk before removing from oven.

PRUNE FILLING:

½ pound dried prunes   ¾ cup corn syrup
water   rind 1 lemon, grated

Wash and soak prunes. Cook until tender in just enough water to cover. Put through sieve.

Return pulp to heat. Add corn syrup and lemon rind. Cook on low heat until thick mixture.

APPLE PIE
Marabel Morgan (Mrs. Charlie)

Make 2 piecrusts. Wrap in wax paper and put in refrigerator several hours.

FILLING:

7 cups sliced apples   ½ teaspoon nutmeg
1 cup plus ¾ cup sugar   dash ground cloves
1 teaspoon cinnamon   squirt lemon juice

Preheat oven to 425 degrees. Toss all ingredients lightly, pour into pie shell; dot with 2 tablespoons butter. Put on top crust. Bake for 50 minutes.

MILE HIGH PIE
Anne Huffman (Mrs. John)

1 package frozen raspberries   1 tablespoon lemon juice
2 large egg whites or 3 small egg 1 cup sugar
   whites   whipping cream

Chill a large mixing bowl.

Combine the above ingredients in an electric mixer. Beat a long time until very fluffy and stiff (5 to 7 minutes once the raspberries are broken up). Whip 1 cup of whipping cream and fold into the first mixture. Pour into a graham cracker crust and freeze.

Makes 8 to 10 servings.

DEAR LORD. Cooking and caring for a family is a job that is as dependent on the leadership of the Holy Spirit as any job can be. If a wife does everything exactly right for her husband and family, but does so only under her own power, the success cannot last long. The task is too difficult, too constant, and too demanding for a woman to meet on a daily basis, alone. But as Jesus lives in her and shines through her, her life takes on a special significance that gives a totally new dimension to the assignment of homemaker.

"You have turned on my light! The Lord my God has made my darkness turn to light." (Psalm 18:28)

Until Christ comes into your life and lights the candle, there is no real love, there is no real communication or real togetherness. There is no higher purpose than dirty dishes, unmade beds, unpleasant community tasks, or just getting through the day.

This light or understanding is a gift of God. It does not come through marriage classes, not through cookbooks, not even through desire or good intentions. Even though these are good, there is not the sustaining power to withstand everyday life.

PART VII

HURRY UPS

CHAPTER 24

PUT IT ALL TOGETHER: CASSEROLE COOKING

This chapter is included for my sister cooks everywhere who enjoy putting a splendid dinner on the table every evening, but can't afford to spend hours and hours in the kitchen every day.

Let's face it—cooking is necessary. It is even a fun and creative adventure; but I don't want to spend all day, every day, cooking. There are a lot of other things I enjoy, too.

It isn't that I don't think my family is worth all that effort—I do! But I think they deserve more of me than my cooking!

Casserole cooking is the busy homemaker's best friend. It is a way to incorporate all the things we crave in modern living. Casseroles are timesaving, economical, eye appealing, nutritious, and offer the minimum of work and cleanup. Now, can you top that for a recommendation?

Casseroles can be made in advance, frozen for a later date, or reheated for the next day. They can be cooked, stored, reheated, and served in the same table-attractive pot.

Truly, the casserole is the invention of clever and ingenious cooks. Casseroles employ the use of the more economical cuts of meat. With the addition of vegetables, herbs, and spices, the flavors can blend gradually while the meat slowly cooks to a delicious tenderness.

A casserole usually needs only a salad, beverage, and dessert to complete the meal. Casseroles can be super-simple dishes for the children or scrumptious, put together for guests. At our house, a casserole goes to the table for most any occasion.

Along with some of our better casserole recipes, I have included a few do-ahead salads that seem to go well with casseroles. Of course, the classic green tossed salad is hard to beat as a casserole companion.

So, put it all together, gals; then go play a game of tennis in your leftover spare time!

SUPER CHICKEN CASSEROLE
Bobbie Evans (Mrs. Norm)

Norm is a tackle for the Miami Dolphins football team.

*4 chicken breasts, skinned,
  boned, and chopped into
  small pieces*
1½ teaspoons Ac'cent
¼ teaspoon pepper
½ cup corn oil
2 packages broccoli

1 cup wild rice, cooked
1 can cream of chicken soup
½ cup mayonnaise
1 teaspoon lemon juice
½ teaspoon curry powder
*1 cup shredded sharp Cheddar
  cheese*

Preheat oven to 375 degrees. Sprinkle chicken with Ac'cent and pepper, sauté in oil until white, drain.

Cook broccoli, add rice, layer with chicken in buttered casserole dish. Mix remaining ingredients. Add to dish, cover with cheese and foil.

Bake for 30 minutes.

Makes 4 servings.

CASSEROLE SOUTH OF THE BORDER

2 pounds ground beef
1 onion, chopped
*1 can (10 ounces) red chili
  sauce*
pinch salt and garlic salt

2 cans cream mushroom soup
1 can water
1 can green chili, chopped
1 package tortillas
¾ pound cheese, grated

Brown meat and onion. Add chili sauce and salt. Simmer until tender. Heat soup plus 1 can water and green chili. Line casserole with tortillas. Add about 1-inch layer meat, then cheese and broken tortilla pieces. Cover with 1 cup soup mixture. Repeat until casserole is filled. Top with cheese. Let stand overnight in refrigerator.

Bake 1 hour at 350 degrees.

Makes 8 servings.

CHICKEN CASSEROLE FAMILY FARE
Bernice Sonnenberg

1 can (10½ ounces) cream of
    mushroom soup
1 can (10½ ounces) cream of
    chicken soup
½ of a 14½ ounce can of
    evaporated milk

1⅓ cups instant rice
1 frying chicken, cut up
1 envelope dry onion soup mix

Preheat oven to 325 degrees. Heat the soups with milk, stirring until smooth. Do not add water to soup.

Remove from heat. Stir in uncooked rice and pour into 13 × 9 × 2-inch greased baking pan.

Lay pieces of chicken on top of rice mixture. Sprinkle dry soup mix over top. Cover pan with foil and seal tightly. Bake for at least 2 hours. Keeps well until serving time. If you wish, you may use only chicken breasts or thighs in this recipe.

LASAGNA IN A HURRY

1 pound ground beef
3 small onions, chopped
2 cans (8 ounces each) tomato
    sauce
1 teaspoon salt
¼ teaspoon oregano
¼ teaspoon basil
dash coarse ground pepper

1 clove garlic, minced
1 package (8 ounces) wide
    noodles, cooked and well
    drained
1 cup cottage cheese
1 cup sour cream
½ cup shredded Cheddar
    cheese

Preheat oven to 350 degrees. Brown beef and drain. Add onions and cook about 2 minutes. Add tomato sauce and seasonings. Cover and simmer for 10 to 15 minutes.

In a baking dish, alternate layers of noodles, cottage cheese, sour cream, and meat mixture. Top with shredded cheese.

Bake for 25 minutes.

Makes 6 servings.

CHICKEN MACARONI BAKE

1 can mushrooms
1 can cream of chicken soup
1½ cups shredded cheese
2 cups elbow macaroni, cooked
2½ cups cooked and diced
   chicken
1 cup canned peas

¼ teaspoon thyme
¼ teaspoon poultry seasoning
dash paprika
1 teaspoon soy sauce
½ cup fine bread crumbs, mixed
   with 1 tablespoon butter
¼ cup grated Parmesan cheese

Preheat oven to 350 degrees. Mix together all ingredients except
bread crumbs and cheese in a large mixing bowl. Pour into a baking
dish. Top with bread crumbs and Parmesan cheese. Sprinkle with
another dash paprika. Bake for 30 minutes.

Makes 6 servings.

MUY PRONTO

1 pound ground beef
1 onion, chopped
½ cup chopped celery
1 small can sliced mushrooms
1 can cream of mushroom soup
1 teaspoon salt

¼ teaspoon oregano
dash pepper
1 package frozen peas
1 package refrigerated biscuits
1 cup shredded Cheddar cheese

Preheat oven to 350 degrees. Brown beef, onion, celery, and mushrooms in fat in a skillet. Drain fat. Stir in soup, seasonings, and peas.
Simmer 5 minutes. Pour into shallow baking dish. Top with biscuits
and cheese.

Bake for 20 minutes.

Makes 6 servings.

BEEF 'N' MACARONI

1 cup elbow macaroni
½ pound ground beef
1 small onion, chopped
½ green pepper, chopped
¼ teaspoon basil

¼ teaspoon thyme
1 teaspoon Worcestershire sauce
1 teaspoon salt
1 can Cheddar cheese soup

Preheat oven to 300 degrees. Cook macaroni. Brown meat and chopped onion and pepper. Add seasonings.

Combine meat and macaroni in a casserole. Pour Cheddar soup over mixture.

Bake 30 minutes.

Makes 6 servings.

SUNDAY NIGHT CASSEROLE
Chef Lee H. Gibson

1 pound lean ground beef
salt and pepper to taste
1 can golden mushroom soup
1 can onion soup

¼ can white wine (optional)
1 package long grain and wild
* rice mix*

Preheat oven to 350 degrees. Brown hamburger in a skillet, season with salt and pepper in the casserole, bring both cans of soup and the wine to a boil.

Stir in the seasoning from the rice package and add rice.

Bring this all to a boil and cover.

Bake in the oven for 45 minutes.

Makes 6 servings.

PORK CHOP CASSEROLE
Judi Griese (Mrs. Bob)

Bob Griese plays quarterback with the Miami Dolphins.

9 to 10 center-cut pork chops
salt and pepper
6 medium large potatoes

2 to 3 cans cream of mushroom
* soup*
1 can Cheddar cheese soup

Preheat oven to 275 degrees. Brown pork. Place in large baking dish. Salt and pepper. Cover with thin-sliced peeled potatoes. Add non-diluted cans of soup. Salt and pepper again.

Bake for 2 hours, until tender.

Makes 6 servings.

FROZEN PINEAPPLE SALAD
Judi Griese (Mrs. Bob)

12 large-size marshmallows	½ cup chopped pecans
1 cup hot milk	½ cup chopped maraschino
½ pint whipping cream	cherries
1 cup crushed pineapple, drained	2 tablespoons cherry juice

Dissolve marshmallows in milk, using double boiler. Let cool. Whip cream, then add to marshmallows and rest of ingredients. Freeze.

A good match up with casseroles.

Makes 10 servings.

Along with her many duties as pastor's wife of Northwest Baptist, Peggy Chapman finds time to raise three sons and do some of the best cooking I have ever eaten.

The Tamale Casserole is really a recipe from Mrs. Addie Hardin in our church. One summer her family stayed in a cabin in North Carolina the week before we were to occupy the same cabin. When we arrived, dinner was on the stove awaiting us. Included was this casserole, and I have made it ever since.

TAMALE CASSEROLE
Peggy Chapman (Mrs. Bill)

1 pound ground beef	1 can (16 ounces) tamales
1 medium onion, chopped	1 can (8 ounces) whole grain
salt and pepper	corn, drained
1 can (8 ounces) tomato sauce	grated Cheddar cheese

Preheat oven to 350 degrees. Brown ground beef and onion, season with salt and pepper, add tomato sauce and juice from tamales. Simmer on low heat. Cut tamales into small cubes, add to corn, and heat until warm through.

Butter casserole, add one layer of tamale mix and one layer of meat mixture. Repeat (2 layers of each), sprinkle top with cheese and bake for 40 minutes.

Makes 6 servings.

Our friend and former secretary Kathie Epstein has eaten with us so many times, she knows what kind of food we like most. So she suggested this sea food casserole. It is easy and very tasty.

ILI ILI CASSEROLE
Kathie Epstein

2 *pounds lump crab meat, fresh* or canned	2 *cups cooked rice*
2 *pounds small cooked shrimp*	2 *cups mayonnaise*
½ *green pepper, chopped*	1 *package frozen peas*
⅓ *cup chopped parsley*	*salt and pepper to taste*

Preheat oven to 350 degrees. Toss together all ingredients lightly. Place in buttered casserole.
Bake 1 hour, covered.
Makes to 6 to 8 servings.

John Huffman was President Nixon's "sometime" pastor at the Presbyterian Church in Key Biscayne. Now he is pastor at the historic First Presbyterian Church of Pittsburgh. He and Anne are just the finest people and ones we have thoroughly enjoyed a friendship with. Both of Anne's recipes are natural companions to casseroles.

BLACK CHERRY MOLDED SALAD
Anne Huffman (Mrs. John)

1 ⅞2 *can black pitted cherries*	1 *bottle (12 ounces) Coke*
2 *cans (8 ounces) crushed pineapple*	1 *package (8 ounces) cream cheese*
1 *package cherry-flavored gelatin*	½ *cup chopped walnuts*
1 *package raspberry-flavored gelatin*	

Heat juice from fruit and dissolve gelatin. Add Coke and chill till rather thick. Mash softened cheese (use the electric mixer) and fold in fruit, cherries, and nuts.

Makes 6 servings.

SAUERKRAUT SALAD
Anne Huffman (Mrs. John)

1 large green pepper	1 medium-size jar pimiento,
1 large onion	drained
2 cups chopped celery	1 quart sauerkraut

Cut the above ingredients fine and add:

¼ cup water	2 cups sugar
½ cup cooking oil	1 heaping teaspoon celery seed
¾ cup white vinegar	

Mix well. Cover solids with liquid, and push down solids that tend to rise to the top. Let stand in refrigerator at least 24 hours before using. Keeps well.

Rather different, and quite tasty with chicken dishes or casseroles.

Makes 6 servings.

SPICED PINEAPPLE
Peggy Chapman (Mrs. Bill)

3 cups sugar	sprinkle mustard seed
⅔ cup vinegar	3 #2 cans pineapple chunks,
3 sticks cinnamon	drained
about a dozen cloves	

Boil sugar, vinegar, cinnamon, cloves, and mustard seed 15 minutes (covered) and pour over 3 cans pineapple chunks (#2 can, 1 lb. 4½ oz., drain juice from pineapple.) It is possible to pack these hot and seal if desired. If not, keep refrigerated. The longer, the better!

Being able to work with the Billy Graham crusades has been a blessing that can never be topped. Part of this good experience is meeting and working with the staff. T. W. Wilson and Mary Helen are the behind-the-scenes power; T.W. as Mr. Graham's associate, managing the Montreat office, and Mary Helen with her prayer support.

This Apricot Salad looks a little complicated at first, but when it is finished, you really have a spectacular menu entree.

APRICOT SALAD
Mary Helen Wilson (Mrs. T. W.)

2 packages orange-flavored
   gelatin
2 cups boiling water
1 cup pineapple juice and
   apricot nectar

1 heaping cup puréed canned
   apricots
1 heaping cup crushed
   pineapple, drained
¾ cup small marshmallows

Dissolve gelatin in boiling water. Mix all ingredients in bowl and place in refrigerator until congealed.

FROSTING:

1 cup pineapple juice and
   apricot nectar
½ cup sugar
2 level tablespoons flour
1 egg, beaten

2 tablespoons margarine
1 cup whipped cream
grated Cheddar cheese, mild or
   medium

Cook juice, sugar, flour, egg, and margarine on medium heat until thick. When cold (room temperature), add whipped cream, slightly sweetened. Spread over firm gelatin and top with grated Cheddar cheese.

Makes 8 servings.

DEAR LORD. I'm like most women, I guess. I'm pretty good at complaining some about my motherly and wifely chores and responsibilities, but the opportunities for these chores are really gifts from you. Help me, not just to know, but also to feel that my stewardship of these responsibilities becomes my gift to you.

CHAPTER 25

SOUP'S ON

Whatever happened to the old-fashioned soup bone that used to simmer on the back of the stove all day? The rich, meaty aroma would work its magic all through the house. By suppertime everyone who had been caught in the spell would be weak with hunger. Just smelling that soup cooking throughout the afternoon could turn a regular eater into a lumberjack.

Use to, the first crisp breezes of autumn heralded the official opening of homemade soup season. In Florida, with the use of delicately flavored iced soups and chowders, we can include soups on the year-round menu.

In old-time Swedish cooking, substantial soups were the backbone of the family's diet.

In some parts of Europe, many farmers have a breakfast of soup, which, I'm sure, is a grand boost to the day nutritionally.

In French cooking, soups are sometimes referred to as "simple peasant fare." Meaning, I assume, plain food for the working class, because French soups are far from simple.

In *Modern Domestic Cookery* and *Useful Recipe Book* (copyright 1845) the following observations are given for "managing" to get soups and stews to the table "in the highest state of perfection."

When you make any kinds of soups, more especially portable, vermicelli, or brown gravy soup, or, indeed, any other that hath roots or herbs in it, always observe to lay the meat at the bottom of your pan, with a good lump of butter. Cut the herbs and roots small, lay them over the meat, cover it close, and set it over a slow fire: this will draw all the virtue out of the roots or herbs, turn it to a good gravy, and give the soup a different flavour from what it would have on putting the water in at first. As soon as you find the gravy is nearly dried up, then fill the saucepan with water, and when it begins to boil skim off the fat, and pursue the directions given for the soup intended to be made. In making peas soup observe, that if they are old, you must use soft water; but if green, hard or spring water, as it will greatly contribute to the preservation of their colour. One principal thing to be observed in making all kinds of soup is, that no one ingredient is more powerful in the taste than another, but that all are as nearly as possible equal, and that the soup be relished in proportion to the purpose for which it is designed.

GRANNY'S GARDEN SOUP

1 pound ground beef
1 large onion, sliced
1 can tomatoes
1 can (18 ounces) tomato juice
1 can water
½ cup chopped celery
3 carrots, sliced
2 bunches celery leaves (to be removed before serving)

2 medium potatoes, peeled and cut into 2-inch cubes
1 teaspoon salt
1 teaspoon pepper
¼ teaspoon each marjoram, thyme, crushed bay leaves
2 tablespoons soy sauce

Brown meat in a large Dutch oven and drain. Add onion slices and cook until tender.

Add tomatoes, tomato juice, and water. Add celery, carrots, celery tops, potatoes, and seasonings.

Bring to a boil, reduce heat, and simmer for 1 hour or until vegetables are done.

Remove celery tops.

Serve with corn bread and a gelatin salad.

Makes 8 to 10 servings.

BROWNED CABBAGE SOUP (Vitbalssoppa)

1 large head cabbage
¼ cup bacon drippings
6 cups beef or beef and vegetable stock

¾ tablespoon dark corn syrup
6 whole allspice
6 white peppercorns
salt

Trim cabbage and slice into bite-size sections. Cook the cabbage slowly in the bacon drippings until soft and slightly brown. Stir constantly. Remove cabbage and drain on paper towels.

Heat the vegetable stock in a large stew pot. Add drained cabbage, corn syrup, and seasonings. Cover and simmer for 30 minutes.

Serve with seasoned croutons and a sprinkling of Parmesan cheese. Makes 4 servings.

TOMATO CONSOMMÉ

3 cans (10½ ounces each) beef
  broth
1 can (1 pound) tomatoes
1 package (3 ounces) cream
  cheese, softened

1 tablespoon milk
3 tablespoons chopped parsley

In saucepan, combine beef broth and tomatoes. Bring to boil; reduce heat and simmer to heat through. Combine cheese, milk, and parsley; blend until smooth. Serve consommé in bowls; top each with about 1½ teaspoons cheese mixture. Serve with wheat thins and a tossed green salad.

Makes about 6 cups.

When seasoning soups and casseroles, use whole spices whenever possible. Whole spices can be added at the beginning of the cooking time.

However, when I have only ground spices and herbs available, I usually add them near the end of the cooking time so the flavor of the herb is not destroyed in long cooking.

GREEN PEA SOUP

1 pound green split peas
3 quarts water or part water
  and part vegetable stock
1½ teaspoons salt
½ teaspoon pepper
¼ teaspoon allspice
¼ teaspoon marjoram

2 pounds spareribs
2 beef bouillon cubes
1 large onion, sliced
1 cup celery, cut in ¼-inch
  pieces
3 to 4 carrots, cut in ¼-inch
  pieces

Place peas and water with vegetable stock in a large soup pot. Bring to a boil. Reduce heat, cover, and simmer for 1 hour.

Add spices, ribs, and bouillon cubes. Mix well and continue to simmer for 30 more minutes.

Next add the onion, celery, and carrots and cook for an additional 30 minutes.

Serve in deep soup bowls.

Makes 6 to 8 servings.

The following beef stew recipe is by far an all-time favorite. It can even be served to guests on cool evenings for an old-fashioned family dinner. The blend of spices gives this stew a flavor that easily becomes a topic of conversation at the table.

Slices of fresh fruit or a congealed salad really completes this meal since meat, vegetables, and bread appear in the main dish.

SHAKER STEW

⅓ cup flour
2½ teaspoons salt
½ teaspoon pepper
3 pounds chuck or round cut
   into 2-inch cubes
¼ cup butter or oil
1 bay leaf
1½ teaspoons dried thyme
   leaves
½ cup chopped celery tops
1 small onion, stuck with
   4 whole cloves

2 sprigs parsley
8 small onions, peeled
5 medium carrots, pared and
   halved
10 new potatoes, scrubbed with
   jackets left on
2 medium white turnips, pared
   and cubed
1 cup chopped celery

Combine flour, salt, and pepper and place in a clean plastic bag. Drop 4 or 5 pieces of meat into the bag and shake the bag to coat the meat with the flour mixture. Remove the coated meat and add more pieces to the bag until all pieces are covered. Heat the oil in a large Dutch oven or stew pot.

Add the meat and brown evenly on all sides. Add bay leaf, thyme, celery tops, onion with cloves, parsley, and 2 tablespoons of the leftover flour mixture. Stir with a large wooden spoon to combine all ingredients well.

Next add 3 cups of boiling water. Cover and reduce heat to simmer for 2 hours.

Meanwhile prepare the onions, carrots, and potatoes. Add these to the meat mixture and continue to simmer 20 minutes. During this time prepare the turnips and celery and add them to the stew. Recover and simmer 10 more minutes.

Follow the directions for Chive Dumplings below. Drop dumpling batter by large spoonfuls into the top of the boiling stew.

Leave room between the spoonfuls for the batter to rise. Cook uncovered for 10 minutes and then cover for 10 additional minutes.

Serve the stew in the cooking pot and let each guest serve himself.

CHIVE DUMPLINGS BATTER:

2 cups biscuit mix	1 egg
2 tablespoons chopped parsley	½ cup milk
1 tablespoon chopped chives	

Combine the biscuit mix with the parsley and chives. Add the egg and milk. Mix well.

Dick Shack has been my agent for several years. Dick is well known for being one of the best agents around. And his wife Ruth is known for being one of the best family cooks around. Ruth has the belief that good fellowship starts with a family pot cooking on the stove. She tells of some of their finest evenings that have started with this stew in the middle of the table. Ruth serves the stew with a large green salad.

STEW WITH DUMPLINGS
Ruth Shack (Mrs. Dick)

6 *pounds of brisket of beef, cubed*	*½ cup chopped fresh parsley*
½ cup flour	*2 bay leaves*
½ cup cooking oil	*2 teaspoons chopped thyme*
2 pounds onions	*1 tablespoon salt*
6 cloves garlic	*pepper to taste*
¼ cup brown sugar	*2 cans beef broth*
2 tablespoons of vinegar	*3 cups tomatoes, cubed*
	2 tablespoons of vinegar

Coat the beef cubes with flour. Brown in the cooking oil. Remove from oil and set aside. Slice the onions coarsely and crush the garlic cloves. Add to the cooking pot and brown lightly.

Add the browned cubes of beef, sugar, vinegar, parsley, bay leaves, thyme, salt, and pepper. Stir lightly. Scrape bottom of pot with wooden spoon.

Pour broth over all. Add tomatoes. Cover casserole and bake in 325-degree oven for two hours.

Remove casserole from the oven and place on range top. Stir in 2 more tablespoons of vinegar. Cook on medium heat until sauce bubbles.

DUMPLINGS:

Combine 2 cups self-rising cake flour, sifted, ¾ cup milk, 2 tablespoons melted butter. Mix well.

Drop batter by tablespoonfuls into simmering (not boiling) stew. Cover (do not open) and cook for 15 minutes. If a toothpick inserted into a dumpling emerges clean they are ready.

PICADILLO (PEEK AH DEE'YO)
C. G. (Bebe) Rebozo, Key Biscayne, Florida

"For a large family (nine children) of modest means, meal planning had to be economical, nourishing, and plentiful. This recipe, therefore, would serve thirty normal people or twenty hungry ones. My mother's recipe has gone through considerable evolutions with quantities never measured. To the best of my knowledge, these were *substantially* the ingredients and quantities the last time I concocted this palatable porridge":

3 medium-size bell peppers
3 medium-size onions
1 whole garlic
2 large cans tomatoes
1 medium-size jar stuffed olives
1 small can tomato sauce

6 large bay leaves
1 jar capers
3 pounds coarsely ground chuck
   and/or flank
1 cup seedless raisins

Optional: Worcestershire sauce, cooking wine, Tabasco, salt, pepper, oregano, or anything else you can think of

Finely chop bell peppers, onions, and most of the whole garlic. Mash tomatoes. Place all ingredients with the exception of the meat and raisins in a 6-quart pot and simmer for approximately 2 hours. Add ground beef. You may prefer to brown the meat first. Simmer to suit taste. Add raisins and simmer for another fifteen minutes.

Serve over rice.

Don and Dorothy Shula are true family people. Their daughter, Anne, is in Gloria's class at Miami County Day School.

Don is coach of the World Champion Miami Dolphins football team, so when this family "waits on Daddy" it is some wait!

WAIT FOR DADDY CHICKEN SOUP
Dorothy Shula (Mrs. Don)

3½ tablespoons salt
6 quarts water
4 to 6 chicken breasts
6 chicken legs
6 chicken thighs
5 medium onions, peeled

8 carrots, peeled and cut in half
1 teaspoon Spanish saffron
2 large packages egg noodles
   (medium size) boiled
   according to label on package

In a large soup pan, bring salted water and chicken to a boil. After water boils, remove any fatty parts which may rise to surface. Add vegetables and saffron and bring to another boil. Then cover and cook on low heat or simmer for 1½ hours. Pour over prepared noodles, using strainer while pouring. Save meat and vegetables until "Daddy comes home."

Makes 8 servings.

BLACK BEAN SOUP
Columbia, gem of Spanish restaurants

1 pound black beans	½ pound white bacon, chopped
2 green peppers, chopped	3 ounces olive oil
1 onion, chopped	2 bay leaves
1 pod garlic	

Wash beans well, put in pot with 2 quarts of water, green peppers, onion, and pod of garlic that has been chopped fine. When boiling, lower flame and add bacon. When beans thicken get frying pan, put in olive oil, and 2 bay leaves, and fry until well done; then add to beans. Serve with white rice.

For purée, strain the black beans and add 1 ounce of cooking sherry.

FAMILY'S FAVORITE VEGETABLE SOUP—Good for the weekend
Mrs. M. H. Richardson, Florida Citrus Commission

3 pounds lean chuck, cut in 1-inch squares	3 bay leaves
6 cups water	2 teaspoons Worcestershire sauce
1 medium-size bone with marrow	¼ teaspoon chili powder
6 cups tomato juice	1 cup each diced celery, sliced carrots, diced potatoes, chopped cabbage
⅓ cup chopped onion	
1 tablespoon salt	

The day before serving, brown meat well on all sides, drain on paper toweling, and add to large soup pot containing boiling water and soup bone. Add the next six ingredients. Cover and simmer (barely bubbling) for 2 to 2½ hours until meat is tender. Cool, remove bone and bay leaves, refrigerate over night. Next day, remove any fat from top, add four vegetables, and simmer until vegetables are tender. Fine with tossed salad and French bread.

Makes 8 to 10 servings.

Bread and biscuits are such a natural accompaniment to soup that I just can't resist adding a few of my favorites.

CHEESE BISCUITS

¾ teaspoon paprika
½ teaspoon mixed herbs
1 teaspoon each thyme,
    marjoram, and basil

⅓ cup grated Parmesan cheese
1 package ready-to-cook biscuits
½ stick butter, melted

Preheat oven to 425 degrees. Mix the paprika, herbs, and cheese together.

Cut each biscuit into halves. With your hands roll each section into a ball. Dip each one in the butter, then in the herb cheese mixture.

Place on a cookie sheet and bake 10 to 12 minutes.

Makes 30 small biscuits.

This is a very old family recipe from Evelyn Galvin. It was made by her mammy for many years on the farm!

GALVIN'S CORNBREAD
Evelyn Galvin (Mrs. Bill)

1 cup yellow corn meal
1 tablespoon flour
3 teaspoons baking powder
2 eggs

1½ teaspoons salt
1 cup whole kernel corn (fresh
    if available)
1 cup sour cream

Mix ingredients; bake at 400 degrees until golden brown, approximately 30 minutes. Cut into squares. Serve hot. You may double the recipe. Equally good next day.

DILLY BREAD

1 *package yeast*	1 *tablespoon butter*
¼ *cup warm water*	2 *teaspoons dill seed*
1 *cup creamed cottage cheese*	1 *teaspoon salt*
2 *tablespoons sugar*	¼ *teaspoon soda*
1 *tablespoon instant minced*	1 *egg*
onion	2¼ *to* 2½ *cups flour*

Soften yeast in warm water. Combine rest of ingredients in bowl, folding in flour last, to form a stiff dough.

Cover, let rise until about double in bulk.

Stir down and turn into bread pan.

Let rise until double in bulk.

Bake 30 to 40 minutes in 350-degree oven.

Delicious when served with barbecue or soups.

SOUR CREAM CORN MEAL MUFFINS

1 *cup sour cream*	½ *teaspoon soda*
1 *egg yolk, slightly beaten*	½ *teaspoon baking powder*
1 *teaspoon salt*	1¼ *cups corn meal*
1 *teaspoon sugar*	1 *egg white, beaten*

Preheat oven to 450 degrees. Combine the first six ingredients. Blend well. Add corn meal and fold in egg white.

Drop into hot, well-greased muffin pans.

Bake 20 to 30 minutes.

DEAR LORD. *I was so angry today, God, and in that moment of anger the words spilled out. Words that brought a hurt look to my child's eyes and an angry flush to Bob's face. I'm sorry, Lord, for things I said. Forgive me. You and I have talked so often about this temper and my angry feelings. Break up the tightness in my throat that keeps me from admitting that I am sorry. Help the words to again spill out, this time asking for forgiveness.*

PART VIII

ESTABLISHING CHRISTIAN TRADITIONS
ON HOLIDAYS

CHAPTER 26

EGGS FOR EASTER

Long before the resurrection, people celebrated a rebirth of life in the spring. The spring festival was one of great rejoicing to herald the end of winter and the return of flowers, leaves, and grass. God's good earth reminded them that there is life which cannot be killed. Life always returns to the world in the form of spring.

These early celebrations included many symbols to represent this new life. One of the most ancient symbols was the egg. When the shell broke, new life came into the world. Also, the rabbit, being a symbol for the abundance of new life, was used.

It was as if the people of ancient times were celebrating the hope of new life in Christ. After the resurrection, the joy of Christ's promises became mingled with the joys of the spring festival. Both celebrations represented new life and new hopes in the hearts and lives of men.

For Christians, Easter is the most joyous religious holiday of the year. It is the day of victory, the day of joy and promise. He lives, and because He lives, we, too, are reborn to life.

The early Christians used Easter as the time for baptizing new church members. After the Christian baptism, converts put on new white clothes as a sign of their new lives. Probably that custom preceded our desire to wear new clothes on Easter Sunday. Rather than wanting to show off, as some people believe, new clothes on Easter are just another way we represent our new life in Christ.

On Easter Sunday, Christians around the world attend outdoor sunrise services to watch the new day dawning—still another symbol of newness. Then special church services and special music follow. The kinds of services may vary but the message of Easter is the same —life without end.

My gift to the Easter celebration is usually in the form of music. I enjoy attending and singing at sunrise services.

Easter is always a time of rest and reflection at our house. I do not spend extra time cooking, but rather enjoy using that time with the children in special Easter traditions.

We are careful to always talk to the children about the importance of Easter and its meaning. I'm not always sure just how much they are able to retain, but I want to be sure the facts are available.

I remember one year when the twins were four. We went into great detail during the days preceding Easter, explaining the meaning of Easter. By Friday, they were able to parrot back to us, "Jesus Christ died and He arose from the dead on the third day. That is Easter." We were proud that we had done such a fine job of teaching. What we didn't realize was that TV was doing a good teaching job also. The kids had watched a TV special and had learned something from it too.

That Good Friday it was our very special privilege to have Billy Graham and Grady Wilson as dinner guests. What better audience could we have to show off our children's great religious knowledge of Easter?

So I said to my son, in my most motherly voice, "Billy, why don't you tell Mr. Graham what Easter is."

Billy (Graham) was most obliging and joined me in the invitation. "Yes, Billy, tell me about Easter."

Without a moment's hesitation, our little Billy said, "Sure, it is when the Black Easter Bunny comes to leave eggs at your house."

Billy Graham laughed and enjoyed our surprise. I vowed at that moment never to ask my children for a performance again. It was a funny and cute happening. It helped us realize children sometimes don't comprehend a truth even though they can say the words perfectly.

Irene Snider is my neighbor who lives across the street. She lived many years in Cuba with her family. There they had a chance to develop a taste for fine cooking. The following recipe belonged to Irene's grandmother. This delicious delicacy was served during the holidays with all the family together.

EASTER BREAD
Irene Snider

1 cup boiling water
½ cup powdered milk
½ stick butter or margarine
½ teaspoon salt
2 small eggs, beaten

1 package yeast dissolved in 1
   cup warm water
1 cup wheat germ
½ cup sugar
5 to 6 cups flour

Pour boiling water over powdered milk, butter, and salt in a bowl. Cool to lukewarm.

Add eggs, yeast, wheat germ, and sugar. Stir in enough flour to make batter stiff (2 to 3 cups). Beat until smooth. Add more flour (about 3 cups), enough to make dough stiff enough to knead. Knead about 10 minutes.

Place dough in bowl; let rise in warm place until doubled in bulk (1½ to 2 hours). Turn out on floured board and knead lightly. Form into loaves. Let rise until doubled.

Preheat oven to 350 degrees and bake for about 40 minutes, until golden brown.

EGGS BENEDICT

4 English muffins
¼ cup butter
8 slices smoked ham, heated

8 poached eggs
paprika
water cress

HOLLANDAISE SAUCE:

¾ cup butter
6 egg yolks
2 tablespoons lemon juice
¼ teaspoon salt

dash white pepper
2 tablespoons boiling water (if
   needed)

Prepare sauce first and keep warm over hot water until ready to serve: Cut butter into three equal parts. Put egg yolks and one piece butter into top of double boiler over hot, but not boiling, water. Stir quickly with wooden spoon until butter melts. Repeat with remaining two pieces. Remove from heat, beat for a minute. Gradually beat in lemon juice. Add salt and pepper to taste. Replace over hot water and stir until sauce is smooth and slightly thickened. If water becomes too hot, sauce may curdle. If it does, just beat boiling water in until sauce is smooth again.

Now cut muffins into halves and toast. Spread with butter, add ham slices, top with poached egg,* and spoon Hollandaise sauce over the top. Sprinkle with paprika and garnish with water cress. Allow 2 portions for each person.

EGGS REMOULADE

10 hard-cooked eggs, halved lengthwise
1½ cups mayonnaise
2 tablespoons light cream
6 tablespoons chopped dill pickles

1 tablespoon chopped parsley
2 teaspoons prepared mustard
½ teaspoon dry mustard
slivered toasted almonds.

Arrange eggs on serving platter. In small bowl, combine remaining ingredients, except almonds; blend well. Spoon over eggs, top with almonds.

Makes 5 servings (2 eggs each).

SUGAR EGGS

4 cups sugar
2 tablespoons water

food coloring

Measure sugar into bowl. Mix water with a few drops food coloring. Begin mixing the sugar and water together, using your hands.

Pack the sugar into large or small egg-shaped molds. You can use the little plastic eggs from the toy store if other molds are not available. When the sugar is packed tightly, scoop out the center of the two egg halves, leaving at least a ½ to 1-inch shell of sugar. Allow the sugar to dry at least 6 hours. Then gently shake to remove sugar from mold.

---

* To poach eggs easily, fill shallow pan, such as a skillet, with about 1¼ inch of water. Add salt. Bring water to boil, lower heat until it is just simmering. Break eggs (cold from the refrigerator) into a small bowl, one at a time. Pour carefully into simmering water. Cook several at once, simmering until white has become solid and yolk is still soft. Remove from water with slotted pancake turner. To prepare French-style poached eggs, use a small saucepan filled with salted water. When water is simmering, stir rapidly with a spoon to make a small whirlpool. Drop egg into center of whirlpool and simmer. Cook one at a time. This kind of poached egg looks like an oval-shaped white ball.

I usually use the handy, ready-made frosting in a container with the decorative caps to decorate the sugar eggs. A line of frosting around the edge of one half egg will decoratively cement it to its other half. Then add flowers, dots, lines, or whatever with the frosting tubes.

Makes about 6 to 8 small eggs, depending on the thickness.

Larger sugar eggs are delightful to make also. You can use the plastic containers from the hosiery that is sold in supermarkets. The large eggs make beautiful shadow boxes. Before the sugar hardens, cut a small opening in the side of each egg half to form a 2-inch opening when the egg is reconstructed. Use small paper cutouts to form a spring scene inside the egg.

DECORATING EGGS

Part of the ancient spring festival was to give elaborately decorated eggs as gifts to special friends. In Persia, China, and northern Europe, this custom seemed to be most popular.

I think it has merit as a Christian custom for artistic persons who enjoy this delicate art.

Empty eggshells may be used for decorating. Use a knitting needle and puncture a small hole in each end of an egg. Blow the contents out so you can use the egg. Rinse shell with water and allow to dry. Then decorate the shell.

When decorating an egg, it is fun to know the ancient symbols and their meaning so your egg will say what you want it to say. Flowers on an egg stand for love. A deer represents good health, and the sun says good luck. A rooster stands for wishes that will come true.

Many religious eggs from European countries have crosses on them with the message "Christ Is Risen."

EASTER EGG CHEESE SOUFFLÉ

4 eggs, separated
2 packages frozen creamed spinach
5 hard-cooked eggs, peeled and sliced
1 small onion, chopped
½ stick butter
¼ cup flour
½ teaspoon salt
½ teaspoon dry mustard
1 cup light cream
dash Tabasco sauce
1 cup shredded Swiss cheese

Preheat oven to 350 degrees. Beat egg whites to a soft-peak stage and set aside.

Cook spinach, according to package instructions. Cool. Pour into an 8-cup soufflé dish. Arrange sliced eggs over the top of the spinach.

Sauté onion in the butter. Blend in flour, salt and mustard. Cook just until bubbly. Stir in cream and Tabasco. Stir constantly and continue to cook until the sauce begins to thicken.

Use a mixer to beat the egg yolks into the cream sauce mixture. Beat well after each one. Stir in cheese and fold in egg whites.

Pour into soufflé dish on top of spinach and eggs.

Bake for 45 minutes and serve at once.

I can see these beautiful egg bread nests as perfect Easter remembrances for friends, neighbors, and church acquaintances.

EASTER EGG BREAD

1 package (¼ ounce) active dry
    yeast
1 teaspoon sugar
¼ cup lukewarm water
1 cup milk, scalded
¼ cup shortening
1 egg, beaten

¼ cup sugar
1 teaspoon salt
3½ to 4 cups flour
1 jar (4 ounces) maraschino
    cherries, drained and chopped
3 tinted raw eggs

GLAZE:

1 cup confectioners' sugar
1 tablespoon soft butter

2 tablespoons milk
¼ teaspoon vanilla

In small bowl, combine yeast, 1 teaspoon sugar, and water; let stand 5 minutes. In large bowl, combine milk, shortening, beaten egg, the ¼ cup sugar, and salt. Add about 2½ cups flour; mix well. Blend in yeast mixture and cherries. Add enough additional flour to make a stiff dough. Turn onto lightly floured surface; knead until smooth and elastic (about 8 to 10 minutes). Place in a greased bowl, turn to grease top. Cover; let rise in warm place, free from drafts, until doubled in bulk (about 1 hour).

Punch dough down; divide into three equal parts. Roll each piece of dough into a long rope. Braid rope; form into a ring on a greased baking sheet. Form three "nests" in braid; place a tinted egg in each. Cover; let rise in warm place, free from drafts, until doubled in bulk (about 1 hour). Preheat oven to 400 degrees; bake 8 minutes. Reduce heat to 350° F.; bake 20 to 25 minutes. Place on wire rack to cool.

Combine ingredients for glaze; spread over bread.

Makes 1 ring (6 to 8 servings).

BAKED EGGS GRUYÈRE

*6 1-ounce individual Gruyère
    cheese wedges
10 crisp cooked bacon slices,
    crumbled*

*6 eggs
½ cup heavy cream
salt
⅛ teaspoon pepper*

Preheat oven to 350 degrees. Slice cheese wedges and cover the bottom of a generously buttered baking dish. Spread bacon bits in bottom of dish with the cheese. Carefully break eggs over cheese and bacon. Spoon cream over the eggs and season with salt and pepper. Bake for 20 minutes or until the eggs are set.

Makes 6 servings.

BAKED EGGS IN TOMATO SHELLS

Preheat oven to 350 degrees. Scoop out the pulp from 4 medium-size tomatoes. Sprinkle the inside of each shell with salt, pepper, and basil. Break 1 egg carefully into each shell. Place the shells in a baking dish with a little water. Bake for about 20 minutes or until the eggs are set. Sprinkle each with 1 teaspoon grated Parmesan cheese and a dash of paprika. Place under broiler until tops are just bubbly. Serve at once.

Makes 4 servings.

*When someone becomes a Christian
he becomes a brand new person inside.
He is not the same any more. A new life
has begun!* (2 Corinthians 5:17)

DEAR LORD, *at this, the beginning of
a new day, take over my life for today.
Take over my will, my emotions, and
my intellect. Let your light so shine
through me today that my family, my
friends, and my work associates see your
life and light. May I be so totally committed to your leadership that others
may come to know of your great gift of
light to them.*

CHAPTER 27

SHARING THANKS AT THANKSGIVING

One of the nicest things about our end-of-year holiday season is that it usually nudges us all into remembering to say "thanks" to friends we have been needing to thank all year long.

Now this need or desire to give gifts or send reminders of appreciation can lead to a frenzied commercial shopping spree or to the warmth and friendliness of my own kitchen.

A homemade gift is a gift of love. It is a gift of myself—my time, my thoughts, and my creativity. It is the nicest way of saying, "Thanks for being you!"

When I was a little girl, we often got homemade candy or cookies from Grandma Berry for Christmas. She couldn't afford anything else, but we thought it was just about the best gift of all. Even today, I would rather have a homemade or handcrafted gift than any of the most expensive gifts money can buy.

I am trying hard to instill this beautiful custom in my children. Every year we do our "gift baking." It is like a party day of officially opening the holiday season. It is one way I have of bringing the best from my childhood into their world of today. Of course, the children do more sampling than producing, but that is fun, too.

Sometimes I enjoy working with a friend to really turn out a batch of goodies at one time.

Our two top gift items from the kitchen are Chocolate Toes and Peanut Brittle. We often use other things as well.

The recipes in this chapter are especially selected as suitable gift cookery. The fruitcakes in the following chapters are also very good for sharing thanks.

Most of these goodies can be prepared well in advance of the busy part of the holiday season and kept in the pantry or the freezer until time to make your deliveries.

We put our Chocolate Toes and Peanut Brittle in apothecary jars and tie them with beautiful red and green ribbon. The cakes can be wrapped in foil, then in colored cellophane paper and tied with a big bow. An addition of a cutting board, a coffee mug, an unusual kitchen utensil, or a collection of wooden spoons gives real class to your labor of love.

Be sure to label each home-done goodie so the recipients will know what they are eating. If there are special instructions about care of the product, such as refrigeration, be sure to include that, too.

From the youngest person on your gift list to the oldest, or the most esteemed, or the guy who has everything, or the family who has very little, there is not a single category that would not appreciate and enjoy gifts from your kitchen.

By the way, don't forget to leave a few extras on the shelf or in the freezer to say "thanks" or "happy birthday" or "congratulations" or "I appreciate you" all during the year.

Of all Grandma's recipes, this one is my most special! Christmas is never Christmas without Chocolate Toes. Grandma always made them, and now we always make them.

It is a family event. All the children help. They can practically do it themselves now, but I like to be in on the fun.

This is also one of the few recipes Grandma wrote down. She cooked by dabs and pinches, and that just can't be put on paper. I know, because I've tried. I used to write her recipes down, then come home to my kitchen to try them out. More times than not I would end up calling Grandma long distance to see what a "dab" meant, or how big a "pinch."

I am reprinting the recipe for Chocolate Toes exactly as Grandma wrote it down for me. She, of course, was never able to finish school, so she spells phonetically. The letter with this recipe in her own handwriting is one of my dearest treasures.

GRANDMA BERRY'S CHOCOLATE TOES

Anita I don't know if i can rite this to where you can under stand you take a stick of margrine and a Box of Powder sugar and Poot it in a mixen bole and just work it till you can Ball it in one Big ball and Pinch it off in to little Balls and Place them on a Platter and then take one slab of parifean and then take unsweaten chocklet about 4 squars and Poot them in a small stuer and melt them and then take a fork and dip the little sugar Balls in to the melted chock-let and parifean and then sit them out on a wax paper.

It is interesting to me how so many women of Grandma Berry's day liked to use the term, "never fail" to describe their recipes. It seemed to weave a magic around the recipe that guaranteed success every time.

This is one of my favorite Christmas recipes, although I enjoy it at other times of the year.

GRANDMA BERRY'S NEVER-FAIL PEANUT BRITTLE

2 cups sugar
1 cup white corn syrup
½ cup hot water
2 cups raw peanuts (or any kind of nuts)

3 tablespoons butter
1 teaspoon vanilla
2 teaspoons soda

Boil sugar, corn syrup, and water until it forms a hard ball when a little bit is dropped into cold water.

Now add peanuts and butter and stir continuously until the mixture turns a brownish gold color.

Take from fire, add vanilla and soda and pour into a greased platter to cool.

TOASTED PUMPKIN SEEDS

Scoop seeds from a large pumpkin and separate them from the fibers. Wash; allow to dry. Preheat oven to 250 degrees. Toss seeds in melted butter to coat well; spread on baking sheet. Sprinkle with salt; bake 1 hour. Shake and serve; or tie up in small calico sacks for extra gift treats.

PUMPKIN BREAD

3⅓ cups flour
3 cups sugar
2 teaspoons soda
1½ teaspoons cinnamon
1 teaspoon ground cloves
1 teaspoon nutmeg

1 teaspoon salt
1 can pumpkin
4 eggs
1 cup oil
⅔ cup water
1 teaspoon vanilla

Preheat oven to 350 degrees. Mix first seven ingredients. Add pumpkin, eggs, oil, and water. Mix until smooth. Add vanilla, and nuts if desired.

Pour into 4 small greased loaf pans. Bake 45 to 50 minutes.

ORANGE BREAD
Vera Dunton

1 cup orange peel, cut in thin strips	1 cup sugar
½ teaspoon soda	3 tablespoons melted butter
1 cup sugar	pinch salt
1 cup water	3½ cups flour (if not self-rising, add 3 teaspoons baking powder
2 eggs, well beaten	
1 cup milk	1 cup chopped pecans

Preheat oven to 325 degrees. Put orange peel and soda in pan with water to cover. Cook until tender.

Drain off soda water and rinse. Add 1 cup sugar and water, and boil until stiff. Let cool. Mix and add eggs, milk, and 1 cup sugar. Beat all together.

Add butter, salt, flour, and nuts, and mix well.

Put in greased loaf pan. Bake for 1 hour or until done.

Delicious served plain or sliced thin with butter as a sandwich with coffee or tea when friends drop in.

Homer Lindsay, Jr., was our pastor at Northwest Baptist before the Chapmans came. He left just as our family crises came with the twins' premature birth. I couldn't believe the Lord was taking such a tower of strength just when I needed it most. Of course, God filled our void with Bro. Bill; but Homer and Shirley have continued to be very dear to us.

CRANBERRY FRUIT BREAD CAKE
Shirley Lindsay (Mrs. Homer)

2 cups all-purpose sifted flour
1 cup sugar
baking powder
1½ teaspoons soda
1 teaspoon salt
1 egg, well beaten
¼ cup Florida orange juice

1 tablespoon grated orange rind
3 tablespoons liquid shortening
 (salad oil)
½ cup chopped nuts
2 cups fresh or frozen
 cranberries, coarsely chopped

Preheat oven to 325 degrees. Sift together flour, sugar, baking powder, soda, and salt. Combine egg, orange juice, orange rind, and cooking oil. Make a well in dry ingredients and add egg mixture all at once. Mix only to dampen. Carefully fold in nuts and cranberries. Spoon into greased loaf pan (9 × 5 × 3-inches). Spread corners and sides slightly higher. Bake until crust is brown and toothpick inserted comes out clean, about 1 hour. Remove from pan; cool. Store overnight for easy slicing.

"This is a recipe I learned to make in our first pastorate in Northport, Alabama. Those good Alabama cooks taught me a lot!
"This recipe is at its best when made with fresh-picked cucumbers."

CRISP PICKLE SLICES
Peggy Chapman (Mrs. Bill)

Slice 7 pounds of cucumbers ¼ inch thick. Cover with the following solution: 2 cups powdered lime in 2 gallons of water. Soak cucumbers in solution 24 hours, rinse thoroughly, and cover with fresh water. Soak 3 hours. Drain well and cover with the following solution:

2 quarts red vinegar   1 tablespoon salt
4½ pounds sugar

Tie in a bag and add to vinegar:

1 teaspoon celery seed   1 teaspoon mixed pickling spices
1 teaspoon whole cloves

Soak cucumbers in vinegar solution overnight. Be sure the solution covers them. Place container over heat and boil gently for 40 minutes. Pack in jars and seal.

This is another one of Mother's recipes. It is great to keep in the freezer for unexpected company or events. Make a double recipe when you make it.

BANANA NUT LOAF
Lynn Cate (Mrs. George)

¾ cup sugar   3½ teaspoons baking powder
2 tablespoons shortening   1 teaspoon salt
1 egg   1½ cups milk
2 fully ripe bananas, mashed   ¾ cup chopped nuts
3 cups sifted flour

Preheat oven to 350 degrees. Grease and flour a 9 × 5 × 3-inch loaf pan. In bowl, cream sugar and shortening until light and fluffy. Beat in egg and bananas. Sift flour, baking powder, and salt together; add to sugar mixture alternately with milk, beginning and ending with milk. Fold in nuts. Pour batter into prepared pan; bake 1 hour. Cool before slicing.
Makes 1 loaf.

LADY BIRD JOHNSON'S LACE COOKIES
From the LBJ Ranch

½ cup flour
½ cup coconut
¼ cup corn syrup (red or blue label)

¼ cup brown sugar, firmly packed
¼ cup margarine
½ teaspoon vanilla

Preheat oven to 325 degrees. Mix flour with coconut. Cook over medium heat, stirring constantly, syrup, sugar, and margarine until well blended. Remove from heat and stir in vanilla. Gradually blend in flour mixture.

Drop by teaspoonfuls 3 to 4 inches apart on ungreased cookie sheet.

Bake until totally flat and lacy-looking—about 8 minutes. Partially cool before removing from pan.

APRICOT NUT BREAD

2¼ cups biscuit mix
1 cup rolled oats
¾ cup sugar
1 teaspoon baking powder
¼ teaspoon salt

½ cup dried apricots, cut in pieces
1 cup walnuts, coarsely chopped
1¼ cups milk
1 egg

Preheat oven to 350 degrees. Grease and flour a 9 × 5 × 3-inch loaf pan. In bowl, combine biscuit mix, oats, sugar, baking powder, salt, apricots, and nuts; mix to coat fruit and nuts. Combine milk and egg; mix well. Add to dry ingredients; stir just to moisten dry ingredients. Pour batter into prepared pan; bake 1 hour. Cool before slicing.

Makes 1 loaf.

We went to the Strawberry Festival in Plant City, Florida, one year. When the time came to leave, our hosts insisted we take a crate of strawberries home with us on the plane.

I spent the next week making strawberry preserves. Since the strawberries were so good and just right for preserving, my efforts were greatly rewarded.

STRAWBERRY PRESERVES

5 cups ripe berries   ½ cup lemon juice
4 cups sugar

Place berries in pan in which they are to be cooked, add sugar, and allow to stand for 8 to 10 hours. Bring to boil; boil for 3 minutes exactly.

Add lemon juice, bring again to a boil, and boil for 3 minutes exactly.

Remove and cool in pan, then pour into sterilized jars, seal with paraffin.

PECAN-COATED CHEESE BALL

1 large package (8 ounces)   1 small onion, minced
  cream cheese   1 clove garlic, minced
1 small jar (5 ounces) processed   3 tablespoons wine vinegar
  sharp cheese spread   (optional)
2 jars (5 ounces each) processed   chopped pecans
  Roquefort cheese

Let cheese warm to room temperature. Beat together till light and fluffy and blended.

Beat in onion, garlic and vinegar. Chill. Roll into ball. Then roll in chopped nuts until well coated.

Chill again. Makes 1 large ball or 3 small.

Freeze for later use, if you like.

CANDY PEANUTS

2 cups raw peanuts   ½ cup water
1 cup sugar

Put all ingredients in heavy skillet. Cook until all moisture is used up, approximately 20 minutes. Spread out on foil; break up.

A perfect thing to put in old-fashioned fruit jars for gift giving.

DEAR LORD, *thank you for surrounding me with dear and precious people. Friends, family, acquaintances, associates. My world is a much happier place because of them.*

How long has it been since I've said, "Thank you. Thanks for being you. I appreciate what you are doing." How can they ever know how special they are to me unless I tell them so?

I need so desperately what other people can give me—recognition as a person, purpose, community, friendship, and understanding. Dear Lord, help me, in turn to recognize these needs in others also. And once recognizing, guide me to reach out through your love to them. O Lord, Friend to all, help me be the kind of friend that I myself need.

CHAPTER 28

THANKSGIVING TRADITIONS

Thanksgiving and Christmas holidays are the times I miss my Oklahoma family the most. In the early years of marriage, I really had to fight a battle of resentment over this. Thanksgiving was synonymous in my mind with lots of relatives all laughing and talking and eating. When the day arrived and there were no relatives and no Oklahoma family reunions, I would sink into deep despair.

Even though it is not as bad now, I still begin to reminisce around the holidays and remember those special family times.

Now is a new time—a new era. It is time to concentrate on building our own family traditions and warm special feelings for the holidays.

For years, I overcompensated, in a way, for the loneliness I felt. I really went all out cooking for Thanksgiving. Fortunately, my children didn't see the underlying motive for my busy cooking activities. We all enjoyed the big dinners and the piles of home goodies. I would start in advance. Often by Thanksgiving day, I would be so exhausted I could hardly make it through dinner.

On one Thanksgiving I didn't cook. My dad was coming to spend Christmas with us. It was the first time he and I had had a Christmas together since I was a child. Bob and I decided to save as much of my energy and cooking time as we could so I could go into the Christmas season feeling really on top of things. I wanted that Christmas to have my best self.

One of the ways we decided to cut down was to eat Thanksgiving dinner at the country club instead of my cooking it. Frankly, I didn't think the children would notice, much less be disappointed. How wrong I was. The minute Bobby heard the news, he said, "This is going to be the worst Thanksgiving of my entire life." He was right! The food at the club was delicious, but it really wasn't the same to any of us.

However, I had plenty of time and energy at the end of the day to play a game of touch football with the children, so that made up for the lack of Thanksgiving cooking.

Apparently, the traditions of our Thanksgivings are already being firmly ingrained.

Now we have decided to go one step further with Thanksgiving tradition and build our own Florida family reunion. It is not always possible for my relatives to visit at Thanksgiving, so we are making plans with Charlie and Marabel Morgan to become a Thanksgiving family with us.

We usually are fortunate enough to have Bob's parents with us at Thanksgiving, and the Morgans have Charlie's grandmother, parents, brother, and his family with them. That makes a good-size family for a Thanksgiving meal. We have the meal at our house one year and at the Morgans' the next. The host family always is responsible for the turkey and other main dishes. The visiting family brings vegetables and desserts.

The six children between us are delighted at the prospects. They think it sounds like the Indians and the Pilgrims. The men, I think, see it as a way to ease some of the cooking tensions that evolve. I see it as a beautiful way to ease the emptiness I feel for my long ago holidays. Sharing Thanksgiving is just about the nicest way to celebrate a meaningful holiday I can think of.

The plan of offering thanks during the harvest season was a familiar custom to the colonists who came to this country from Europe. But the American Indian is the one who really gave us the Thanksgiving feast tradition we know today. The Indian harvest festival lasted three days and was a ritual to thank their gods for the bounty of harvest. The early menus included roast venison, duck, goose, wild turkey, cranberry sauce, clams, smoked eels, leeks, corn bread, and a large variety of vegetables and fruits.

My own Thanksgiving menus are probably a little fancier but striking in similarity. Many of the holiday recipes in this chapter are used both at Thanksgiving and at Christmas dinners. The main dinner dishes are mostly included in this chapter and the desserts and Christmas goodies are in Chapters 29 and 30. The recipes in all the holiday chapters can be interchanged for superb holiday dining.

THANKSGIVING DINNER MENU

Poached Salmon with Green
Mayonnaise
Roast Turkey with Wild Rice
Stuffing and Giblet Gravy
Twin Duckling, Apple-Butter
Coated
Ham Towers with Cherry Sauce
and Orange Sauce
Cranberry and Orange Salad
Mold
Cranberry Relish
Nutted Sweet Potato Balls
Mashed Potatoes

Fresh Green Beans Vinaigrette
Corn Pudding
Wilted Spinach Salad
Stuffed Mushrooms
Hot Rolls, Assorted Breads,
Butter
Pumpkin Pie
Chocolate Log, Key Lime Pie,
Citrus Cake
Date-Nut Balls
Fruitcake and Cookies
Espresso Coffee, Iced Tea
Carbonated Grape Juice

POACHED SALMON

water
2 ounces red wine vinegar
½ lemon, sliced
1 teaspoon salt

1 teaspoon coarse ground pepper
1 bay leaf
4-pound piece salmon

Fill steamer with water to just below level of tray; add vinegar, lemon, and seasonings. Grease tray of steamer; place salmon on tray; place tray in steamer. Cover; steam 30 minutes. Remove fish to serving platter. Serve topped with Green Mayonnaise.

Makes 8 servings (½ pound each).

GREEN MAYONNAISE SAUCE:

1 cup mayonnaise
⅓ cup chopped fresh spinach

*2 tablespoons finely chopped
chives*
1 tablespoon chopped parsley

In bowl, combine ingredients; blend thoroughly. Chill well.
Makes about 1 cup.

ROAST TURKEY AND GIBLET GRAVY

1 14- to 18-pound turkey
melted butter
1 tablespoon salt
1 teaspoon coarse ground pepper
2 teaspoons seasoned salt
1 teaspoon poultry seasoning
1 teaspoon garlic powder
½ teaspoon ground ginger

1 teaspoon paprika
¼ teaspoon basil
3 tablespoons dried parsley
    flakes
1 stalk celery cut in ½-inch
    slices
1 large onion, chopped
giblets and neck

Preheat oven to 350 degrees. Clean and dry the turkey. Brush with melted butter. Mix the dry seasonings together in a small bowl and thoroughly rub them on the turkey inside and out. Truss and tie the bird and place in a roaster, breast side up. Place the celery, onion, giblets, and neck in the roasting pan. Add about 1½ to 2 cups water. Cover and bake 3 to 4 hours. Or follow the package directions that come with the turkey for length of cooking time.

Remove the turkey and giblets from the pan when done. Reserve the celery, onion, and broth for gravy. Remove to another pan for thickening.

Stuff the turkey cavity with the Wild Rice Stuffing and return it to the roaster. Lower oven temperature to 300 degrees and bake for 30 minutes uncovered.

Meanwhile dice the giblets to add to the broth, along with the onions and celery. Add 2 tablespoons cornstarch and cook over low heat until thickened. Serve as a side dish to the turkey.

WILD RICE STUFFING:

½ pound small mushrooms
2 tablespoons butter
3 tablespoons minced onion
2 cups wild rice, cooked

2 tablespoons blue cheese,
    crumbled fine
½ cup chopped parsley
½ cup slivered almonds

Chop the mushrooms fine. Sauté in butter until tender. Add onion and cook for about 2 minutes more.

Add cooked rice, cheese, parsley, and almonds to the mushroom mixture. Combine well.

Makes enough stuffing for 1 turkey.

TWIN DUCKLING, APPLE-BUTTER COATED

Tried out on Thanksgiving 1967.

2 5-pound ducklings
giblets and necks
salt
1 stalk celery, cut in thirds
1 large onion, peeled
5 cups cooked rice
2 cups finely diced cooked ham

2 tablespoons snipped scallions
pepper
dash garlic powder
½ teaspoon paprika
½ cup apple butter
parsley sprigs

About 5 hours before serving:

Rinse ducklings in running cold water: remove fat cavities and necks; pat dry with paper toweling; remove pinfeathers; refrigerate. In small saucepan combine giblets, necks, 1 teaspoon salt, celery, and onion; simmer, covered, 1 hour. Drain, discarding liquid and celery.

Finely dice giblets and onion; add meat from necks, discarding bones. Then add rice, ham, scallions, ¼ teaspoon pepper, 1 teaspoon salt; mix well.

Start heating oven to 350 degrees. Rub body cavity of each duckling with 1 teaspoon salt; loosely fill both body and neck cavities with rice mixture; sew them up.

In small bowl, combine 1 tablespoon salt, ¼ teaspoon pepper, garlic powder, and paprika; sprinkle over stuffed ducklings.

On rack in large roasting pan, place ducklings, breast side down. Roast 1¾ hours. Then turn, breast side up, and roast 1½ hours, or until drumstick meat is soft when pressed between fingers.

Thirty minutes before ducklings are done, combine apple butter with 2 tablespoon drippings from roasting pan. Use to coat entire ducklings, then complete roasting.

When done, remove ducklings to large platter, garnish with parsley sprigs, and serve, quartered with kitchen scissors.

Makes 4 to 6 servings.

HAM TOWERS (with Cherry Sauce and Orange Sauce)

First tried on Thanksgiving 1967.

2 6-pound fully cooked boned
   ham rolls
1 cup brown sugar, packed
⅓ cup bottled horseradish
lemon juice
1 tablespoon whole cloves
1 can (1 pound) red tart pitted
   cherries
6 tablespoons granulated sugar
½ teaspoon salt

⅛ teaspoon cinnamon
⅛ teaspoon nutmeg
cornstarch
red food color
¼ cup wine vinegar
1½ cups fresh Florida orange
   juice
1 orange peel, thinly sliced
parsley sprigs

When buying hams, ask meatman to cut each crosswise into ½-inch slices, then reassemble it in its original form by tying slices together with cord.

About 2¼ hours before serving:

Start heating oven to 325 degrees. Place hams on their sides, side by side, crosswise, in large roasting pan. Bake, uncovered, 2 hours, turning occasionally.

In small bowl, combine brown sugar, horseradish, ¼ cup lemon juice; set aside. Half an hour before hams are done, insert cloves here and there in the slices. Next, pour brown sugar mixture over them. Then complete the baking, using a pastry brush to baste hams often with liquid in roasting pan, turning occasionally.

Meanwhile, drain juice from cherries into measuring cup; add water to make 1 cup. Pour into small saucepan; add 1 teaspoon granulated sugar, salt, cinnamon, nutmeg, 4 teaspoons cornstarch, and enough red food color to make a bright red. Cook over medium heat, stirring constantly, till thickened and clear. Add cherries, then cook this cherry sauce till heated through. Set aside, keeping warm.

In another small saucepan, combine vinegar, ¼ cup granulated sugar, orange juice, and 5 teaspoons cornstarch. Cook over medium heat, stirring constantly, till thickened and clear; add orange peel; cook this orange sauce till heated through; set aside, covered, keeping warm.

To serve, arrange the two ham rolls upright on their flat ends, side by side, on a large heated platter. Remove cords. Pour some cherry sauce over one of the hams, and orange sauce over the other. Garnish platter with parsley sprigs. Pass remaining sauce in gravy boats. Refrigerate leftovers to serve, hot or cold, later.
Makes 16 servings.

NUTTED SWEET-POTATO BALLS

2 cans (1 pound, 2 ounces each)
    yams, drained
½ teaspoon salt
⅛ teaspoon pepper

¼ cup miniature marshmallows
melted butter or margarine
⅓ cup honey
1¼ cups chopped pecans

Day before:

Mash yams well, then add salt, pepper, marshmallows, and 1 tablespoon melted butter. Form into 10 balls; lay, side by side, in 12 × 8 × 2-inch baking dish, then refrigerate, covered, until needed.

One half hour before serving:

Start heating oven to 350 degrees.
Heat honey with 1 tablespoon melted butter. Then, with 2 forks roll each yam ball, first in honey mixture, then in chopped pecans, and return to baking dish.
Spoon 2 tablespoons melted butter over the yams, and bake them 15 minutes, or until they are all heated through.
Makes 10 servings.

MASHED POTATOES
Betty Irby (Mrs. Bob)

6 medium potatoes
2 cups grated Cheddar cheese
½ cup butter
1 pint sour cream

¼ cup chopped pimiento
1 tablespoon salt
¼ teaspoon pepper

Preheat oven to 350 degrees. Grease a 2-quart casserole. Cook potatoes, with jackets on, until done; cool, peel, and grate. Reserve ⅓ cup cheese for topping. In large bowl, combine potatoes, 1⅔ cups cheese, and remaining ingredients. Beat until blended. Spoon into prepared casserole; top with remaining ⅓ cup cheese. Bake 40 minutes.

Makes 6 servings.

HOT GREEN BEANS VINAIGRETTE

Remove the tips from 1½ pounds fresh green beans. Put the beans in a saucepan with about 1 inch boiling salted water. Bring water to boil and cook beans, uncovered, for 5 minutes. Cover pan and cook them 10 to 12 minutes longer or until tender but crisp.

Drain, if necessary, arrange beans in a vegetable dish, and pour Sauce Vinaigrette over them.

SAUCE VINAIGRETTE:

In a small bowl, combine 6 tablespoons salad oil, 1½ teaspoons wine vinegar, 1 teaspoon each of chopped shallots and parsley. Add ½ teaspoon each of salt and pepper.

Mix the dressing thoroughly.

Makes 6 servings.

OLD-FASHIONED CORN PUDDING

2 tablespoons sugar
1½ tablespoons cornstarch
1 cup milk
3 eggs, beaten
1 can (1 pound) cream-style
  corn

2 tablespoons melted butter
½ teaspoon salt
dash nutmeg

Preheat oven to 300 degrees. Grease a 1-quart casserole. In bowl, combine sugar and cornstarch; add milk; beat until smooth. Add eggs, corn, butter, and salt; mix well. Pour into prepared casserole; sprinkle with nutmeg. Place casserole in pan of hot water; bake 1¾ hours or until custard is set.

Makes 6 servings (about ½ cup each).

WILTED SPINACH SALAD

2 pounds fresh spinach	3 slices bacon, crumbled
3 hard-cooked eggs	1 red onion

Cut large veins from the spinach leaves. Tear leaves into bite-size pieces. Slice eggs and onion. Put all together with bacon in a large bowl and toss. Top with following dressing.

SPINACH SALAD DRESSING:

¾ cup chili sauce	1 tablespoon soy sauce
¾ cup red wine vinegar	¾ cup salad oil
1 cup sugar	

Mix well and serve.

STUFFED MUSHROOMS

12 medium to large mushrooms	½ medium-size onion, chopped fine
1 large clove garlic, mashed	4 slices prosciutto, chopped fine
6 fresh parsley sprigs, leaves only	4 tablespoons sour cream
2 chicken livers, chopped fine	¼ cup fresh creamery butter
2 tablespoons sifted seasoned bread crumbs	salt and pepper
	3 tablespoons olive oil

Preheat oven to 300 degrees. Wash mushrooms and dry. Cut stems completely out of the caps and chop stems fine. Mix garlic and parsley together and add the chicken livers, bread crumbs, onion, prosciutto, and chopped mushroom stems, and mix well.

Add sour cream and butter. Taste and correct the seasoning, if necessary.

Stuff mushroom caps with the mixture. Place caps, stuffed side up, in an oiled baking dish. Sprinkle a few drops of olive oil on top of each mushroom. Bake for about 45 minutes. Check for cooking.

Serve warm as an antipasto, spooning a little Italian salad dressing over top, or serve hot with meat dishes, or as a separate vegetable or as a main course.

The following recipe from Mrs. Alvin Dark produces Alvin's favorite cake. The Darks (he is the former great baseball player and now manager of the Oakland As baseball team) dine on this cake for breakfast, lunch, dinner, and in between.

The lives of Alvin and Jackie are truly an inspiration to all who know them. At one point in their spiritual search, the two of them claimed a promise from God given in Revelation 17:17a: "For God will put a plan into their minds, a plan that will carry out his purposes." Since that time, Jackie and Alvin are able to say, "Everyday, good times and bad, praise the Lord, God is in charge!"

PUMPKIN CAKE
Jackie Dark (Mrs. Alvin)

1 package spice cake mix	*¾ cup oil*
1 can pumpkin	*3 eggs*
¾ cup brown sugar	*½ cup chopped nuts*

Preheat oven to 350 degrees. In a large bowl combine cake mix, pumpkin, brown sugar, oil, eggs, and nuts. Blend at low speed until moistened (about 1 minute). Beat 2 minutes at medium speed. Spread batter in greased, floured 13 × 9 × 2-inch pan.

TOPPING:

½ cup sugar	*¼ stick softened margarine*
½ cup flour	*½ teaspoon cinnamon*

In medium bowl combine sugar, flour, margarine, and cinnamon with a fork. Mixture will be crumbly. Sprinkle evenly over batter. Bake for 40 to 45 minutes.

CHOCOLATE LOG

4 eggs, separated
½ teaspoon salt
½ teaspoon cream of tartar
⅓ cup plus ¾ cup sugar
¼ cup water
1 teaspoon vanilla
½ cup cocoa

½ cup flour
¼ teaspoon soda
1 cup heavy cream
1 can (14 ounces) fudge frosting
1 cup marshmallow cream
cocoa

Preheat oven to 350 degrees. Grease bottom of 15 × 10 × 1-inch jelly roll pan. Line with wax paper and grease again. Beat egg whites with salt and cream of tartar in large bowl until soft mounds form. Gradually add ⅓ cup sugar. Continue beating until very stiff peaks form. Combine egg yolks, ¾ cup sugar, water, vanilla, cocoa, flour, and soda in small bowl. Fold batter gently but thoroughly into beaten egg whites using a wire whip or rubber spatula. Pour batter into pan. Bake at 350 degrees for 20–25 minutes until cake springs back. Turn out immediately onto towel sprinkled with cocoa. Peel paper from cake.

Whip the cream. Add the fudge frosting and marshmallow cream. Spread this filling mixture over the cake. Roll the cake up, jelly roll fashion. Sprinkle top with remaining cocoa.

Makes 8 servings.

AUNT ALVA'S UNBAKED FRUITCAKE
Carolyn Stambough (Mrs. R. J.), former Florida Citrus Queen

¾ cup milk
1 pound marshmallows
1 box (1 pound) graham
    crackers, crushed
1 cup candied cherries, halved

1 cup candied pineapple, cut in
    small pieces
1 box (15 ounces) seedless
    raisins
4 cups shelled Brazil nuts

Line two 9 × 5 × 3-inch loaf pans with wax paper; butter paper. In top of double boiler, scald milk; add marshmallows, stirring until marshmallows melt. In large bowl, combine remaining ingredients. Pour marshmallow mixture over fruit mixture; mix thoroughly (use hands if necessary). Firmly pack into prepared pans; cover top with wax paper. Wrap in foil; store in refrigerator about a month before using.

Makes 2 loaves.

FRUITCAKE COOKIES
Nan Tomlinson

3 cups sifted flour
1 pound dates
1 pound candied cherries
1 pound candied pineapple
1 pound white raisins
6 cups chopped pecans
½ pound butter

1 cup brown sugar
3 teaspoons soda dissolved in 3
   tablespoons milk
4 eggs, separated
1 teaspoon cinnamon
1 teaspoon nutmeg
¼ cup cooking sherry

Preheat oven to 300 degrees. Mix ½ cup flour with fruit and nuts. Cream butter, sugar, soda, and well-beaten egg yolks. Add remaining flour, spices, and sherry. Combine with fruit and nuts.

Beat egg whites and fold into the batter. Drop in very small amounts on cookie sheet and bake for 20 minutes.

DATE-NUT BALLS

My children really enjoy using the hand grinder and can spend most of one afternoon working on this recipe.

1 cup figs
1 cup dates
1 cup raisins

1 cup chopped pecans
1 tablespoon lemon juice
1 cup crushed graham crackers

Grind the figs, dates, and raisins in a hand-turned grinder.

Mix the ground fruit, the nuts and lemon juice, also the cracker crumbs. Shape into small balls and roll in powdered sugar or more cracker crumbs.

SPICY PUMPKIN PIE
Mrs. Jeannette Brown, Washington, D.C.

CRUST:

1½ pints butter pecan or vanilla ice cream, softened

FILLING:

1 cup pumpkin
1 cup sugar
1 teaspoon cinnamon
¼ teaspoon ginger

¼ teaspoon nutmeg
¼ teaspoon salt
½ pint heavy cream

Line bottom and sides of a 9-inch pie plate with ice cream, smoothing with spoon to make an even generous coating; freeze. In saucepan, combine pumpkin, sugar, cinnamon, ginger, nutmeg, and salt. Cook over low heat 3 minutes (to dissolve sugar). Remove from heat; cool. Whip the cream; fold into cooled pumpkin mixture. Spoon into ice cream "crust"; return to freezer; freeze. If desired, just before serving, sprinkle top with additional nutmeg.

Makes a 9-inch pie (6 servings).

How we thank you, Lord! Your mighty miracles give proof that you care.

Then I will praise God with my singing! My thanks will be his praise—

Sing out your praises to our God, our King.

Go through his open gates with great thanksgiving; enter his courts with praise. Give thanks to him and bless his name. For the Lord is always good. He is always loving and kind, and his faithfulness goes on and on to each succeeding generation.

CHAPTER 29

THE SPIRIT OF CHRISTMASES PAST

Thanksgiving and Christmas holidays always meant family reunions, first at the Berrys and sometimes at the Bryants. My Grandma Bryant died when I was quite young, so the family times I remember at her house were really in the early years.

Since I had lived with the Berrys for a while, they always seemed more special and more like home.

But whichever place we went, there were great clans of relatives and great cooks in both families. I remember everyone would bring his own specialty. Usually Grandma would bake the turkey. She would get up in the wee hours of the morning to get the turkey on. By the time we all got there, the smell of that Christmas turkey met us halfway down the road.

She also made a homemade corn bread dressing. It was made with a pinch here and a pinch there. I always tried to get that recipe but she would say, "Well, I reckon as how I don't remember jes' how I made that."

Grandma would go ahead and prepare an entire Christmas dinner just as if no one were bringing a thing. All the vegetables were home grown. None of the food was fancy, just plain out-of-the world cooking! The aromas were overpowering. It was torture having to smell all that cooking—especially since none of it was ready until three in the afternoon. Even though these Christmas dinners took time and were hard work for Grandma, I never one time heard her complain or talk about how tired she was. Any time we went in that kitchen, she always had time to love on us and to talk to us. I remember she had one of the old wooden swings on the front porch. There were big oak trees and a yard to run in and woods to play in.

If the holiday took us over a Saturday night, we would all sit around the living room and listen to the Grand Ole Opry. That was the entertainment highlight of the week.

The kids always had a separate table, of course. There wasn't enough room at one table for all of us. I don't ever remember eating at the "big" table until after I was married.

We never got a lot of gifts at Christmas. We did always get one thing we really wanted, and I know Mother and Daddy really had to sacrifice to get that.

Sandy and I always got the same thing for Christmas. I can remember one year we both got these beautiful big dolls with red and white dotted swiss dresses on. I remember those dolls so well because they were the biggest dolls I had ever seen. They were huge.

Also the biggest treat we ever got in our stocking was an orange. They were such a treat because they were imported to Oklahoma, of course, and we couldn't have them too often. So an orange was always one of the best of our Christmas goodies. I loved those oranges so much that I even ate the peeling. (How little did I know that I would be representing Florida oranges someday!) There was also a candy cane, an apple, and some nuts in the stocking. Certainly not a store-bought toy or gift like my children expect in their stockings.

Now, Florida oranges are so commonplace around our house that our kids would think Santa Claus was off his rocker if he left an orange in their stocking. So instead the kids leave a Florida orange, cookies, and milk for Santa to snack on after coming down our chimney.

Christmas holidays meant family togetherness in the biggest sense of the word. I mean it was all for one and one for all in those big family events. I loved those holidays. It was a warm, wonderful family madhouse.

Bob was raised so differently, and yet his parents are so close; but it was a different kind of closeness than my very large family had. He has really had to learn to open up to my family. He was an only child and an only grandchild. That has made it difficult for him to understand these giant family reunions.

There were so many parts of my childhood that were not happy. I guess that is why I cling so tightly to these parts that were just so wonderful. I think that is also why holidays and holiday cooking are so vitally important to me.

I go wild cooking for the holidays. In a way, I am trying to re-create or duplicate what it took 6 or 8 good cooks to prepare at

Grandma's. Unconsciously, it is my way of bringing back those happy memories of my childhood.

As the Christmas traditions of my own little family begin to evolve, I feel this obsession lessening a little each year. Slowly, I am beginning to see that I must be free to enjoy the traditions developing now. Before, I was trying to *make* tradition happen without realizing traditions slowly grow and develop with each new family unit. The warm holiday feelings are not gone, and never will be. They are just changing. Merry Christmas, Bob, and Bobby, and Gloria, and Billy and Barbara.

Here is a punch that is served hot, and one especially designed for non-drinking Christians.

FLORIDA CITRUS WASSAIL
Lottie McCall (Mrs. Ronald), Vero Beach, Florida

6 Florida oranges	*1 gallon apple cider*
1 box cloves	*½ cup lemon juice*

Preheat oven to 350 degrees. Clean oranges; stud with cloves every few inches. Use a pick or fork to pierce small holes in the oranges in between cloves. Place oranges in a 7 × 5 × 2-inch baking pan; bake 30 minutes. In large kettle, heat apple cider and lemon juice. Slowly pour into punch bowl (so heat will not break glass). Add spiked, baked oranges.

Makes about 1 gallon.

Doris Niles is a voice and a name out of my distant past. In Will Rogers High School, in Tulsa, Oklahoma, she diligently taught me and the other high school kids through the years. Now she is a legend in her own time. I am including a portion of her conversation since it shows what a special "people" person she is.

"When you were in high school, our staff compiled a book, *W.R. Faculty Recipes*. Betty Rutherford, the secretary, duplicated it and the art department created the cover design. The Will Rogers staff are the best cooks I know. I can attest to this because we have a pot luck dinner once a year, when, naturally, everyone wants to show prowess in the kitchen as well as in the classroom. Frequently we duplicate recipes of popular dishes.

"In the recipe book is one by Lola Lockwood called, 'Aunt Bill's Brown Candy.' As with every recipe that I use, I have modified it considerably, and every Christmas season, upon request from my family, I make it at least a half a dozen times in order to have plenty for Christmas giving and serving. Our friends always expect us to have it on hand when they come to pay their Christmas calls. What is not consumed I store in plastic bags in metal cans in the freezer. It's fun to have it in the summer or even the next Christmas.

"I must explain the change in name of the recipe. You may remember that your generation called me "Auntie Dodo," the name given me by my niece when she was learning to talk. It stuck. When Carol went to Will Rogers, she let it slip that I had the nickname. To make a long story short, a neighbor child at home who likes the candy declares that it doesn't make sense to call it 'Aunt Bill's Brown Candy.' She has changed it to 'Uncle Dodo's Brown Candy.' Here it is."

UNCLE DODO'S BROWN CANDY
Doris Niles

3 cups white sugar	⅛ pound margarine
½ pint whipping cream	2 teaspoons vanilla
⅛ teaspoon soda	2 cups cut-up pecans

Put 2 cups of sugar and the cream in a large saucepan. Start bringing it slowly to a boil. At the same time, start melting the remaining cup of sugar in a heavy skillet and stir constantly to prevent scorching. When it is melted, pour it slowly into boiling sugar and cream mixture. Test it frequently in ice water until it reaches a firm softball stage. (It doesn't take long.) Remove from the heat and immediately add the soda, and stir vigorously until it foams. Then add the margarine allowing it to melt as you stir. Leave the mixture off the burner but in a warm place for exactly 10 minutes; add the vanilla and begin beating. When the mixture is thick and heavy with a dull appearance, add the nuts. Turn into an 8 × 8-inch buttered pan. Cut into squares when slightly cooled.
Note: If we've had a good pecan crop, I add even more nuts.
Makes about 3 pounds.

This is one of those Christmas recipes that leaves you with the feeling of high accomplishment. It takes hours to do, but really looks great when it is finished. I usually try to do two at one time. What little isn't eaten during the season can be frozen and served later.

Bake this cake in November and let it set until Christmas. Time causes a slight fermentation which greatly enhances the flavor.

THE VILLAGERS FRUITCAKE

First used Christmas 1968.

2⅓ cups sugar	1 pound golden raisins
2¼ cups butter	1 pound dark raisins
10 egg yolks	1 pound dates, pitted and
½ cup sifted all-purpose flour	chopped
1 pound pecans, broken	2 teaspoons cinnamon
1 pound almonds, blanched and	2 teaspoons cloves
chopped	2 teaspoons allspice
1 pound candied cherries,	10 egg whites
chopped	4 cups plus 2 tablespoons sifted
1 pound glazed pineapple,	all-purpose flour
chopped	1 teaspoon soda
1 pound citron, chopped	¼ cup warm water

Preheat oven to 250 degrees. Cut brown paper to fit bottom and sides of 10-inch tube pan and 2 9½ × 5 ×3-inch loaf pans. Grease pans, fit in paper, and grease again.

Cream sugar and butter together. Add egg yolks, beat well after each addition. Flour nuts and fruits with the ½ cup flour. Add nuts, fruits, and spices, mixing well.

Beat egg whites stiff and sift in the 4 cups plus 2 tablespoons flour a little at a time, adding alternately with beaten yolks. Add soda to warm water and mix into batter.

Fill prepared pans. Smack on hard surface to settle batter. Bake in very slow oven for about 3½ hours for tube pan and 2 hours for loaf pans, or until cake tests done when a toothpick comes out clean.

PEANUT PATTI
Mrs. Paul Fleming

Paul's my first cousin, Aunt Gola Mae's youngest son.

2½ cups sugar
⅔ cup white corn syrup
1 cup half and half
2 cups peanuts

½ stick margarine
1 teaspoon vanilla
red food coloring

Mix first five ingredients and cook on low heat to soft-ball stage. Add vanilla and a drop or two of red food coloring. Beat by hand until cool. Drop on wax paper by spoonful.

Dollye and Kent are friends from my Breakfast Club show days. Dollye should be a master of easy family recipes. She has raised four boys and has been a secretary to Kent.

This salad recipe comes from her holiday collection.

FESTIVE 3-TIERED GELATIN MOLD
Dollye Tomlinson (Mrs. Kent)

Use large circular mold.

1ST LAYER:

1 small package lime-flavored gelatin
1 can (16 ounces) sliced pears

2ND LAYER:

1 small package lemon-flavored gelatin
1 package (8 ounces) cream cheese

1 small can crushed pineapple, drained
½ pint heavy whipping cream

3RD LAYER:

1 small package strawberry-flavored gelatin

1 small can fruit cocktail, drained

Mix lime gelatin and pour into mold. When partly jelled, arrange pears in circular design. This will be top of mold when finished. Chill completely.

In separate bowl, mix lemon gelatin with 1½ cups water and partly chill. Break cream cheese in small chunks and mix well into lemon gelatin, add pineapple. Whip cream and fold into gelatin mixture. Pour into mold for 2nd layer and jell completely.

Mix strawberry-flavored gelatin in separate bowl and pour gently into mold for 3rd layer. When partly jelled, press fruit cocktail pieces with spoon into this layer. Chill completely.

Makes 18 to 20 servings.

This fruitcake recipe was given to me by my aunt Mrs. Betty Callen. Aunt Betty is mother's youngest sister and has really perfected some of Grandma Berry's recipes.

LEMON FRUITCAKE
Aunt Betty Callen

1 pound butter	3 cups all-purpose flour
2 cups sugar	2 ounces pure lemon extract
6 egg yolks, beaten	1 teaspoon soda dissolved in
1 pound white raisins	1 tablespoon warm water
1 quart pecans	6 egg whites, beaten

Preheat oven to 350 degrees. Mix all the ingredients well. Lastly fold in the egg whites. Bake in a tube cake pan which has been lined with brown paper. Bake 2¾ hours. Allow cake to cool before removing from pan.

This recipe belonged to Aunt Marie's mother Mrs. Forrest. It was the standard "special event" cake and was always on hand for Thanksgiving and Christmas.

FAVORITE APPLESAUCE CAKE
Aunt Marie Berry

½ cup shortening
1 cup sugar
1 egg, well beaten
1½ cups sweetened applesauce
2 cups flour
2 teaspoons cocoa
1 teaspoon cinnamon

½ teaspoon cloves
⅛ teaspoon salt
¾ cup raisins
¾ cup chopped nuts
2 teaspoons soda
¼ cup hot water
1 teaspoon vanilla

Preheat oven to 350 degrees. Cream shortening and add sugar gradually. Cream together until light and fluffy. Add egg and the applesauce. Mix well. Sift flour, measure and sift again with cocoa, cinnamon, cloves, and salt. Mix with raisins and nuts. Add gradually to apple mixture and beat well. Combine soda and hot water. Add to mixture and mix well. Add vanilla. Bake in two greased and floured layer-cake pans for 35 minutes. Top and spread layers with the following Caramel Nut Frosting.

CARAMEL NUT FROSTING:

1½ cups light brown sugar
    firmly packed
½ cup granulated sugar
¼ teaspoon salt

¾ cup top milk (cream)
2 tablespoons butter
1 tablespoon cream
½ cup chopped nuts

Combine sugars, salt, milk, and butter in saucepan and bring to a boil, stirring constantly until sugar is dissolved. Cook slowly, keeping crystals washed from sides of pan. When small amount forms a soft ball in cold water, remove spoon and set pan aside to cool. Do not move pan until mixture is lukewarm. Beat until mixture thickens. Add cream and beat until thick enough to spread. Add nuts and spread between layers of cooled applesauce cake.

"I like to bake this cake because it reminds me of the pear trees Grandma Berry had in her front yard. We ate pears from those trees all our lives and didn't know until we were half grown that we were not supposed to eat the green ones."

PEAR CAKE
Sandra Bryant Page (Mrs. Sam)

3 cups flour	1 cup oil
1 teaspoon soda	2 cups sugar
1 teaspoon vanilla	2 eggs
1 teaspoon cinnamon	1 cup nuts
½ teaspoon salt	3 small pears, chopped

Preheat oven to 350 degrees. Mix the flour, soda, vanilla, cinnamon, and salt together. Add the oil, sugar, eggs, and nuts. Mix well. Add pears. Bake in loaf pans for about 1 hour.

"This is a recipe I use around Christmas when we have parties for the Sears staff and their wives. I got the recipe from Sam's secretary in Kansas City. Last Christmas the guys at the office requested that I send some to them for the pre-Christmas days at work."

SNOWBALLS (Russian Tea Cakes)
Sandra Bryant Page (Mrs. Sam)

2 sticks margarine	large pinch salt
6 well-rounded tablespoons confectioners' sugar	2 cups flour
2 teaspoons vanilla	2 cups or more cut-up pecans

Preheat oven to 250 degrees. Mix margarine, sugar, vanilla, and salt until consistency of whipped cream. Add flour and nuts. Form balls about the size of walnuts. Bake 45 minutes. Be careful not to let them brown. Roll in confectioners' sugar when taken from the oven. When cool, roll in sugar again.

DEAR LORD. *Thank you, God, for my past and for what it gives to my present. Thank you for the past which taught me what family love is all about.*

Thank you for my now Christmases which are teaching me what all family love can become.

CHAPTER 30

THE JOYS OF CHRISTMASES PRESENT

Food is a great socializer. That is why all great social events and all Christian holidays require a shared meal which is often the central feature of the occasion.

Our big Christmas dinner is on Christmas Eve night. I start a month in advance preparing the do-ahead kinds of things. A typical Christmas dinner menu includes several salads, five or six vegetables, at least two entrees, and four or five desserts. It varies only slightly from year to year.

I must be honest and say that when we have suckling pig on the menu I order it ready to serve. Although it is a fascinating and delicious addition to a Christmas dinner, I have not felt confident to tackle such an adventurous undertaking along with all the other dishes I prepare. But every other dish on our menu I do myself with help from visiting family members. (The recipes for many of these main dinner dishes are found in Chapter 29.)

When my sister and her family visit for Christmas, Sandra really enjoys pitching in on the cooking. One time I remember the two of us staying up until three in the morning working on stuffed mushrooms. Of course we were so tired the next day we could hardly remember anything. But the hours we spent in the kitchen were marvelous make-up hours for the long months we are not able to be together.

CHRISTMAS DINNER MENU

Appetizer: Poached Salmon with Green Mayonnaise Sauce
Salads: Cranberry-Orange Salad Mold
      Cream Cheese Mold
      Relish Tray

Vegetables: Asparagus Delight
    Corn Pudding
    Stuffed Baked Mushrooms
    Sweet Potato Balls
    Black-eyed Peas
    Green Beans
    Mashed Potatoes
Entree: Roast Turkey with Wild Rice Stuffing and Gravy
    Suckling Pig with Cherry Sauce
    Goose with Orange Sauce
Bread: Hot Assorted Rolls with Butter
Drinks: Catawba Juice, Ice Tea, Coffee
Desserts: Chocolate Pies
    Citrus Cake
    Pumpkin Pie
    Apple Pie
    Key Lime Pie
    Gloria's Brownies
    Ice Cream
    Chocolate Log
    Homemade Fruitcakes

After dinner we go to the music room. One year Bob got our whole family an organ. Now Bobby plays the organ while Gloria plays the piano. Billy and Barbara sing together. We all join in on Christmas carols.

Then the children get to open the gifts from their friends.

Santa Claus comes on Christmas morning and the family gifts are opened. We always have a gigantic tree in the living room, decorated with traditional ornaments—both store-bought, hand-made, and collected from the overseas Bob Hope tours.

Children and Christmas go together, because children still have the imagination to believe in and enjoy the mysteries and the simple moments and are able to see beauty where it is often unnoticed by adults.

We are very emphatic about teaching our children the true story of Christmas. We always point out that gifts and Santa Claus are a very fun part of Christmas. We use gifts to show our love and friendship for each other, but the true meaning of Christmas is, of course, God's great gift to the world.

We are honest to tell them that we really don't know the exact date Jesus was born. In fact, it probably was in the spring, but December 25 is the date that is set aside to celebrate this miraculous birth.

The Christmas Eve time in the music room is a natural time for us to read and retell the story from Luke of the first Christmas. We build onto the story each year adding more details, more background, and more Scriptures as we feel the children are ready to absorb more.

One of the nicest holiday celebrations we have in our family is the event of decorating the Christmas Advent tree. Our friend Edith Beers has designed and written a beautiful poem book and Advent tree celebration. Beginning with December 1 we add one ornament to the tree each day in December as we read the accompanying poem. Each day describes one aspect of a Christmas tradition. It is an ideal way to teach the right meaning of the different traditions associated with our observance of Christmas. And it is a meaningful way to lead children through the maze of pre-Christmas brassiness to a warm religious experience on the twenty-fifth.

Although it is not possible to reproduce her lovely poems here, different Scripture verses or Christian tradition discussions could be used instead. Design your own Advent celebration.

There are people who woefully sigh that the meaning of Christmas is gone. But Christmas can only exist in spirit in the hearts and minds of persons. Once found it can be passed on to others both young and old. My role in our family Christmas is to introduce and nurture these traditions in our children in such a way that the spirit of the Christ child will live forever with them.

Christmas needs *children* to constantly rediscover the joys and simple delight of the season. Christmas needs *tradition* to insure its continuance from year to year. And Christmas needs parents to bring these two ingredients together.

Changing, renewing, growing, Christmas is old and new at the same time and full of deep spiritual meaning for the Christian. Christmas is an individual affair, with each person bringing his own hopes, dreams, and prayers to the celebration. But at the same time, Christmas is a celebration to be shared in the community of family and close friends.

Christmas is a time of reaching out to others to show Christ's love for the world. And it is a time for looking inward to re-evaluate the blessings of our Christmases past, the joys of Christmases present, and the hope of Christmases to come.

ANITA'S KEY LIME PIE

CRUST:

1 cup graham cracker crumbs
2 tablespoons sugar

2 to 3 tablespoons melted butter
or margarine

FILLING:

1 can (15 ounces) condensed
milk

3 egg yolks
½ cup lime juice

TOPPING:

½ pint heavy cream
2 teaspoons confectioners' sugar

1 teaspoon vanilla

Preheat oven to 350 degrees. In a bowl, combine ingredients for crust; firmly press into bottom and sides of a 9-inch pie plate. Bake 10 minutes; cool.

To make filling, in a bowl, combine all ingredients; blend well. Pour into cooled crust; refrigerate at least 1 hour.

To make topping, in bowl, beat heavy cream until stiff peaks form; blend in sugar and vanilla. Spread over pie. Refrigerate before serving.

Makes a 9-inch pie (6 servings).

Tom and Margie Ruggiero are friends through Northwest Baptist Church. Their daughter Jeannette was in my Sunday school class last year.

MANGO NUT BREAD
Margie Ruggiero (Mrs. Tom)

½ cup butter
¾ cup sugar
2 eggs
2 cups sifted flour
1 teaspoon soda

¼ teaspoon salt
⅔ cup raw mangoes, cut fine
½ cup nuts
1 tablespoon lime juice

Preheat oven to 375 degrees. Cream butter and sugar. Add eggs. Stir in dry ingredients. Add mangoes, nuts, and lime juice. Mix well.
Bake in loaf pan for 1 hour.
Wait until second day to slice.

This recipe is the traditional Christmas Eve dessert at the George Wilson home in Minneapolis, Minnesota. This handsome dish follows a Swedish smorgasbord that all relatives and guests have enjoyed.

STEAMED PRUNE PUDDING
Mrs. George Wilson

2 eggs
1 cup brown sugar
1 cup melted shortening
2 cups cooked, diced prunes

1 cup flour
½ teaspoon salt
1 teaspoon soda
1 tablespoon cold milk

Beat eggs well. Dissolve brown sugar in melted shortening, add to eggs. Add prunes. Add flour and salt to prune mixture. Dissolve soda in milk and add last. Mix well. Put in well-greased muffin tins and place in pan of water (cookie sheet with sides). Steam 1 hour uncovered.

SAUCE FOR PUDDING:

Beat 1 egg until foamy. Add 5 tablespoons melted butter slowly. Add 1½ cups confectioners' sugar. Mix very well. Blend in 1 cup whipped cream. Add 3 to 4 tablespoons sherry flavoring (or vanilla, if preferred). Spoon over individual puddings.

For a festive look, sprinkle red or green sugar over the sauce and place a candle in each and light as they are served.

In some families, Christmas time is more than trees, gifts, reunions, or Santa Claus. Holiday time means football time on television. So to a family like the Howard Twilleys, the holiday recipe file includes snacks to watch TV with. Howard plays end for the Miami Dolphins.

FAMOUS FOOTBALL FUDGE
Julie Twilley (Mrs. Howard)

4½ cups sugar
1 can evaporated milk
¼ pound margarine
4 large bars (16 ounces each)
   chocolate

2 packages (6 ounces each)
   chocolate chips
1 pint marshmallow cream
2 cups pecans
2 teaspoons vanilla

Boil together sugar, milk, and margarine. Let come to a boil and boil for 8 minutes, stirring constantly. Cut chocolate into small pieces and mix with chocolate chips in a large mixing bowl. Pour hot mixture over the chocolate and beat well. Then add marshmallow cream, nuts, and vanilla. Beat until cool. Pour into buttered pan.

From the Don Shula family. Don is coach of the Miami Dolphins.

"Many years ago, my great grandmother, Bridget Fitzgerald, taught her children how to make the Christmas Event Cookies.

"In Ireland, after the last Advent candle burned, the Christmas Event Cookies were passed around to each member of the family to begin the great event celebration of the birthday of Jesus Christ."

THE CHRISTMAS EVENT COOKIES
Dorothy Shula (Mrs. Don)

4 cups all-purpose flour	*1½ teaspoons nutmeg*
1½ cups granulated sugar	*1 cup shortening*
1 teaspoon baking soda	*2 eggs*
1 teaspoon baking powder	*1 teaspoon vinegar*
½ teaspoon salt	*¾ cup milk*

Preheat oven to 450 degrees. Mix dry ingredients together. Add shortening and blend thoroughly. In 1-cup measuring cup, crack eggs, add vinegar and milk, and stir. Then add to dry ingredients and blend well. Cover mixing bowl with a damp dish towel and put in refrigerator for 1½ hours or overnight. Then, remove from refrigerator and let stand until room temperature. On a slightly greased cookie pan, put each cookie after rolling out mixture with rolling pin, cutting with a heart-shaped cutter (signifying love of Christ), then sprinkle with white sugar, and green- and red-colored sugar.

Bake each pan for 4 to 5 minutes.

Makes 8 dozen.

This is a family Christmas candy recipe from Bill Chapman's mother and grandmother. When his mother was living, she mailed us a box every year. Since her death, I have learned how to make it.

WEEKEND CANDY
Peggy Chapman (Mrs. Bill)

3 cups sugar	*½ cup cut candied pineapple*
1 cup light corn syrup	*½ pound shelled pecans*
1½ cups coffee cream	*½ pound shelled walnuts*
1½ teaspoons vanilla	*½ pound shelled Brazil nuts—*
½ cup cut candied cherries	*optional*

Boil the sugar, corn syrup, and cream in a saucepan to the soft-ball stage (238 degrees). Cool to lukewarm, about 30 minutes. Add the vanilla, stir until beginning to thicken. Add the fruit and nuts. Press into a buttered square pan. Work quickly!

When cold (just a very few hours), cut into squares.

A perky traditional holiday salad from the Grady Wilson family. Grady, along with Billy Graham, has visited in our home for dinner. He and Wilma are absolute towers of strength and faith.

HOLIDAY JOY SALAD
Wilma Wilson (Mrs. Grady)

1 tablespoon unflavored gelatin
½ cup cold water
½ cup heavy cream
½ cup sugar
1 package (3 ounces) cream
* cheese, softened and creamed*

2 tablespoons mayonnaise
½ cup chopped maraschino
* cherries (red and green)*
½ cup drained crushed
* pineapple*

Soften together the gelatin and cold water. Dissolve over hot water. Cool. Whip cream and add sugar, creamed cheese and mayonnaise. Add gelatin. Fold in fruits. Pour into oiled rectangular baking dish or six individual molds. Chill until firm. Unmold onto crisp lettuce. Top each with a red or green maraschino cherry.

Variations: A small can of drained fruit cocktail can be added and/or ½ cup chopped nuts.

Makes 6 servings.

CRANBERRY SALAD-DESSERT MOLD

8 Florida oranges
4 cups coarsely chopped, fresh
* cranberries*
2 cups granulated sugar
4 packages (3 ounces each)
* strawberry-flavored gelatin*

3 cups boiling water
1 tablespoon lemon juice
15 to 16 fresh whole cranberries
Orange Peel Mum

Day before serving:

In medium bowl, combine 5 oranges (peeled, seeded if necessary, then cut into pea-size pieces) with chopped cranberries and sugar. Mix with rubber spatula until sugar dissolves.

In large bowl, dissolve gelatin in boiling water; then add 3 cups cold water, lemon juice, and cranberry-orange mixture. Refrigerate until mixture thickens to an egg-white consistency, stirring occasionally. Then pour this thickened mixture into a 3-quart bundt cake pan and refrigerate.

20 minutes before serving:

Set bundt pan, just to rim, in water water for 10 seconds. Lift from water, hold upright, and shake slightly to loosen gelatin from mold; then invert large round platter on bundt cake pan, invert pan and platter together, then gently lift off pan.

Using a sharp knife, cut 1 orange into 5 crosswise slices; then cut each orange slice in halves. Arrange the halves around cranberry mold, then top each half with one or two whole cranberries. Also, if desired, place Orange Peel Mum in center of cranberry.

Makes 16 servings.

ORANGE PEEL MUM:

Slice top from 1 orange, about ¼ of the way down. With sharp knife, cut out all orange sections, reserving them for fruit salad next day. Then, with kitchen scissors, carefully snip orange shell from top rim down about ¾ inch intervals, forming a fringe; also, if you wish, with scissors trim top of each strip in the fringe so it tapers to a sharp point. Repeat this with a second orange, then nest one in the other.

A great Christian family are the Marvin Watsons from Texas. Marvin was Postmaster General during the Johnson administration. We were fortunate enough to have them in our home for dinner one evening. It came at a time when I was able to do all the cooking for the dinner myself—and for me, that is always fun.

Marvin and Marion have three children and are a beautiful picture of the Christian family.

Three out of five of the Watson birthdays are in December, so the official December birthday cake is beautiful as well as good to eat.

THE RED CAKE
Marion Watson (Mrs. Marvin)

½ cup shortening
1½ cups sugar
2 eggs
2 tablespoons cocoa
2 ounces red food coloring
1 teaspoon salt

1 cup buttermilk
2¼ cups sifted cake flour
1 teaspoon vanilla
1 teaspoon soda
1 tablespoon vinegar

Preheat oven to 350 degrees. Cream together shortening, sugar, and eggs. Make paste with cocoa and coloring and add to sugar and eggs. Add salt and buttermilk with flour and vanilla. Add soda and vinegar. (Add soda to batter first and blend. Then add vinegar last.) *Do not beat hard*—just enough to blend vinegar and soda. Pour into two 8-inch cake pans. Bake for 30 minutes. Cool and split each layer. Frost with your favorite white icing. I prefer the Seven-Minute Icing.

SEVEN-MINUTE ICING:

2 unbeaten egg whites
1½ cups sugar
5 tablespoons cold water

¼ teaspoon cream of tartar
1½ teaspoons light corn syrup

Place ingredients in top of a double boiler over rapidly boiling water. Beat constantly for 7 minutes. Remove the icing from the fire. Add 1 teaspoon vanilla, continue beating until icing is right consistency to spread.

HOLIDAY CHESS PIE

8 packages (3 ounces each)
    cream cheese
4 egg whites

1 cup sugar
1 teaspoon vanilla
⅔ cup zwieback crumbs

Preheat oven to 350 degrees. Cream the cheese well to soften. Beat egg whites until stiff. Blend in sugar and add to cheese. Stir in vanilla.

Pour into 8-inch spring pan, 3 inches deep, buttered and dusted with zwieback crumbs. Bake for 25 minutes.

ICING:

2 cups sour cream   ½ teaspoon vanilla
2 tablespoons sugar

Preheat oven to 475 degrees.
Mix ingredients together and spread over top of cake. Bake 5 minutes. Chill 2 hours. Garnish with fresh fruits if desired.
Makes 8 servings.

A beautiful Christmas punch . . .

TOPAZ PUNCH

½ cup red maraschino cherries   1 can (6 ounces) frozen Florida
½ cup green maraschino   orange juice concentrate,
   cherries   thawed
1½ quarts lemon sherbet   1 quart water
1 can (6 ounces) frozen   ¼ cup sugar
   lemonade concentrate, thawed   2 bottles (½ pint each)
                                                   sparkling catawba juice

Arrange red and green cherries in bottom of a 5-cup ring mold. Stir lemon sherbet to soften; spoon into mold over cherries, pressing to make firm ring. Freeze. In large bowl or pitcher, combine lemonade concentrate, orange concentrate, and water; stir until blended. Add sugar and stir until dissolved. Chill.
To serve, dip sherbet mold in hot water; invert and unmold ring into empty punch bowl.
Pour in chilled juice mixture. Slowly add catawba juice and mix until blended.
Makes 20 5-ounce servings.

DEAR LORD. O God, even in the early Christmas
        morning stillness of this hour, help me too to be
        still and know.
To know that you are God.
To know that peace can reign in this household today.
To know your love will totally enfold each of us as the
        day leads us into new experiences and relation-
        ships.
Be still and quietly know . . .
        the strength, the assurance, and the peace of God.

GENERAL INDEX

friendship, 263; for God's perfect
love, 201; groups, 157; for guidance,
28, 112; for husband, 125; for
kitchen togetherness, 185; after
meals, 82; before meals, 195–96;
morning, 19, 44, 104, 164, 254, 299;
partners in, 127–28; for patience, 59;
projects, 65; for a special day, 104;
for strength, 142; by Teddy Moody
Heard, 132; of thanks, 35, 164, 263;
287; on wonders of creation, 87, 91
Pressures, 92, 93, 126
Prince, Mrs. Milford W., 79
Psalms: 18:28, 219; 47:6, 277; 69:30,
277; 75:1, 277; 92:1–5a, 164; 100;
4–5, 277; 103:1–5, 209; 118:24, 44

Radio, xiv, 102, 283
Rebozo, C. G. (Bebe), 238
Recognition, 263
Re-evaluation, 291
Religious training, 14
Remington, Billie, 121
Resurrection, 247
Retreats, 166
Revelation: 17:17a, 273
Rewards, for weight loss, 144
Richardson, Mrs. M. H., 146, 189, 240
Roberts, Evelyn (Mrs. Oral), 76, 77
Roberts, Oral, 76
Role-playing, 93, 94
Ruggiero, Jeannette, 291
Ruggiero, Maggie (Mrs. Tom), 291,
292
Ruggiero, Tom, 291
Rutherford, Betty, 280

Salter, Mrs. Minnie, 98, 99
Sanders, Colonel Harland, 214
Sanders, Mrs. Harland, 214
Sanford, Peggy Noel, 129
Savell, Taris, 79, 180
Sawakwa, Oklahoma, 106
Sawyer, Bill, 171
Sawyer, Dody (Mrs. Bill), 139, 171,
172, 183
Scotland (Scots), 169
Scriptures, 57, 171, 211, 290
Sears', 101, 286
Semel, Sandy, 64, 136
Semel, Vera (Mrs. Sandy), 64–65, 136
Seminole, Oklahoma, xii

Service, adventure of, 173
Shack, Dick, 237
Shack, Ruth (Mrs. Dick), 237, 238
Shepherd, Bettie (Mrs. David), 146
Show business—Christian
responsibility, relationship, xiii–xiv
Shula, Anne, 239
Shula, Don, 239, 293
Shula, Dorothy (Mrs. Don), 239, 294
Simon. See Peter
Singers, 115; -music, relationship, 5
Snider, Irene, 248, 249
Snider, Jim, 158
Snider, Pat (Mrs. Jim), 158
Socialization, 93, 94, 151–52. See also
Churches, Family and Togetherness
Sonnenberg, Bernice, 40, 94, 225
Sonnenberg, Mrs. Esther, 40
South America, 193
South Pacific, 85
Spiritual meaning, 290
Spiritual search, 273
Spiritual truths, 12–14
Stambough, Carolyn (Mrs. R. J.), 274
Staton, Audrey, 122
Stone, Marlene (Mrs. Richard), 205
Strawberry Festival (Plant City,
Florida), 261
Strength, source of, vii
Sunday School: luncheons, 156–57
Swedes, 115, 117, 233, 292

Talent, Christian, nurturing of, 126
Tallahassee, Florida, 162
Tanzania, 100
Television, xiii, 76, 248, 293
Tennessee, 97
Texas, 37, 118, 121, 138, 296
Thanksgiving, 255–56, 278; menu, 266;
traditions, 264–65
Thessalonians, First: 5:16–24, 45
"Till There Was You," xiv, 115
Time-marriage, relationship, 116
Timothy, First: 3:18–33, 166
Tishomingo, Oklahoma, xii
Tithes, 166
Togetherness, 3, 93, 120, 219; in
cooking, 178–79; family, 37, 50,
279, 288, prayer, 43; kitchen, 177–
78, prayer, 185
Tolerance, 14
Tomlinson, Dollye (Mrs. Kent), 283

RECIPE INDEX

egg bread, 252–53
egg cheese soufflé, 251–52
Easy fruit pie, 192
Eggplant soufflé, 54
Eggs:
    baked, Gruyère, 253
    baked, in tomato shells, 253
    Benedict, 249–50
    breakfast (3 variations), 47
    decorating, 251
    deviled egg sauce (*see under* Asparagus)
    Easter egg cheese soufflé, 251–52
    poached, 250 *note*
        French-style, 250 *note*
    quiche lorraine, 205–6
    remoulade, 250
    as snacks, 25–26
    stuffed, 25–26
    sugar, 250–51
    See also Soufflés
Enchiladas, Lady Bird Johnson's, 180

Festive 3-tiered gelatin mold, 283–84
Fish and seafood:
    chowder, Florida, 109
    crab meat: Baltimore imperial crab, 107
        crab burgers, 42
        -lobster casserole, 108
    dolphin, 110
    ili ili casserole (seafood), 229
    lobster-crab casserole, 108
    red snapper with hollandaise sauce and mushrooms, 108–109 (*see* snapper)
    salmon grapefruit mousse, 206–7
    salmon, poached, 266
    salmon steaks, baked, 107
    shrimp curry, 139–40
    shrimp hors d'oeuvres, 137
    snapper bonne femme, 106–7 (*see* red snapper)
    snook, 110
    oysters and wild rice, 118–19
Florida:
    chocolate sauce, 67
    citrus cake, Anita Bryant's, 152
    citrus wassail, 280
    fish chowder, 109
    orange cake, 73–74
    orange juice glaze, 74

sunshine salad, 162
    Waldorf salad, 162–63
Frankfurters:
    salad, 154
    See Hot dogs
French-fried:
    hot dogs, 95
    liver, 213
French-style poached eggs, 250 *note*
French toast de luxe, 46
Fresh:
    apple cake, 158
    apple pie, 155–56
    fruit ice cream, 102
Fried:
    chicken, 90
    tomato sandwiches, 89
Frostings. *See* Cake frostings and fillings
Frozen:
    pineapple salad, 228
    strawberry cake, Mrs. Michael's, 131
Fruit:
    apple cake, fresh, 158
    apple cobbler, Mother's, 99–100
    apple dumplings, 183–84
    apple pie, 217; fresh, 155–56
    apricot nut bread, 261
    apricot salad, 231
    avocados, stuffed, 159–60
    banana breakfast bread, 46–47
    banana French toast de luxe, 46
    banana grapefruit dips, 192
    banana ice cream, Luther's, 103
    banana nut loaf, 260
    banana and peanut butter, 32
    berries and cream pie, 98
    blackberry cobbler, 100
    black cherry molded salad, 229–30
    blueberries (*see* cherry delight)
    cherry delight, 156
    cranberries: fruit bread cake, 259
    date-nut balls, 275
    dessert, brown sugar, 215
    fresh:
        ice cream, 102
    fresh poppy seed dressing, 183
    grapefruit:
        dips, 192
    grapefruit peel (*see* Sugared orange rinds)
    grapefruit pudding, 99

french-fried, 95
wiener casserole, 97
yum yums, 191
Hunger quencher, 144

Ice cream:
banana, Luther's, 103
chocolate, 102
first, 101
fresh fruit, 102
orange Alaska, 47–48
peanut butter topping, 32
peppermint, 102
strawberry, 102
strawberry pop, 103
vanilla, 101–2
vanilla-lemon, 101
See also Sherbet
Ice cubes, decorative, 66
Ideal:
chocolate cake, 78
cocoa, 78
Ili ili casserole, 229
Instant:
chocolate mousse, 130
pudding fingerpaint, 6
Italian cream cake, 167

Jam, strawberry preserves, 262
Jelly roll pancakes, 49
Juice:
mint cooler, 27
orange, hot spicy, 24–25
See also Beverages

Kabobs, cheese burger, 41
Key lime pie, Anita's, 291
Kid-tested recipes, 1–59
Knishes: meat, 16–17

Lace cookies, Lady Bird Johnson's, 261
Lasagna, 153–54
in a hurry, 225
Lemon:
bubble loaf, 207–208
cake bars, 191
fruitcake, 284
or orange pudding, 192
Lettuce salad, shredded, 181
Lima bean casserole, 54–55
Lime sherbet, 100–101
Liver, french-fried, 213

Lobster-crab casserole, 108
Lollipops, 66–67
Longhorn loaf, 96–97
Luncheon recipes, 157–63

Macaroni:
chicken bake, 226
'n' beef, 226–27
Mango nut bread, 292
Marshmallow stacks, 31
Mashed potatoes, 270–71
Matzo:
balls, 16
ball soup, 14–15
Mayonnaise:
green, sauce, 266
mustard, 162–63
Meat:
accompaniments: Florida sunshine
salad, 162
beef: bramalough, 179
deviled short ribs, 146
ground: bitter balls, 136–37
casserole south of the border,
224
'n' cheese nibbles, 136
cherry tomato treats, 137
grilled hamburger meal, 95–
96
hamburger stroganoff, 182
hot pot pie, 96
lasagna, 153–54
longhorn loaf, 96–97
mushrooms caliente, 159
muy pronto, 226
stuffed cabbage rolls, 118
tarts, 179
'n' macaroni, 226–27
stew (see Shaker stew and Stew
with dumplings)
tarts, 179
corned beef: barbecue, 98
sandwich spread, 87–88
deviled short ribs, 146
enchiladas, 180
grilled hamburger meal, 95–96
ground meat (see under beef and
hamburgers)
ham: bake, upside down, 117
and cheese on rye, 88–89
towers (with cherry and orange
sauce), 269–70

Peaches and cream pie, 98
Peanut brittle, Grandma Berry's, 257
Peanut butter: and bananas, 32
  cookies, 90
  cream of peanut soup, 33
  dough, 31
  drops, Gloria's, 190
  honey balls, 31
  marshmallow stacks, 31
  pancakes, 31
  sandwiches, 30, (adults), 33–34
  shapes, 32–33
  tarts, 31–32
  topping, 32
Peanut patti, 283
Pear cake, 286
Peas and green beans, 56
Pecan(s):
  -coated cheese ball, 262
  squash with, 55
Peppermint ice cream, 102
Peppers, stuffed, 40–41
Picadillo, 238–39
Pickled brussels sprouts, 55
Pickle slices, crisp, 259–60
Picnics, 85–92
  activities, 86–87
  sandwiches, 87
  sandwich spreads, 87–91
Pie crust:
  Marabel Morgan's, 122
  pie dough kisses, 7
Pie dough kisses, 7
Pies:
  apple, 217; fresh, 155–56
  berries and cream, 98
  cherry delight, 156
  cherry pecan, 140
  chocolate, 73, 168
  chocolate angel, 123–24
  chocolate cream, 190
  coconut cream, 122–23
  crust: Marabel Morgan's, 122
    pie dough kisses, 7
  fruit, easy, 192
  holiday chess, 297–98
  hot pot, 96
  key lime, Anita's, 291
  mile high, 217–18
  peaches and cream, 98
  peanut butter tarts, 31–32
  pumpkin, spicy, 276

See also Cobblers and Tarts
Pineapple:
  ice box dessert, 157
  salad, 213–14; frozen, 228
  sandwich spread, 88
  spiced, 230
Plantation grilled chicken, 94–95
Poached:
  eggs, 250 note
    french-style, 250 note
  salmon, 266
Popcorn, 193
  -balls, 193
Poppy seed dressing, 183
Pork:
  chop casserole, 227
  sweet and sour, 139
Potatoes:
  mashed, 270–71
  refrigerator rolls, 214
  scalloped, 129–30
  sculpture, 57
  See also Sweet potatoes
Poultry:
  accompaniments: Florida sunshine
    salad, 162
  stuffings: wild rice, 267
  See also Chicken, Cornish hens,
    Duckling and Turkey
Poundcake:
  chocolate, 168
  150-year-old, 156
  sour cream, 75–76
Praline squares, 184
Pretzels, 6
Prune:
  filling, 217
  pudding, steamed, 292–93
Pudding:
  boiled custard, 169–70
  corn, old-fashioned, 271
  grapefruit, 99
  instant, fingerpaint, 6
  lemon or orange, 192
  noodle, 15
  pineapple ice box dessert, 157
  Scottish trifle, 169–70
  steamed prune, 292–93
Pumpkin:
  bread, 257–58
  cake, 273
  pie, spicy, 276

Snapper bonne femme, 106–7
See also Red snapper
Snook (fish), 110
Snowballs (Russian tea cakes), 286
Soda biscuits, 49
Soufflés:
  Easter egg cheese, 251–52
  eggplant, 54
Soup, 233–40
  accompaniments, 241–42
    matzo balls, 16
  black bean, 240
  browned cabbage, 234–35
  chicken, 239–40
  cream of peanut, 33
  garden, Granny's, 234
  green pea, 235–36
  hunger quencher, 144
  matzo ball, 14–15
  seasoning, 235
  tomato, 145
  tomato consommé, 235
  vegetable (family's favorite), 240
  See also Chowder, Consommé *and*
    Stew
Sour cream:
  coffeecake, 171
  cookies, 10
  cornmeal muffins, 242
  poundcake, 75–76
Spaghetti:
  homemade, 199–200
  sauce à la Verrocchi, 197–99
Spareribs, bar-b-cued, oriental, 180
Spiced:
  asparagus, 146–47
  hot chocolate, 48
  pineapple, 230
Spicy pumpkin pie, 276
Spinach salad:
  dressing, 272
  wilted, 272
Spread, whipped orange butter, 48–49
Spud and spice cake, 79
Squash:
  McDonald, 58
  with pecans, 55
Steamed prune pudding, 292–93
Stew:
  beef (*see* Shaker stew)
  with dumplings, 238
  picadillo, 238–39

shaker, 236–37
vegetable soup (family's favorite),
  240
Strawberry:
  cake, frozen, 131
  ice cream, 102
  pop ice cream, 103
  preserves, 262
Stuffed:
  avocados, 159–60
  breast of veal, 16
  cabbage rolls, 118
  mushrooms, 272–73
  mushrooms in cream, 120
  onions, 40–41
  peppers, 41
  tomatoes, 40–41
Stuffings:
  for celery, 145
  hamburger, 40–41
  wild rice, 267
Sugar:
  cookies, 6–7
  eggs, 250–51
Sugared orange rinds, 66
Sunday night casserole, 227
Sweet and sour pork, 139
Sweet-potato balls, nutted, 270

Tamale casserole, 228
Tarts:
  beef, 179
  peanut butter, 31–32
  See also Pies
Toasted:
  pumpkin seeds, 257
  waffle sandwich, 89
Tomato(es):
  cherry tomato treats, 137
  consommé, 235
  sandwiches, fried, 89
  soup, 145
  stuffed, 40–41
Topaz punch, 298
Trifle, Scottish, 169–70
Turkey, roast, and giblet gravy, 267
Twin duckling, apple-butter coated,
  268
Two-layer gelatin salad, 130–31

Unbaked:
  cookies, 188–89